Critical Perspectives on Work and Employment

Series editors:
Irena Grugulis, Bradford University School of Management, UK
Caroline Lloyd, School of Social Sciences, Cardiff University, UK
Chris Smith, Royal Holloway University of London School of Management, UK
Chris Warhurst, University of Strathclyde Business School, UK

Critical Perspectives on Work and Employment combines the best empirical research with leading edge, critical debate on key issues and developments in the field of work and employment. Extremely well-regarded and popular, the series is linked to the highly successful *International Labour Process Conference*.

Formerly edited by David Knights, Hugh Willmott, Chris Smith, Paul Thompson, each volume in the series includes contributions from a range of disciplines, including the sociology of work and employment, business and management studies, human resource management, industrial relations and organisational analysis.

Further details of the *International Labour Process Conference* can be found at www.ilpc.org.uk.

Published:
Maeve Houlihan and Sharon Bolton
WORK MATTERS

Alan McKinlay and Chris Smith
CREATIVE LABOUR

Chris Warhurst, Doris Ruth Eikhof and Axel Haunschild
WORK LESS, LIVE MORE?

Bill Harley, Jeff Hyman and Paul Thompson
PARTICIPATION AND DEMOCRACY AT WORK

Chris Warhurst, Ewart Keep and Irena Grugulis
THE SKILLS THAT MATTER

Andrew Sturdy, Irena Grugulis and Hugh Willmott
CUSTOMER SERVICE

Craig Prichard, Richard Hull, Mike Chumer and Hugh Willmott
MANAGING KNOWLEDGE

Alan Felstead and Nick Jewson
GLOBAL TRENDS IN FLEXIBLE LABOUR

Paul Thompson and Chris Warhurst
WORKPLACES OF THE FUTURE

More details of the publications in this series can be found at
http://www.palgrave.com/business/cpwe.asp

Critical Perspectives on Work and Organisations Series

Series Standing Order ISBN 978-0230-23017-0

You can receive future titles in this series as they are published by placing a standing order. Please contact your bookseller or, in case of difficulty, write to us at the address below with your name and address, the title of the series and the ISBN quoted above.

Customer Services Department, Macmillan Distribution Ltd, Houndmills, Basingstoke, Hampshire RG21 6XS, England

---

Work Matters

Critical Reflections on Contemporary Work

Edited by
**Sharon C. Bolton &
Maeve Houlihan**

palgrave
macmillan

First published 2009 by
PALGRAVE MACMILLAN

Palgrave Macmillan in the UK is an imprint of Macmillan Publishers Limited,
registered in England, company number 785998, of Houndmills, Basingstoke,
Hampshire RG21 6XS.

Palgrave Macmillan in the US is a division of St Martin's Press LLC,
175 Fifth Avenue, New York, NY 10010.

Palgrave Macmillan is the global academic imprint of the above companies
and has companies and representatives throughout the world.

Palgrave® and Macmillan® are registered trademarks in the United States,
the United Kingdom, Europe and other countries

ISBN-13: 978-0-230-57639-1
ISBN-10: 0-230-57639-7

This book is printed on paper suitable for recycling and made from fully
managed and sustained forest sources. Logging, pulping and manufacturing
processes are expected to conform to the environmental regulations of the
country of origin.

A catalogue record for this book is available from the British Library.

A catalog record for this book is available from the Library of Congress.

10   9   8   7   6   5   4   3   2   1
18   17   16   15   14   13   12   11   10   09

Printed and bound in China

*To the lyrical field respondents of all our collective research
projects to whom, so clearly, work matters.*

Contents

List of Figures and Tables

Figures

Tables

Acknowledgements

Work Matters is one of a series of collaborations between us that has involved some extraordinary adventures, long and late nights, and more than the odd question from one to the other along the lines of 'what possessed us?' However, such moments are soon and quickly replaced by moments of pride and pleasure in the work that we get to read and write, and in the stories that are told through volumes such as this.

This volume is inspired in part by papers presented at Work Matters – the 26th International Labour Process Conference, University College Dublin, from 18–20 March 2008. We proposed the title Work Matters for the conference because we wanted to capture something of the passion and urgency so many of us feel about just how much work *matters* to a thriving society and how it can make, break, and shape individual lives. Our hope was to generate accounts that give voice to this lived experience. We believe that this volume casts light on some of the places where this is happening, and tells stories that need to be heard.

Now that our work on this volume is done it's time for us to reflect and acknowledge the enormous amount of help we have received in making it happen; from ILPC through Paul Thompson, Irena Grugulis and the organising group; from our respective home teams at Quinn and Strathclyde, and from all the participants at the Work Matters conference, who made the experience of running this conference a delight. We'd like to particularly acknowledge Carolin Grampp, who was a pillar of support throughout the conference journey and beyond. And we'd like to also acknowledge the space Sharon's Marie Curie Fellowship gave us to work together in Dublin over the summer.

We are above all indebted to the contributors whose work forms the heart of this volume, and whose dedication to unearthing the truth of today's workplaces echoes and dances from the pages of their work. Each has been patient and even enthusiastic in working with a demanding deadline, and, it has to be said, a demanding editorial team.

Warm thanks are due to Ursula Gavin, Mark Cooper and all at Palgrave Macmillan for their great support and enthusiasm for the project. And as ever, we thank our families, friends and colleagues for their continual support and interest in what we do, and for their reminder to us, when our belief occasionally falters, that this work too, matters.

SCB and MH

Notes on the Contributors

Alicja Bobek is a research student on the Migrant Careers and Aspirations project and a PhD candidate in the Department of Sociology, Trinity College Dublin. She has an MA in Sociology and an MA in Migration and Ethnic Studies from the Jagiellonian University in Krakow. Her research is on highly skilled Polish workers in Ireland, their migrant networks and their performance on the labour market.

Marcia Bok is Professor Emeritus from the University of Connecticut School of Social Work where she taught social welfare policy and research for many years. While at the University of Connecticut she co-edited a journal on HIV/AIDS and Children and conducted research on Puerto Rican women, Latino Children in Foster Care and Adoption, and Latino/a Workforce Issues in Social Work. In addition to teaching and research, Dr. Bok has been a board member, agency administrator, planner, and programme evaluator in the areas of child welfare, HIV/AIDS and homelessness. She has had a long standing interest and currently advocates for low-income women in the community and at the state legislature in Connecticut. Her long career as a social worker and her background from a blue-collar, union family have demonstrated the importance of good jobs, with good wages and benefits for working class people and that these goals are achievable.

Sharon C. Bolton is Professor of Organisational Analysis at Strathclyde University Business School, Glasgow, UK. Her research interests include the emotional labour process, public sector management, the nursing and teaching labour process, gender and the professions and the Human in Human Resource Management. Research is published widely in leading sociology and management journals such as *Work, Employment and Society*; *Sociology*; *Journal of Management Studies*; *Gender, Work and Organisation*. A sole authored book *Emotion Management in the Workplace* was published by Palgrave in 2005 followed by two edited collections in 2007: *Searching for the Human in*

Human Resource Management (with Maeve Houlihan) and *Dimensions of Dignity at Work*. Sharon loves her work, it matters to her and would like to think that it matters to others too.

Carol Boyd-Quinn worked as a lecturer in human resource management at the University of Glasgow until 2003 when she undertook a five-year medical degree at the same university. She has recently qualified as a medical doctor and plans to pursue further research into the labour process of doctors. Other research interests include occupational health and safety and emotion work in the airline, railway and nuclear power industries. She has published in leading sociology and management journals including *Work, Employment and Society* and has a sole-authored book *Human Resource Management and Occupational Health and Safety* published in 2003.

Isobel Calder is a recently retired lecturer from the Department of Educational and Professional Studies, University of Strathclyde. Her last job before retiring was as Director of the Professional Development Unit of the Faculty of Education. Before joining the Faculty in 1999, Isobel spent nearly thirty years teaching in Scottish primary, secondary and special schools, latterly as Head of a large Learning Support Department. The experience of collaborating with others to try to make school life easier for all children led to Isobel's research interest in how adults from different professional backgrounds, and sometimes with no professional training at all, can work together in schools and classrooms to support the educational needs of children, especially those who are experiencing learning difficulties.

David Coats joined The Work Foundation as Associate Director – Policy in 2004, having previously been Head of the Economic and Social Affairs Department at the TUC from 1999–2004. From 2000–04 David was a member of the UK's Low Pay Commission and was appointed as a member of the Central Arbitration Committee (the UK's industrial court) in 2005.

Johanna Commander is a research fellow at the University of Strathclyde, in the department of HRM. She has a BA (Hons) in Community Arts and an MSc in Human Resource Management both from the University of Strathclyde, as well as an MBA from Queen Margaret University. At present she is also working on her PhD which examines the management of creative workers and has an international comparative focus.

Vaughan Ellis is a Lecturer in Human Resource Management at Napier University in Edinburgh. Before embarking on an academic career he worked in the private sector for six years, in a number of clerical and managerial roles. He was recently awarded his Doctorate by the University of Stirling for research into the changing organisation and experience of clerical work at Scottish Gas, following privatisation and the subsequent introduction of the call centre. He has published in *Work, Employment and Society and New Technology, Work and Employment*. His main research interests include the transformation of work, trade unions and research methodologies.

Mary Gatta, a faculty member at the Department of Labor Studies and Employment Relations and the Center for Women and Work at Rutgers University, has written extensively on service workers, gender equity, and welfare reform. Her book, *Juggling Food and Feelings: Emotional Balance in the Workplace*, investigates how individuals maintain and manage their emotions in an attempt to rebalance them as they are interacting in the workplace. Using the setting of the restaurant, Dr. Gatta explores differences in emotional balancing practices among waitstaff, the use of emotion scripts by restaurant managers, and degrees of agency among servers. Her second book, *Not Just Getting By: The New Era of Flexible Workforce Development*, chronicles thinking and research on workforce development initiatives that delivers skills training to single working poor mothers via the Internet. Dr. Gatta's interest in service work and workers stems from her many years working in retail and restaurants during college and graduate school. Those experiences instilled a keen understanding of the hard work service workers perform daily.

Kay Gilbert is a senior lecturer in the Department of Human Resource Management at Strathclyde University. Kay has a keen interest in enabling fairness and equity in the workplace and her main areas of research are equal pay and job evaluation. Kay is ACAS designated Independent Expert under the Equal Pay Act Amendment Regulations.

Carolin Grampp lectures and researches in a variety of subjects in management at University College Dublin. Originally from Germany, but living and working in Ireland for the past ten years, her main interest is in knowledge, learning and social processes in organisations. She is currently undertaking a PhD having realised that this is work that matters to her, and to those who she researches and works with. Carolin was conference administrator for Work Matters ILPC 2008.

Christine Guégnard is a senior research sociologist at the French Center for Research on Education, Training and Employment, and at the Institute on Sociology and Economics of Education (Iredu), associated with the French National Center for Scientific Research (CNRS) and the University of Burgundy, Dijon. Her research activities focused on the training and employment relationships, especially the youth transition, the tensions on the labour market, and the policies of education or employment in terms of equal opportunities, related to gender.

Ian Hampson works in the School of Organisation and Management, in the Australian School of Business at UNSW. His teaching and research interests include the political economy of skill, training and learning. Dr. Hampson has worked for the past three years on a project funded by the New Zealand Government to detect 'invisible' service work skills, and has published on work organisation and training policy.

Benjamin Hopkins is a doctoral student in the Industrial Relations Research Unit, University of Warwick. Having read Economics and Management at St Hugh's College, Oxford he worked for Cadbury Schweppes (which does not form the case study featured in this book), spending time at the company's factories in both Bournville and Sheffield. Following this, he worked for BBC News in London before completing an MA in Industrial Relations at Warwick. His doctoral research investigates the use of short-term work in low skill jobs in food manufacturing in the UK. As well as the chocolate factory described in this book he has spent time at a ready meals factory, a spice factory, a turkey factory and a brewery.

Maeve Houlihan is a senior lecturer in Organisational Behaviour and Work at UCD Business Schools, University College Dublin. Her research and publications focus on contemporary working lives, management practices, and their links with society. She recently co-edited *Searching for the Human in Human Resource Management* with Sharon Bolton (2007). Prior to life as an academic, Maeve has worked as a personnel officer, call centre agent, receptionist, kitchen orderly and office cleaner. Although she sometimes wonders, she is lucky to have been able to mostly find truth in her father Michael's maxim that if you love what you do, you'll never work a day in your life.

Scott A. Hurrell has recently taken up a post as lecturer in Human Resource Management at Aston Business School Work and Organisational Psychology Group, having previously worked as a researcher for the Scottish Centre for Employment Research at Strathclyde Business School, Dept of HRM. His research interests include skills and work organisation, recruitment and selection, low wage work and the interactive service sector and he has published in academic and practitioner journals including the *Human Resource Management Journal*. Work matters to Scott as he is finally in the real (well academic!) world after what seemed like a lifetime as a student. Scott greatly values being in a job which can add insight to, and hopefully improve, the working lives of others.

Anne Junor works in the School of Organisation and Management (The University of New South Wales) and is deputy director of the Industrial Relations Research Centre and an editor of *The Economic and Labour Relations*

Review. She has been a school and university teacher, union official and unpaid care-giver. Her research fields include skill, precarious employment, public sector management, diversity and pay equity.

Paul McGrath lectures in organisation behaviour and organisation theory at the UCD School of Business, University College Dublin. His current research interests include multiple organisational identities, and the dynamics and historical emergence of cellular organisational design. His research on monastic communities and knowledge intensive firms has been published in journals including *Organization and Management History*. He is curious about the frequently unrealised positive potential between the needs of workers wanting to do their jobs, and the numerous organisational artefacts and control systems imposed on their activities.

Sylvie-Anne Mériot is a senior research sociologist at the Céreq, the French Center for Research on Education, Training and Employment, located in Marseilles. She has worked on several government projects, and has played an important role in several reforms especially in the French education system.

Elaine Moriarty is a post doctoral researcher on the Migrant Careers and Aspirations project at Trinity College Dublin where she also teaches research methodology and social policy on the MPhil in Ethnic and Racial Studies. Her teaching and research interests include migration, citizenship, labour markets, qualitative research methods, race and ethnicity and cultural studies. She has published articles on racism and citizenship in Ireland.

Kate Mulholland teaches Employment Relations at Bristol Business School, University of West England. She has previously taught Sociology at the Queen's University, Belfast, and has held research posts at Warwick Business School, University of Warwick, Royal Free Hospital, London and the Central Policy Unit, London. She has researched and published work on work organisation in the privatised utilities, entrepreneurialism, class gender and family politics, call centre employment, and presently employment relations in food distribution. Her book, *Class, Gender and the Family Business* (2003) was nominated for the BSA Philip Abrams Memorial Prize.

Kirsty Newsome is a senior lecturer in the department of Human Resource Management at the University of Strathclyde, Glasgow, UK. Her research, writing and teaching encompasses employee relations and industrial sociology. Her current research interests are in the area of changing inter-firm relations and labour process change in supply organisations.

Dennis Nickson is Professor of Service Work and Employment and Head of the Department of Human Resource Management, University of Strathclyde.

He researches and writes in the broad area of human resource management in the interactive service sector. He has published numerous articles, including in *Human Resource Management Journal, International Journal of Human Resource Management and Work, Employment and Society*. Sole and co-authored books include *Human Resource Management for the Hospitality and Tourism Industries* (2007) and *Looking Good, Sounding Right* (Industrial Society, 2001). Having spent six years working in a job he hated in the civil service, Dennis is aware of how lucky he is now to be working in a job he loves; and hopes his research can contribute to improving the work of others.

Kaye Robyn Ogle is a Senior Lecturer within the School of Nursing at Deakin University. She has worked within the health field in a variety of clinical, educational and administrative roles for over 25 years. Her research predominantly involves health services and health workforce issues, particularly experiences of managing and being managed.

Anna Pollert is Professor of the Sociology of Work at the Centre for Employment Studies Research at Bristol Business School, the University of the West of England. Prior to this, she was a professor at the Working Lives Research Institute, London Metropolitan University and Principal Research Fellow at the Industrial Relation Research Unit, University of Warwick. She has published widely in the areas of class, gender, workplace relations, worker representation and the transformation of the former 'Communist' countries of Central Eastern Europe to capitalism. Her books include *Girls, Wives, Factory Lives* (1981), *Farewell to Flexibility?* (1991) and *Transformation at Work in the New Market Economies of Central Eastern Europe* (1999). She is currently focusing her research on the experience of non-unionised, low paid workers.

James Richards is a Lecturer in Human Resource Management at Heriot-Watt University in Edinburgh. His research interests include the possibilities for employee expression through internet communication technologies, as well as the study of more conventional forms of organisational misbehaviour. He completed his Doctorate at University of Stirling and has published in Employee Relations and New Technology, Work and Employment.

Justyna Salamońska is a research student on the Migrant Careers and Aspirations project and a PhD candidate in the Department of Sociology, Trinity College Dublin. She has a BA in Philosophy and an MA in Sociology from the University of Warsaw and was also an Erasmus student at the University of Rome 'La Sapienza'. Her research interests include migration, mobility, labour markets, and the sociology of organisations.

Louise Simmons is an Associate Professor of Social Work at the University of Connecticut School of Social Work and Director of the University's Urban Semester Program. Her research interests and publications involve urban social and political movements, community organising, community-labour coalitions, welfare reform and urban policy issues. Dr. Simmons is the author of *Organizing in Hard Times: Labour and Neighbourhoods in Hartford* (1994) and editor of *Welfare, the Working Poor and Labour* (2004). She is an editor of the *Journal of Community Practice*. She has been an activist in civil rights, labour and community struggles in Hartford, Connecticut for over 35 years and served a term on the Hartford city council with a local third party in the early 1990s. She continues to be involved in struggles for rights of low wage and immigrant workers.

Paul Thompson is Professor of Organisational Analysis in the Department of Human Resource Management at the University of Strathclyde. Amongst his recent publications are A *Handbook of Work and Organization* for Oxford University Press (co-edited with Stephen Ackroyd, Pam Tolbert and Rose Batt, 2004) and a Fourth Edition of *Work Organizations* (with David McHugh). His research interests focus on skill and work organisation, control and resistance, organisational restructuring and changing political economy. He is Research Notes, Debates and Controversies Editor of Work, Employment and Society and an editor of the Palgrave Series – *Management, Work and Organization.*

Chris Warhurst is Professor of Labour Studies and Director of the Scottish Centre for Employment Research at the University of Strathclyde in Glasgow. He is also co-editor of the British Sociological Association journal *Work, Employment and Society*. His research and publications focus on labour process and labour market issues and developments. Current research examines aesthetic labour, knowledge work and union-led workplace learning. He has published numerous articles, including in Administrative Science Quarterly, *Journal of Organizational Behavior and Sociology*. Sole and co-authored and co-edited books include *Work Less, Live More?* (2008) *The Skills that Matter* (2004) and *Looking Good, Sounding Right* (2001). He regards the task of sociology as contributing not just to understanding but also the improvement of work and employment.

James Wickham is Jean Monnet Professor of European Labour Market Studies and Director of the Employment Research Centre in the Department of Sociology at Trinity College Dublin (TCD). He is principal investigator of the 'Migrant Careers and Aspirations' research project within the Trinity Immigration Initiative. His research interests focus on work in its social, technological and institutional context: employment and the European Social Model, transport and employment (especially business air travel), and trans-national careers of the highly skilled.

Work, Workplaces and Workers: The Contemporary Experience

Sharon C. Bolton and Maeve Houlihan

This book has a very simple ambition: to explore the matter of work and why work matters from the perspective of a range of workers engaged in different forms of work in a wide variety of workplaces. These accounts link their telling from the workplace to the globalised economy, with disconnected capitalism firmly in their sight. The many authors of this collection introduce us to voices from the supermarket floor, the factory floor, school rooms, taxi cabs, hotels, restaurants, care homes, public sector blogs, junior doctors on their rounds, and more. They are voices that tell of how we work today. They tell us of the systems and procedures and rules and regulations and bureaucratic structures. They tell us of the persistent growth of work routinisation. And yet they tell of flexibilisation – most particularly of the employment relationship – and of the personal consequences of casualisation. They tell us of intensifying management regimes, new technologies and changing, and often unmet, expectations and at the same time they tell of passion for and joy in work. They tell us of the story of the individual – and as structure rears its head – of choices and lack of choices, of a desire to work as a means to an end, and for a whole host of other reasons too. These are accounts that determinedly bring forth the voice and humanity of people in relation to their work experiences. The threads that tie these diverse narratives together present a picture of commonality across all sorts of regimes around one central point – the increasing pressure of the workplace under vigorous capitalism.

Why work matters

Whilst we write about work matters the irony is not lost that as we study we are also our own subjects. Sat in an airport lounge, laptops balanced on knees, working in the short hour between clearing Immigration and flying to an American conference, we find ourselves in the unlikely position, given we are editing a book entitled work matters, of looking at each other and wondering if, and why, work matters to the extent it appears to do. Questions borne of fatigue and frustration summed up in the challenge 'whose idea was this book anyway?' Lacking immediate inspiration we sit and stare around us and observe the actions and interactions of passengers and airport workers. The shuffling cleaner who with stooped shoulders drags her bucket along the floor. The officious, and somewhat overenthusiastic, immigration officer. The 'suit' sat opposite shouting orders into his mobile phone and another suit nearby also balancing a laptop on his knee.

The results of our musings are not very profound: we work and our work matters to us and it matters for others too. At its most basic work matters because in a market-based economy we need to sell our capacity to labour as a means to survival (even though, as many of the chapters to follow remind us, sometimes it barely fulfils that function). But casting our fatigue aside for a moment, there is more: work matters because it is rarely only that; it is about esteem and disrespect, status and subordination, opportunity and cost, commitment and alienation. If we listen to people talk about their work we are reminded that work and workplaces are fields of struggle where interests can both coincide and clash, and personhood is both attacked and maintained (Sayer, 2005: 41). And, perhaps most importantly, that work is a fundamental requirement of humanity but the capacity for its achievement essentially relies on factors external to the individual. Do they receive adequate pay? Are they involved in interesting work? Do they experience reasonable conditions? Have they security of tenure? Are they offered equality of opportunity? Thinking in terms of work matters recognises that work has both material and subjective dimensions rooted as it is in a moral economy (Sayer, 2005); a world where the *social* and the economic are immutably symbiotic and interdependent. Thus the experience of work relies on the material conditions of 'decent work' *and* the support of the human ties that generate respect and dignity (Bolton and Houlihan, 2007; Bolton, 2007). The economic world depends on social abilities to oil its wheels. This is very different than simply making the best of a bad job and generating a positive attitude to work, as some commentators would see it (Reeves, 2001; Knell, 2000). Rather, the economy depends on the full spectrum of social life – in all its messiness. In recognising that work matters, work becomes a political issue; a means of analysing the wellbeing of society through a telling lens.

So back to the question 'whose idea was this book?'. Actually we cannot lay claim to the idea at all. It is an idea generated by all of us who work, and the stories that we tell about it. Listening to these stories restores a sense of clarity. We believe in good work. Work that brings connection and fulfilment.

Work that fulfils potential. And we believe in people's capacity to derive joy from work. And yet also we are concerned that work can be miserable, toxic, soul destroying, inadequately rewarded, and at times dangerous. Examining closely these accounts of contemporary work, workplaces, and workers reveals a rich and varied picture of the ways in which these aspirations – these rights – are afforded, and the concerning degree to which they are under pressure.

As we settle into a new millennium, the question of whether work is getting better, or indeed, worse; whether we are improving in the act of organising work; and whether our needs and expectations as workers are changing, has never been more pertinent. Time perhaps to reflect on the evidence, as we turn now to each: *work, workplaces* and *workers*.

Work

If some things have changed but much has stayed the same then this is reflected in critiques of contemporary work that highlight the inequalities in access to well-paid work and safe and secure working conditions. Polly Toynbee's study of the working poor spans 30 years (1971, 2003) and highlights how structural inequalities have changed little over that period with vast numbers of people working for barely, if not less, than the minimum wage whilst carrying out work that should be socially valued but is not. Similarly Fran Abrams' (2002) account of living 'below the breadline' in the UK and Barbara Ehrenreich's experiences of low pay work in the US points out that often it is only the non-material rewards that make work bearable (2001). These accounts reflect ever present concerns about the general availability of 'good work' (Coats, 2007; Green, 2006; Moynagh and Worsley, 2005; Powell and Snellman, 2004; Sennett, 1998, 2003; Thompson, 2005). Concerns that are echoed worldwide with common themes emerging from all advanced and developing economies as people are feeling under pressure in today's world of work and reporting that work has grown more stressful for all categories of employees from senior managers to manual workers and most people saying that they are working more intensely and clocking in for more hours than in the recent past (Eurofound, 2007; Coats, 2007; Green, 2006; OECD, 2007).

And yet policy-makers continue to propose a unitarist vision of equality of opportunity in a high skill, high reward economy where there is a general conception of a radical break from the past with the introduction of new types of creative, technology and knowledge led work – work that is ideally presented as 'infomated': virtual, clean and value-adding. The upbeat theme is represented by the focus on the 'high road' of management which includes the development and utilisation of new skills and the increasing availability of 'good' work along with the move towards the utilisation of soft, tacit knowledge and even its long overdue recognition as a quantifiable skill (DTI, 2004; Coats, 2007; Westwood, 2002). While indeed higher skilled work is increasing in advanced economies (Ghose *et al.*, 2008), there appears to be little recognition that whilst some jobs – notably manufacturing and information processing – have moved from advanced to developing economies (thus triggering the notion of only high skill jobs remaining), a vast majority of 'routine' jobs remain, particularly those at the human interface: shelves still need stacking, noses wiping, tables clearing and wounds dressing. And flexibilisation is hitting these workers hard, most particularly lower-skilled workers, assigned to the margins with non-standard work arrangements, and less and less security (Ghose *et al.*, 2008). The continual pressure to push costs down an ever lengthening supply chain is wreaking its work, with large companies squeezing smaller companies into agreeing impossible contract terms which are then reflected in the pay and conditions of workers. And this is not simply a reality for the private sector, as the public sector too adopts the business model, creating its own internal markets. Healthcare, education, and state services each one by one have become marketised, in the process creating an army of contracts and agency workers, these institutions divorcing themselves ever more blindly from their embeddedness in moral economy.

Meanwhile, the jobs flowing from shifts towards services and 'new' forms of work are proving just as gruelling, monotonous, tightly controlled and poorly rewarded (Thompson, 2005). Empirical studies highlight the poor conditions of work in call centres, retail and hospitality; the emotional pressures front-line service workers face and the health risks involved in the new 'clean jobs' (Bolton and Houlihan, 2005; Boyd, 2003; Callaghan and Thompson, 2002; Houlihan, 2002; Taylor *et al.*, 2002, 2003). Nor can we say that 'dirty work' has disappeared. On the contrary, the growth in 'personnel services'[1] partially represents a new 'upstairs and downstairs' (GMB quoted in *Guardian*, 2005) where the cash rich but time poor contract out domestic work – cleaning, gardening, childcare – and a 21st century servant class emerges who regularly earn less than the minimum wage and have no employment rights or protection (Greg and Wandsworth, 2000; Philpot, 2000; The Work Foundation, 2005). This is also spawning a very much understated informal economy, and here too the most vulnerable members of society are to be found – particularly home workers and migrant workers employed on the fringes of legality.

Contemporary critical accounts of work offer a balance to the hyperbole of the Knowledge Economy rhetoric and question what the realities of work are for the majority of people (Ackroyd *et al.*, 2005; Baldry *et al.*, 2007). Whilst recognising that 'bad' work is unlikely to disappear (Coats, 2007; Philpot, 2000; Taylor, 2002) there is a call to ensure that policy makers and companies worldwide recognise what the ingredients of good work might be – a recipe that clearly reflects the ILO's definition of 'decent work' in its emphasis on equality of access, employee voice and just reward: (Coats, 2007; ILO, 2006; Moynagh and Worsley, 2005; Taylor, 2002; Westwood, 2002).

Whatever the approach, there is a growing consensus that at the present time 'good' work appears to be the preserve of those clearly defined as 'knowledge workers'; a privileged band involved in the professional, high tech and creative industries who fare well in the new economy, at least on the face of it enjoying continual opportunities for growth and development and increasing levels of pay, whilst the largest majority of the global workforce are subjected to lesser terms and conditions at the sharp end of the economy, in mundane, yet demanding, support and service occupations. While many of the occupations explored in this book bear the flat characterisation 'low-skilled', as the chapters amplify, this captures little of the level of dexterity, emotion work and not least, toleration, that is involved. Boxing off work as low skilled has persisted for too long because of the voicelessness of certain groups, and part of the work of meaningful research is to create a vocabulary and understanding that can tangibly change this.

And of course it is vital to put all this in context: Ghose *et al.*'s latest report (2008) *The Global Employment Challenge*, reminds us that 73 percent of the world's workers live in developing economies, coping with underemployment and mere survival, that the world's labour force is growing rapidly, and mainly in developing economies, and that there is a serious world crisis of insufficient productive jobs. So while our concentration here is on issues pertaining to advanced economies where the vast majority of the world's capital and 'skills' are located, it is shameful to note that here, as worldwide, the first challenge remains providing economically sustaining work with the promise of decent work remaining lower down the agenda.

The conclusions? While the distribution, technologies and locations of work may be changing, the nature of work that is to be done in our world, remains largely unchanged. There is a deficit of decent work, and fundamentally this revolves around core issues of pay, equity, security and dignity. Critical sectors such as education, health and care work are vastly undervalued, and while the volume of high skilled or knowledge work is increasing, it too may be driving a schism whereby lower skilled work is yet further marginalised.

Workplaces

So are we getting better at organising work and the way in which we manage it? For some 30 years or more the debate on changing organisational forms has been dominated by the argument of whether we have moved into a post-bureaucratic, post-Fordist world as new forms of creative and service-orientated labour takes over from routinised manufacturing type jobs. At the most basic, post-bureaucratic organisational forms are defined in opposition to modernism which is identified as resting on a rationalistic, positivistic, technocratic knowledge base that seeks efficiency through standardisation, order and control. If organisations are the form of our modern condition, one cannot help but note that this is frequently represented less as an opportune or benevolent phenomenon but more as something which is constraining and repressive. Organisations 'do' (define) us, rather than we 'doing' (defining) organisation.

On the other hand it is proposed that we now have networked, non-hierarchical, flexible and learning organisations, something celebrated as offering cleaner, safer and more supportive, even liberating working environments (Reeves, 2001; Bickham, 1995). All of which entails new management practices often presented as high commitment human resource management, involving mechanisms of employee empowerment and offering opportunity and development within a learning environment. The basic message being that employees are to be treated as valuable resources rather than merely commodities – as assets, as human capital. This is clearly demonstrated with the advent of so called exemplary organisations such as Google, Microsoft, Starbucks, Goldman Sacks and the many more that top the world wide 'Best Places to Work' lists (Great Places to Work Institute, 2008).

However, what ample empirical studies tell us is that the radical change envisaged (from old to new, from control to liberated, from modern to post, from structured to flexible) has not actually materialised: organisations are still rule bound and demanding, and most usually rely on a fundamental division of labour and spoils. Forms of control may be more subtle, bound up in psychological contracts and modes of comportment, but they are control nevertheless. Despite some changes, there is not a lot of evidence to support the image of the 'new' workplace. Where are the 'winning teams', the managers as coach, the empowered workplaces, where is the work-life balance?

Instead, when some employers talk about flexibility and new forms of work organisation they mean the freedom to hire and fire workers, employ them on a variety of contractual terms and require them to work antisocial hours (Moynagh and Worsley, 2005). Rather than working less, employees report working longer and longer hours with intensified work routines resulting in over 25 percent of men and women across Europe reporting that their job left them feeling exhausted most or all of the time (Eurofound, 2007). In effect, claims of empowerment, learning and development, teamwork and flexibility are slotted into workplaces where little has changed: jobs are not redesigned, work is not reorganised, and attempts to work flexibly are more about organisational efficiency than personal benefit or opportunity. And most fundamentally, as this volume attests, there is strong evidence that too many businesses are competing on the basis of the low road: low pay, low skills, yet a continual drive for greater productivity and flexibility, with the burden borne by employees.

This is a formula for increasingly desperate measures of control rather than empowerment, as companies struggle to harness and direct their efforts to compete, and face few real choices. As a result workplaces more generally are experiencing a decline in voice mechanisms (for both participation and protection) and trade union influence with an associated sharp increase in pay inequalities, work intensity and insecurity (Kelly, 2005). The individualisation of employment relations continues apace, notwithstanding variation in collective bargaining and partnership strategies cross-nationally. The absence of strong employee side control mechanisms leaves workers increasingly vulnerable to flexibilisation and work intensification, and all the tariffs they pay to support the new economy. And yet, in some sense, new voice forums are emerging, with the democratisation of information and access presented by technology and networks, as Ellis and Richards will describe later in this book.

And what of community, and the notion of the workplace as the site of such a significant portion of our life and experience? The workplace is still structured in traditional ways, though greater numbers are working flexibly in the form of agency, off site, and off shore work. New technologies have both enabled and constrained occupational community. Long hours and the requirement for dual income has put pressure on home life, and most fundamentally, communities, creating an unprecedented level of fragmentation of social life. The impact of work is shown, throughout the chapters that follow, to bear consequences not only for the individuals who work, but for those they care for, drive, heal, feed and more. Quality of work and workplace, has implications for itself, for those that do it, and for the society we live in. It inscribes the quality of our care, our goods and services, our livelihood.

Workers

What does all this mean for workers in this brave new world of work? A range of available survey data that asks people about their experiences of work (BHPS, 2004; Eurofound, 2004, 2007; OECD, 2007; Ghose et al., 2008) endorses existing accounts of growing divisions in the global economy (Taylor, 2002; Thompson, 2005). For instance there appear to be two extremes in the experiences of different occupational groups – those clearly thriving at the top end of the labour market and those merely existing at the bottom. Data from the UK British Household Panel Survey (BHPS, 2004) tells us that 'personal service' occupations (very often relegated to the informal economy) are least likely to experience security in work, promotion opportunities, flexible work practices and trade union membership; 'sales and customer service' occupations are least likely to feel that a fulfilling job is more important than money or to be a member of a trade union; and 'elementary occupations' are least likely to enjoy promotion or training opportunities, autonomy over working hours, feel secure about work, be employed on a permanent contract and earn adequate pay. On the other hand, 'professional occupations' are the most likely to receive adequate pay, company pension, trade union membership, promotion opportunities, work-related training and feel that a fulfilling job is more important than money, but least likely to have a permanent contract and more likely to work unpaid overtime; and 'managers and senior officials' are most likely to have a permanent contract, be satisfied with job security, enjoy promotion opportunities and autonomy over working hours (BHPS, 2004). This last group are also likely to attract typical FTSE company CEO salaries of around £2.5m, representing the huge gap between those at the top of the labour market and those at the bottom.

Less surprising, amongst claims from Trade Unions that employees in UK supermarkets would have to work 94 hours a week to earn the national average wage, is that 'elementary occupations' and 'sales and customer services' are the least satisfied with their work (Haurant, 2004). However, as we suspect, economic reward is not the only reason work matters. Work involved in personnel services, which is mostly made up of different types of 'care work', offers opportunities for meaning that are clearly missing from the mainly 'dirty work' done by cleaners (Cottell, 2005; The Work Foundation, 2005; Tomlin, 2005; Toynbee, 2003), cold call telephone sales (Ronson, 2006) and front-line 'McJobs' (Lindsay and McQuaid, 2004), where the biggest complaint from workers, other than low pay and unsociable hours, is the lack of respect from either employers or the public despite feelings of pride in the work itself (BHPS, 2004).

Similar polar messages emerge from European data. Notably, gender emerges as a key dimension shaping very different experiences of men and women (BHPS, 2004; Eurofound, 2004, 2007): men are least likely to feel satisfied with work, or job security and least likely to work reasonable hours but enjoy adequate pay, promotion opportunities, trade union membership and be a member of a company pension; whilst women are most likely to feel satisfied with work and job security and work reasonable hours but least likely to enjoy promotion opportunities, earn adequate pay, be a member of a company pension or be a member of a trade union.

Interestingly, despite the many bleak accounts of work it is extraordinary that, when asked to take a global perspective of their working lives, respondents express a high level of satisfaction (BHPS, 2004; Eurofound, 2004, 2007). It is especially striking that women, so clearly disadvantaged with regard to pay, benefits and opportunities for development, report significantly higher levels of satisfaction than men. Women's still recent ascendance to full participation in the labour market would seem to be influencing job satisfaction figures. Some commentators (Edwards and Burkitt, 2001) claim that high rates of job satisfaction are related to low rates of expectation. Highly paid workers (and men who dominate these positions) fully expect an array of benefits including interesting and meaningful work, whilst those who are lesser paid (substantially women) would like all of these things but rarely expect to receive them – and therefore report that they are satisfied with what they already have. A sad indictment of the divided labour market that is further supported by BHPS data which shows that 'personal services' workers, which we might also read as 'women' as they constitute 86.2 percent of this occupational group, are significantly more satisfied with their work than other groups. Despite low pay and poor working conditions this occupational group is continually reported as deriving meaning from their work via caring labour (Bolton, 2001, 2005; Rainbird, 2007; Stacey, 2005). It would seem that the will to care carries a price. It is no accident that it is those who are prepared to sacrifice material expectation, or those who have little choice in the work they do, are the ones paying it. This volume pays particular attention to women at work, women's work and where they are working, and from housekeeping to deft factory work, and from classroom assistance to the supermarket floor; the presence of an army of middle aged women with families, earning less than a fully viable economic wage, and yet keeping the wheels of industry going, is apparent. What is just as relevant is how men are working, and where they are not.

Survey data captures the experiences of those in formal employment but what of those who work on the margins of the employment system, and in fact society? Apart from sensationalist reports of migrant workers draining national resources and tragic accounts of the deaths of migrant workers such as the UK's Morecambe Bay Cockle Pickers, we are only beginning to track the experiences of this group of workers who are paid less than the minimum wage and are afforded no employment rights. A group of workers referred to as the Cinderella of the labour market due to their invisibility (Cooper and May, 2007) and the difficulties in capturing their experiences of work. Too little is known about these, and all workers, trapped in the informal economy. The experience of migrant workers, and the realities of increasingly multicultural workplaces unsurprisingly emerges several times in this volume. We hear from migrants speaking pragmatically about their hopes and intentions. And we hear from workplaces defined by their multiculturalism. Sometimes such accounts are littered with the ugly image of 'us and them', mapping racial division as workers struggle to claim some form of control over the increasingly tight spaces they occupy.

Workers today are also experiencing significantly the effects of casualisation. Statistics on contingent work are fragmented, making it notoriously difficult to paint a definitive picture. However it is clear that the use of agency, contract and temporary employment is widespread in Europe (EIRO, 2005) and the United States (Kalleberg, 2000; Smith, 2001) and affects a significant proportion of the working population. The latest figures for Europe indicate that approximately 23 percent of employees have some type of non-standard employment contract (primarily a fixed-term contract), and that for the most recent entrants to the labour market (those who have spent less than four years in paid employment), the proportion of non-standard contracts reaches almost 50 percent (Eurofound, 2007). The implications speak for themselves, with many younger workers facing an unprecedented level of insecurity, urged simply to grasp the opportunities and self-realise (Peters, 1999; Crainer and Dearlove, 2000; Knell, 2000), notwithstanding the potentially detrimental effects of precarious and low-quality contingent work (McGovern *et al.*, 2004; Kalleberg, 2000) and the challenges contingent workers face in attempts to navigate 'the great divide' of risk and opportunity (Smith, 2001). Many of the chapters to follow in this book give voice to the lived reality of non-standard work.

In summary, the picture for today's workers is one of divisions: gender, occupational skill levels, race and migrant status, full time and contingent workers. The complex findings emerging around job satisfaction reveal, it would seem, only part of the story. The movement of labour worldwide adds another dimension to that story, with tensions among all workers heightened by individualisation.

Work matters: making sense of contemporary work

What this brief review of contemporary work, workplaces and workers tells us is that work does indeed matter but the reasons why and for whom are complex. Survey data reveals patterns nationally and internationally with many recurring themes and many dilemmas not addressed by the rhetoric of overwhelming opportunities under global capitalism. It tells us of patterns of supply chains that contract out work to armies of women and migrant labour who are among the lowest-paid and most exploited members of the workforce. It tells us of growing disparities in income and continued inequalities in access to decent work. It tells us people feel both insecure and yet imprisoned by their work resulting in high levels of stress and normlessness. And, yet, paradoxically it also tells us that people, on the whole, express high levels of satisfaction with their work, revealing that survey data can only tell us so much. What is missing are nuanced accounts of why work matters. What are the experiences of the people who work at the bottom of the supply chain, who provide support and care to others, who wait tables relying on customers' benevolence to make up meagre wages, who work alone driven by new technology, who leave their home countries in the hope of a better life only to take work far below their skill levels? The chapters in this book provide many missing pieces of this picture. They present contextual data but also insightful accounts of what it is to work in these settings, what are the experiences and consequences. They put work firmly in its place – as a social as well as economic reality. They air voices usually too little heard. They open our eyes wide to work matters.

Moving from the macro to the micro, each of the chapters of this volume has something to say about the nature of contemporary work, and the sense that is to be made of it. In Chapter 2, David Coats offers a landscape account of today's workplaces, drawing on UK and European datasets to ask is today's work getting better? – and articulates a refreshingly frank account of why we should care. While the chapter reflects on the competing portraits of sunlit uplands (skilled, knowledgeable workers with all boats rising in a market economy bridged by good practice HRM), and the 'bleak house' view of a race to the bottom, David is not prepared to let us wallow in such schismic metaphors and instead takes us through the evidence: questioning assumptions and interpretations to arrive at a picture of significant variation in job quality across Europe, and a level of informed optimism regarding future prospects; concluding that we need a more subtle understanding of the implications of liberal, corporatist or inclusive national employment regimes, and a stronger engagement with the political, social and economic choices we are making.

For Chapter 3, Marcia Bok and Louise Simmons take us across the Atlantic, and in their review of the experiences of low wage workers in the US – the very poor, the working poor, the near poor, and those in medium-level skill jobs, quickly becoming 'disposable', it is clear that very little is getting better about this particular world of work. Their account is a compelling confrontation of the realities of life under vigorous capitalism, reinforcing how economic polarisation, the result of three decades of neoliberal policy, robs so many of the chance of decent work and a realistic livelihood. Marcia and Louise weave an account of current US labour statistics with the individual voices of a cross-section of American citizens struggling at the margins. Their chapter sets out the impetus for much needed strategies for change that involve putting the needs of the individual, and most particularly the vulnerable worker, at their heart. However, the vulnerable worker retains, at least, a right to act. In Chapter 4, Anna Pollert takes up this story by reporting on a particular category of vulnerable worker in the UK – the non-unionised employee experiencing problems at work. Anna's account details the playing out of employment problems such as being unpaid, victimised or unfairly dismissed, and how such incidences cut across workplaces from small to large MNCs, where in many cases, Human Resource departments collude against the individual. The study shines particular light on a selection of workers who sought to address such problems utilising the help of Citizen Advice Centres (which, significantly, they were more likely to do than to go to a union). Here the positive story turns bleak, with almost half of respondents finding no resolution to their problem, in many cases due to insufficient CAB resources. The insights from this research are, however, heartening in one sense, reflected by the majority who have sought to address their situations and, indeed, the surprising proportion who took joint action with other employees. Anna's research raises questions about the adequacy of formal (internal) grievance procedures and the impartiality that is possible regarding them.

Introducing a strong theme of the volume, James Wickham, Elaine Moriarty, Alicja Bobek and Justyna Salamońska turn to the issue of migrant workers in Chapter 5, where they investigate the choices and motivations informing young Polish workers who have moved to Ireland and work in the hospitality sector. Their research displays how many respondents had well articulated, conscious and principally financial reasons for making this move; although the point is not lost that such reasoning is fundamentally driven by lack of equivalent earning opportunities at home, and is demonstrably associated with underemployment relative to skill level. James and colleagues' account also fleshes out some less than best practice behaviours of employers in a 'gold rush' economy, including rampant casualisation, 'on call' hours and low pay. While lending partial credence to a mutual choice view their accounts of the realities of casualised work suggests that for many, these conditions are less a matter of advantage than of toleration and, their analysis suggests that after the 'gold rush' ends much will change.

The casualisation of the hospitality sector is explored in a different light by Christine Guégnard and Sylvie-Anne Mériot in Chapter 6, through their discussion of the experiences of hotel housekeepers in France. Although implicitly acknowledging the elements of quality employment regime in France mapped by David Coats, the authors draw our line of sight to a definite secondary labour market: hotels and housekeeping. The low-paid and (not for the last time in this volume) female characterisation of this sector is epitomised in the job of housekeeper or room attendant, and the voices of several in this chapter articulate with compelling acuity, the challenges of their work. Christine and Sylvie-Anne chart the effect of hotel ownership structure and strategy on employment practices, and observe islands of high-road practice that in some ways provide avenues of change, which more paradoxically perhaps, further isolate those working for the low-road majority. And so the account makes clear how structural characteristics and industry conditions set in train the continued evidence of precarious employment contracts and low wages which combined, it would seem, leave housekeepers very little traction to 'escape their professional destiny'. Staying in the hospitality sector, but this time in the USA, for Chapter 7, Mary Gatta takes us through the 'ubiquitous and invisible' daily grind of life as a restaurant server. Wait staff are a growing workforce worldwide, and as Mary reminds us, represent one occupation that can never be outsourced. In the American context in particular, low-wages and tipping are key dimensions of this story, but through this ethnographic account of life on the restaurant floor, we also learn more about the physicality of the job, its emotional content, and its multidimensionality. This narrative account of working a shift in the tightly controlled and routinised environment of a managed chain of restaurants draws the reader into the world of those who serve us our food and speaks volumes about agency and pride in work, and the ways in which restaurant servers, though under pressure, shape their world, all the while skilfully 'balancing trays and smiles'.

Chapter 8 turns to a rather different but equally traditional workplace, as Benjamin Hopkins takes us on a tour of the contemporary English chocolate factory. What he finds there is an indication of little advance from Taylorist assembly line organisation and deskilled work. And yet what has changed is employment relations, with heightened levels of multiethnicity, and multiple employment forms (agency, contract, temporary and part-time) co-existing in a state of unsurprising antipathy. The case of ChocCo is an important, if uncomfortable, opportunity to witness the reality of this experience through the eyes of its participants: the relationships, and relationship breakdowns between routinised workers from home and abroad, and tellingly, to find this road no easier for their supervisors and managers. This field story points to deepening fragmentation and distrust not only between employers and employees, but among and within employees.

In Chapter 9, Kirsty Newsome, Paul Thompson and Johanna Commander take us to an old yet new realm of factory work: food processing companies at the end of supermarket supply chains. Though little thought might be given to the work behind those shiny bags of lettuce, neatly prepared vegetable trays and ready meals that now populate our shopping bags, reading this chapter brings the reality of that hidden, forgotten world firmly into consciousness. Their account captures employee perceptions of and responses to working within varied but, ultimately, tightly controlled factory regimes. However, this account begs a question of who is in control, as the 'seemingly insatiable customer', the supermarkets that drive production targets (revised on a daily basis) and set the performance standards and sanctions, leave the managers and owners, and most particularly the workers, of these factories substantially powerless in setting the agenda. Moving on from well-established accounts, Kirsty and her colleagues ask if resistance is an insufficient framework for analysing the possibilities for engagement in such contexts and explore the concept of dignity at work as an alternative path. While the denial of dignity is, to paraphrase the authors, unlikely to be a major strategic goal of management, it is undoubtedly an operational framework which enables distinction of good work from bad. It is the external determination of employee 'hyper-flexibility' that leads the authors to conclude that ensuring dignity at work is substantially beyond management control. Kate Mulholland steps to the other side of the supermarket supply chain in Chapter 10, in her tale of working life as a shelf stacker or 'replenishment assistant'. Here we find that the pressures experienced at the production end of supermarket supply are mirrored on the retail floor, with employees at both ends paying the price. Kate's account is shaped by the introduction of one of many management efficiency tools: just-in-time systems, and the chapter bears testament to the fallibility of such systems and indeed to employees' avenues of resistance. It is a strong account of the frustrations unleashed on the journey to a net result of increased individualisation and direct control.

Moving to the realm of public sector social and community work for Chapter 11, Chris Warhurst, Scott Hurrell, Kay Gilbert, Dennis Nickson, Johanna Commander and Isobel Calder explore the role of classroom assistants working in Scottish primary schools. Their account reveals that in many senses, classroom assistants (who are mainly female, and mothers) are now doing many duties previously held by teachers, yet without due recognition or reward. Interviews with the classroom assistants display how they are attached to their role and to the children they support but are acutely aware of the under-valuation of what they do and they themselves link this to their life role as being 'just mothers really'. The authors compellingly explore the nature of classroom assistants' and wider society's acceptance of the role as commanding a 'second salary' and as offering convenient working hours as though this is sufficient reward, despite the upskilling and role stretch so firmly illustrated. Chris and colleagues question this acceptance bemoaning the lack of priority given to key social roles and displaying how such important work is patently undervalued as 'women's work'. Staying with care-related work, in Chapter 12, Anne Junor, Ian Hampson and Kaye Robyn Ogle take us to another 'unseen but everywhere' occupation in their examination of care and support work in New Zealand and Australia. Their recently completed sector spanning study confronts the poorly valued nature of care and support skills head on and has led them to attempt to create a vocabulary and taxonomy around care and support related skills. In this chapter, the authors concentrate on one group from within their larger study; taking us right to the heart of eight care assistants' daily lives with vivid accounts that not only give a deep insight into the nature and challenge of this unseen work, but also show just how clearly care and support workers themselves articulate what it is that they do. The ensuing taxonomy seeks to move beyond loose or 'tick-box' understandings, and firmly questions the reductionism of 'soft skills'. Continuing the healthcare theme, Chapter 13 explores what is it like to 'become' a doctor? Carol Boyd-Quinn shares this experience with us in a vivid and merciless ethnographic account of life as a junior doctor. The demanding physical and intellectual challenges and the relentless work intensity resonating from this account will come as little surprise to readers (and yet, our seeming acceptance of this must also be questioned). In addition, however, the chapter imparts frank and moving insights to the underwritten emotional burden of this work, and what Carol tellingly describes as the 'emotional debt' involved. The author conceptualises an emotional bank account, that may or may not have the credit needed from broader life experiences, personal traits and social and structural context; and shows how these resources are drawn by the exacting nature of emotional spending encountered in medical work. Carol goes on to draw out the implications of emotional debt both organisationally and personally though a series of compelling personal and researched accounts.

Chapter 14 changes context substantially, as Carolin Grampp, Maeve Houlihan and Paul McGrath introduce us to the culture, relationships and changing contexts of taxi work, with a case study of the introduction of GPS technology to an Irish taxi firm. Their account charts the individualistic and isolated character of taxi work, and despite this, the formal and informal means by which drivers forge and navigate an occupational community. The authors explore the paradox of these drivers' sole trader status, and yet their dependence on taxi companies, and how in this case, the dual locational and control properties of GPS technologies have subtly transformed relationships between drivers and the firm. The story of these developments illustrates much about the nature of taxi work, but also, about technology and control. What is interesting about this account is the relative lack of resistance these changes have met among drivers, and what this may say about relationships between agents and contractors, and about the dynamics of power and powerlessness.

But lest we fear it, employees are not silent on any of the issues raised in these accounts. With technology as a continuing theme, our final chapter explores the emerging phenomenon of work blogging, what it means and what it does. The interactive capacity of the internet has created a stunningly accessible medium for individuals to directly voice their realities, not least in relation to their work. Vaughan Ellis and James Richards offer a compelling snapshot of just how dynamically this medium is used to make hidden worlds of work publicly visible and understood, in their exploration of the motivations and practices of work bloggers within the UK public sector. Through their eyes, we learn the ways in which many workers are choosing to voice their experiences of work: at times to create, at times to connect, and indeed, at times to correct. Vaughan and James, through in-depth (and online) dialogue with nine active bloggers, get under the skin of this activity and push past easy assumptions about blogs as 'mere' forums for venting, complaining, exposing or resisting corporate ideology, under the canvas of anonymity. The authors build a nuanced understanding of its uses, behind which, we get a telling glimpse of the degree to which, echoing one theme of this volume, work matters in peoples' lives. From a research methods perspective, Vaughan and James also usefully examine the opportunities and issues relating to work blogging as a means of accessing direct workplace accounts, and discuss online methods of research more generally. In doing so, they signpost emergent dimensions of research practice as yet not well appreciated, and assuredly set to expand.

All in all, we hope you fill find that these chapters tell a diverse but thought provoking set of stories from the contemporary workplace and sign-post perennial and emerging issues that *matter*, not just as research practice or an expanding base of understanding the world of work, but matter to individuals, to workers all across the world, as their lived reality.

Work really does matter

The assembled stories from the field give us an opportunity to consider what work means to people, how it is experienced, the key trends that are shaping the experience of work, and the relationship between work and society. They make it possible to dialogue with management practice and contemporary rhetoric, to probe the degree to which rhetoric is meeting reality.

The stories seem to point, yet again, to the urgent need for better manage-ment. And yet, they also highlight the ways in which managers in so many ways are constrained, not free to act in the interests of employees as they might wish to. And when and where they do act, their actions are so often inadequate. As Sennett (2006) has argued; it is not so much the effects of globalisation *per se*, but their consequences for daily life. For instance, the ways in which the constant movement of managers and organisational forms leads to the disablement of human relating in the workplace leaving so many workers without a sense of *witness* in their work, creating a systemic sense of perceived lack of fair play.

This being true, there remains a series of choices, personal, organisational, social and political. Many of these accounts cross all four boundaries, as we see the palpable links between personal choice and social consequences, between social organising and organisational practice, between organisational choice and social dynamics, and between political choice and organisational actions – to take but some examples. What is also clear is the direct link between our choice as consumer and our experience as worker and one is forced to reflect whether in the future it is consumer power rather than voting power which has the greatest prospect of affecting change. That is however, not to let any of the institutions off the hook. As David Coats puts it in Chapter 2, the job is both making the cake bigger, *and* ensuring a fair distribution. Work matters enough for this to be our most vital organisational, social and political policy objective and our personal practice.

Notes

1 According to National Statistics-Standard Occupational Classification (NSOC) 'Care work', i.e. childcare and healthcare assistant are categorised as 'personnel services' and cleaning as 'elementary occupations'. http://www.statistics. gov.uk/methods_quality/soc/structure.asp.

REFERENCES

Ackroyd, S., Batt, R., Thompson, P. and Tolbert, P. (2005) *The Oxford Handbook of Work and Organisation*, Oxford: Oxford University Press.

Bickham, W. (1995) *Liberating the Human Spirit in the Workplace*, New York: McGraw Hill.

Bolton, S. (2001) 'Changing Faces: Nurses as Emotional Jugglers', *Sociology of Health and Illness*, 23(1): 85–100.

Bolton, S. (2005) *Emotion Management in the Workplace*, London: Palgrave.

Bolton, S. (2007) *Dimensions of Dignity at Work*, London: Butterworth Heineman.

Bolton, S. C. and Houlihan, M. (2005) 'The (Mis) Representation of Customer Service', *Work, Employment and Society*, 19(4): 685–703.

Bolton, S. and Houlihan, M. (2007) *Searching for the Human in Human Resource Management: Theory, Practice and Workplace Contexts*, London: Palgrave Macmillan.

Boyd, C. (2003) *Human Resource Management and Occupational Health*, London: Routledge.

British Household Panel Survey (2004) *Waves 13, 2004*, accessed from the UK Data Archive www.data-archive.ac.uk.

Baldry, C., Bain, P., Taylor, P., Hyman, J., Scholarios, D., Marks, A., Watson, A., Gilbert, K., Gall, G. and Bunzel, D. (2007) *The Meaning of Work in the New Economy*, Basingstoke: Palgrave Macmillan.

Callaghan, G. and Thompson, P. (2002) 'We Recruit Attitude: The Selection and Shaping of Routine Call Centre Labour', *Journal of Management Studies*, 39(2): 233–54.

▶

▶

Coats, D. (2007) Respect at Work: Just how good are British workplaces? In Bolton, S. (ed.) *Dimensions of Dignity at Work*, London: Butterworth Heinemann.

Cooper, N. and May, C. (2007) 'The informal economy and dignified work, in Bolton, S. (ed.) *Dimensions of Dignity at Work*, London: Elsevier, pp. 99–105.

Cottell, C. (2005) 'It's time rich city firms cleaned up their act', *The Guardian*, May 7, http://www.guardian.co.uk/money/2005/may/07/workandcareers.jobsandmoney.

Crainer, S. and Dearlove, D. (2000) *Generation Entrepreneur: Shape Today's Business Reality, Create Tomorrow's Wealth, Do Your Own Thing*, London: Financial Times Publications.

DTI (Department of Trade and Industry) (2004) *Five Year Programme: Creating Wealth from Knowledge*, London: Department of Trade and Industry.

Edwards, L. and Burkitt, N. (2001) 'Wanting more from work? Expectations and aspirations of people in low- and middle-paid jobs', *Labour Market Trends*, 109(7): 375–9.

Ehrenreich, B. (2001) *Nickel and Dimed: Undercover in Low-Wage USA*, London: Granta Books.

EIRO (2005) 'Temporary agency work in an enlarged European Union: Final Questionnaire', *European Industrial Relations Observatory*, www.eurofound.europa.eu, accessed July 2008.

Eurofound (2004) *Quality of Life in Europe: First European Quality of Working Life Survey*, www.eurofound.europa.eu/pubdocs/2004, accessed July 2008.

Eurofound (2007) *Fourth European Working Conditions Survey*, European Foundation for the Improvement of Living and Working Conditions, www.eurofound.europa.eu, accessed July 2008.

Fran Abrams (2002) *Living Below the Breadline: Living Below the Minimum Wage*, London: Profile Books.

Ghose, A. K., Majid, N. and Ernst, C. (2008) *The Global Employment Challenge*, Geneva: International Labour Organisation.

Great Places to Work Institute (2008) Best Companies to Work For Lists: Europe, USA, http://www.greatplacetowork.com, accessed July 2008.

Green, F. (2006) *Demanding Work: The Paradox of Job Quality in the Affluent Society*, Princeton, NJ: Princeton University Press.

Gregg, P. and Wadsworth, J. (2000) 'Mind the Gap, Please: The Changing Nature of Entry Jobs in Britain', *Economica*, 67(268): 499–524.

Guardian, The (2005) *Report reveals Upstairs-Downstairs Workforce*, http://www.guardian.co.uk/business/2005/may/23/executivesalaries.executivepay, accessed July 2008.

Haurant, S. (2004) 'Average wage "out of reach" for supermarket workers', *Guardian*, Monday May 17, 2004 www.guardianonline.co.uk.

Houlihan, M. (2002) 'Tensions and Variations in Call Centre Management Strategies', *Human Resource Management Journal*, 12(4): 67–86.

▶

▶

ILO (2006) The Decent Work Campaign: What is Decent Work?, Geneva: International Labour Organisation, www.ilo.org/public/english/decent.htm accessed July 2008.

Kalleberg, A. (2000) 'Non-standard employment relations: Part-time, temporary and contract work', *Annual Review of Sociology*, 26: 341–65.

Kelly, J. (2005) 'Labour Movements and Mobilisation', in Ackroyd, S., Batt, R., Thompson, P. and Tolbert, P. (eds) *The Oxford Handbook of Work and Organisation*, pp. 283–305. Oxford: Oxford University Press.

Knell, J. (2000) *Most Wanted: The Quiet Birth of the Free Worker*, London: Industrial Society.

Lindsay, C. and McQuaid, R. W. (2004) 'Avoiding the 'McJobs': unemployed job seekers and attitudes to service work', *Work, Employment and Society*, 18(2): 297–319.

McGovern, P., Smeaton, D. and Hill, S. (2004) 'Bad jobs in Britain: Non-standard Employment and Job Quality', *Work and Occupations*, 31(2): 225–49.

Moynagh, M. and Worsley, R. (2005) *Working in the twenty-first century*, ESRC and the Tomorrow Project.

OECD (2007) *Babies and Bosses Reconciling Work and Family Life: A Synthesis of Findings for OECD Countries*, Paris: OECD.

Peters, T. (1999) *Reinventing Work: Brand You 50 Ways to Transform Yourself from an 'Employee' into a Brand That Shouts Distinction, Commitment, and Passion!*, New York: Random House.

Philpot, J. (2000) 'Behind the Buzzword: The new economy', *Economic Report*, 14, Employment Policy Institute.

Powell, W. W. and Snellman, K. (2004) 'The knowledge economy', *Annual Review of Sociology*, 30: 199–220.

Rainbird, H. (2007) 'Can training remove the glue from the "sticky floor" of low paid work for women?', *Equal Opportunities International*, 26(6): 555–72.

Reeves, R. (2001) *Happy Mondays: Putting the Pleasure Back into Work*, London: Pearson Education Ltd.

Ronson, J. (2006) 'Cold Sweat', *The Guardian*, Jan 26, http://www.guardian.co.uk/money/ 2006/jan/28/workandcareers. weekendmagazine.

Sayer, A. (2005) *The Moral Significance of Class*, Cambridge: Cambridge University Press.

Sennett, R. (1998) *The Corrosion of Character: The Personal Consequences of Work in the New Capitalism*, New York: W. W. Norton.

Sennett, R. (2003) *Respect in an Age of Inequality*, London: Penguin.

Sennett, R. (2006) *The Culture of the New Capitalism*, Boston, MA: Yale University Press.

Smith, V. (2001) *Crossing the Great Divide: Worker Risk and Opportunity in the New Economy*. Ithaca, New York: Cornell University Press.

Stacey, C. (2005) 'Finding dignity in dirty work: The constraints and rewards of low-wage home care labour', *Sociology of Health & Illness*, 27(6): 831–54.

▶

▶

Taylor, R. (2002) 'Britain's World of Work – Myths and Realities', *Economic and Social Research Council*, www.esrctoday.co.uk.

Taylor, P., Mulvey, G., Hyman, J. and Bain, P. (2002) 'Work Organisation, Control and the Experience of Work in Call Centres', *Work, Employment and Society,* 16(1): 133–50.

Taylor, P., Baldry, C., Bain, P. and Ellis, V. (2003) 'A unique working environment: Health sickness and absence management in UK call centres', *Work, Employment and Society*, 17(1): 435–58.

Thompson, P. (2005) 'Skating on Thin Ice. The Knowledge Economy Myth', University of Strathclyde.

Tomlin, P. (2005) 'The Night Visitors', Monday September 19, 2005, *The Guardian.*

Toynbee, P. (1971) *A Working Life*, London: Peacock Books.

Toynbee, P. (2003) *Hard Work. Life in Low Pay Britain,* London: Bloomsbury.

The Work Foundation (2005) *Domestics: UK Domestic Workers and their reluctant employers*, London, http://www.theworkfoundation.com/pdf/Domestics.pdf, accessed July 2008.

Westwood, A. (2002) *Is New Work Good Work?* London: The Work Foundation. http://www.theworkfoundation.com/publications/.

The Sunlit Uplands or Bleak House? Just How Good are Today's Workplaces?

2

David Coats

Introduction

In this short essay I want to interrogate two competing views about today's workplaces. On the one hand we have the argument that things are getting better. After all, we know, don't we, that skill levels are rising; that more jobs involve complex cognitive tasks; and that job content is much more fulfilling than in the past? Equally, we know that the rise of knowledge work demands a different approach from both operational managers and HR professionals. In tight labour markets workers have plenty of bargaining power and can simply exit for a better job if they are dissatisfied with their present employer. The changes sweeping across the economies of developed countries help to explain why many if not most organisations have adopted a model of enlightened human resource management (HRM), which puts the employee back at the centre of the business. This account falls some steps short of the view that all is for the best in this best of all possible worlds, but it assumes that the sunlit uplands are well within reach. There can be no doubt that both employers and employees can look forward to a bright and prosperous future.

On the other hand, we have an equally widespread view that the quality of work is rapidly deteriorating. It is said that working conditions are being driven downwards under the irresistible pressure of globalisation, with its 'race to the bottom' of wages and conditions. Multinational corporations are engaging in regulatory arbitrage, compelling governments to weaken employment rights, impose restraints on union freedom of action and cut taxes to avoid capital flight. The supposed realities of the situation are captured by the words of Lord Jones of Birmingham, the UK's trade promotion minister, that if the developed world is not lean, mean and deregulated then 'China and India will eat our lunch'. The phrase may lack subtlety, but it packs a powerful ideological punch and confirms the left-populist case against globalisation – even though Lord Jones himself is an enthusiastic free trader and an advocate of open markets. Sometimes it seems that the proponents and opponents of globalisation deserve each other. Both have a tendency to make an extreme case using emotive language when there is more to be gained from a forensic inspection of the evidence. That is the purpose of this chapter.

Why should we care about the quality of work?

An obvious place to start out this discussion is with a simple question: why should we care about the quality of work? Those on the political right might say that the concern is wholly misplaced because people are willing to tolerate almost anything as long as they receive a fair day's pay for a fair day's work. Moreover, there are some jobs that are always going to be seen as less desirable than others. It is difficult to envisage a society in which toilets are not cleaned, bins not emptied and burgers not flipped. A natural consequence of this line of argument is that high quality employment or even 'decent work' is a nice idea but little more than wishful thinking. We should therefore accommodate ourselves to the unavoidable brutalities of the world of work and drop the pointless daydreaming.

It is easy to succumb to pessimism, but a rather ungenerous view of the possibilities for change allows us to tolerate phenomena that might, with a little imagination, be seen as intolerable and amenable to improvement. More seriously perhaps, the argument amounts to little more than a restatement of the old saw that 'the poor are always with us', failing to recognise that the depth and extent of poverty are in large measure matters of social and political choice rather than the consequence of forces of nature (Zartouloudis, 2007).

We might offer some more profound objections to this line of argument. For example, we might say that work has to be seen as a fully human activity (Budd, 2004; Bolton and Houlihan, 2007) and as a social act. In other words, the labour market is a market in people rather than things and the process of work engages all of our skills, talents, capabilities and emotions. Moreover, it is equally wrong to view the workplace as an autonomous realm, where workers surrender their rights as citizens as soon as they cross their employer's threshold. That is why the rights to freedom of association and to establish collective bargaining are identified as core labour standards in the conventions of the International Labour Organisation (ILO). In principle this means that we should retain the freedom to speak truth to power even when subject to a contract of employment; and collective voice is central to our case as the only route to correcting the imbalance of power that exists between the employer and individual employee.

But the most powerful argument that we can deploy, trumping all those used so far, is that the quality of work has an impact on health, life expectancy and opportunity (Marmot, 2004). This case is based on robust epidemiological research and it suggests that the following workplace factors are particularly important:

- Employment security.
- Autonomy, control and task discretion.
- Whether work is boring or monotonous.
- Whether employees possess the skills they need to cope with periods of intense work pressure.
- Whether there is an appropriate balance between the effort that workers make and the rewards that they receive.
- Whether the workplace is seen to be fair. Do workers believe that the employer respects the principles of procedural justice (Kivimaki *et al.*, 2007).
- The strength of workplace relationships – or what some analysts have described as social capital.

Some of these characteristics deserve a little more elaboration. For example, one might say that it is absurd to talk about the importance of employment security when 'jobs for life' have disappeared and Generation Y are footloose, opportunistic and uncommitted to their employers.

Yet whether jobs for life have 'disappeared' is a moot point – the best evidence shows that average job tenures in the UK have been stable for around 20 years (Taylor, 2002); and there is a strong case for saying that the classic job for life only ever existed in a small range of occupations. Moreover the supposed Generation Y phenomenon is best explained by the strong employment growth of the last 15 years and a tight labour market for those with graduate level qualifications. Young people have always had short job tenures up to the age of 24 and this supposed new phenomenon may simply be a consequence of the long boom that some Western economies have enjoyed since the early 1990s. When unemployment begins to rise it will be difficult, if not impossible, for Generation Y to retain a value set that only makes sense during a period of low unemployment.

More importantly, perhaps, the notion of security described here has much more to do with a sense of belonging or rootedness in the workplace than with the formal length of job tenure. It captures the idea that employees are secure when they are participants in change rather than the victims of change. It embraces the idea, which will recur throughout this chapter, that job influence and collective voice are both critical contributory factors to the belief that employment is secure.

The importance of the effort-reward balance also requires some explanation. 'Reward' in this context includes all those elements in the employment relationship that contribute to an employee's belief that their efforts are being recognised. Pay is obviously an important factor, especially if a worker is low paid; but 'reward' also embraces the notion of praise for good performance, being treated with respect by your manager and receiving appropriate recognition from colleagues and senior managers.

Returning to the importance of high quality workplace relationships, social capital is the foundation stone of the trust that needs to exist between colleagues and between workers and their employer. In the jargon, what workplaces need is both *bonding* social capital (good relationships between colleagues) and *bridging* social capital (effective relationships between the employees and their employer) (Putnam, 2000). Both collective and individual voice seem to be important here (Sisson, 1997), with the evidence pointing conclusively to the positive impact of individual employee involvement running in parallel with good collective employment relations through a union or a works council.

My suggestion therefore is that judgments about whether we have reached the sunlit uplands or are living at Bleak House have to be viewed through the lens of job quality – or 'good work', to use The Work Foundation's summary formulation. There is plenty of evidence available that allows us to test these competing conceptions, and it is to the evidence from the UK and the EU that we now turn.

Just how much labour market change have we seen?

At first glance, there is some support for both the sunlit uplands and Bleak House stories in the data on labour market change. So far as the UK is concerned the official figures and projections to 2014 show a decisive shift towards employment in higher skill occupations and a significant decline in the percentage of elementary jobs in the economy (see Figure 2.1). By 2014, almost half the employed workforce will either be managers, professionals or associate professionals (workers like teachers or nurses). On this basis we might conclude that job quality has improved. After all, there seems to be more room at the top, there are more high level jobs and fewer people in low skill employment. Can we therefore conclude that the restructuring of the economy has been positive for all those affected?

It may leave few readers unsurprised to learn that there are other aspects of the story that offer a less positive account. One analysis looking at the period 1979–1999 found evidence of significant labour market polarisation – more good jobs, more bad jobs and fewer middling jobs – often described

Figure 2.1   Occupational change in the UK 1984–2014 (% of all employment)

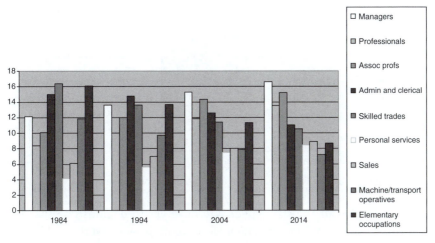

Source: UK Sector Skills Development Agency 2006.

as the emergence of an hour glass labour market (Goos and Manning, 2003). In part this can be explained by the shake-out of employment in manufacturing, with large numbers of skilled and semi-skilled men finding themselves consigned to a life on unemployment or incapacity benefits. But we might reasonably question whether the trend has continued over the recent period of strong growth. For example, a later analysis using the same methodology as Goos and Manning has revealed that the number of really awful jobs fell over the period 1998–2005 (Fitzner, 2006). In part this was a consequence of the success of the UK's National Minimum Wage, which offered a significant boost to the earnings of the lowest paid. But it must also be the case that the slowdown in the process of polarisation reflected the fact that the reduction of manufacturing employment had already taken place.

Another way of approaching the polarisation question is to look at the share of employee jobs by levels of hourly pay relative to the median (the mid-point of the earnings distribution). By this measure there has been no significant evidence of polarisation since the middle 1990s (Figure 2.2).

All that one can conclude perhaps is that there was a process of polarisation taking place in the 1980s and early 1990s that the trend has ended and to a degree has been reversed. But before we also conclude that this endorses the sunlit uplands story, we should remember that all these measures take the level of pay as a proxy for job quality (the higher the pay, the better the job). While this has some intuitive or commonsense appeal, we might also observe that it is quite possible for a skilled and apparently well paid employee to believe that their job is insecure, that they lack autonomy and control, that the workplace is unfair and that they cannot rely on either

Figure 2.2   Share of employee jobs by hourly pay relative to the median

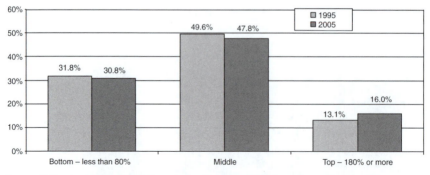

Source: Estimates by The Work Foundation from the UK Labour Force Survey.

their colleagues or their employer. We have yet to demonstrate that the growth of higher level jobs inevitably leads to more 'good work'.

Some phenomena believed to be widespread are often more myth than reality

Whatever one makes of these slightly contradictory data, we can be confident in saying that the trends in job quality in the UK are not being driven by a growing number of contingent workers employed on short-term or agency contracts. Indeed in 2007 there were fewer workers with contingent employment than in 1996. It is striking that the structure of the UK labour market has scarcely changed for 20 years if we take the categories of permanent, temporary, full-time, part-time and self-employed (UK Labour Force Survey, 1986–2006). This is not to suggest that no change has happened (as we have already seen in our discussion of the changing occupational structure); the number of women in the workforce has continued to rise (partly as a result of more generous maternity leave and flexibility policies, often mandated by legislation) and average female job tenures have risen. But it would be quite wrong to conclude that a tsunami of casualisation is washing across the UK labour market, sweeping away all the 'good jobs' in its path.

Of course, rather different trends can be seen in other EU member states. Spain continues to have a very large number of workers employed on temporary contracts – around a third of all those in employment. Sweden, the Netherlands, Germany and France all have higher percentages of contingent work than the UK (which has the lowest percentage in the EU 15). Some readers may find this surprising, but there seems to be an inverse relationship between the extent to which standard employment is regulated and the level of contingent work. In other words, the more stringent the level of employment protection regulation the higher the level of contingent work. This suggests that countries have considerable room for manoeuvre in the extent to which they regulate their labour markets – the Netherlands, Sweden and Denmark all have employment performance that are as good as the UK's, have achieved more equitable social outcomes and have achieved these results despite the supposed rigidities of strong trade unions, strong welfare states and a decent floor of employment protection. Perhaps the Danes have achieved the optimum outcome, with a relatively low level of employment protection legislation (although it is twice as strong as in the UK), a low level of contingent work and high reported levels of employment security, despite the fact that Danish workers have shorter average job tenures than workers in the UK.

Job security and job quality

This brings us to a fascinating set of questions about the relationship between the strength of employment protection legislation, job security and job quality. It is often said, for example, that job security is low in the UK because the labour market is regulated with a light touch, employment rights are weak and employers have a free hand. Yet job security in the UK has been higher in recent years than in countries with a more rigorous approach to labour market regulation – France, Germany and Spain for example (Paugam and Zhou, 2007). To some extent this may reflect the fact that all of these countries have higher unemployment than the UK. Perhaps the most interesting finding is that Denmark (again) seems to have achieved the highest level of employment security. A natural conclusion therefore is that simply legislating to limit employer prerogatives to hire and fire is no guarantee that perceived employment security will improve.

On the other hand, it would be equally wrong to believe that a stronger employment protection legislation (EPL) leads to increased unemployment that leads in turn to reduced employment security. As the OECD has pointed out, there is no strong evidence to show that tighter EPL leads to higher unemployment over the course of the economic cycle (OECD, 2004). It is possible to achieve a golden mean – as the Danish experience proves – where moderately strict EPL, combined with a high level of labour market flexibility and strong, effective trade unions generates good employment performance, secure jobs and high quality work.

Another way of approaching this question is to explore the relationship between employment security and job quality (Paugam and Zhou, 2007). In other words, do workers say that their jobs must be secure before they say that they enjoy quality employment and, in the alternative, do workers who say that their jobs are high quality also say that their jobs are secure? Job security and the quality of employment are most closely correlated in Germany – which means that most workers believe that only secure jobs are decent jobs. One explanation might be that Germany has an 'insider/outsider' labour market, with those employed in traditionally strong sectors (manufacturing for example) enjoying the protection of both employment law and effective collective agreements. Those in other parts of the economy, where collective bargaining is much weaker and where employers have a freer hand, might reasonably conclude that they are both less secure (because they have fewer opportunities to influence workplace change) and enjoy lower quality employment.

Of course, it could be said that the most important factor here is the level of unemployment. But this fails to explain why in France there is a much lower correlation between job security and job quality – put simply, less secure jobs are not necessarily seen as awful jobs, even though French unemployment has been at comparable levels to German unemployment. This is confirmed by the findings for the UK where, *despite* the low level of unemployment, there is a close relationship between job security and job quality (a good job is a secure job and a secure job is a good job). The lowest correlation is to be found in Denmark, once again suggesting that it is possible to generate high quality employment for all – even for contingent workers (around 8 percent of jobs in Denmark are temporary, compared with 6 percent in the UK and around 15 percent in Germany and France). We will return to the factors influencing the quality of employment later in this chapter.

Job satisfaction

At this point it might be useful to review some of the data on job satisfaction. The European Working Conditions Survey 2005 (Eurofound, 2005), which covers the EU 27, gives us a measure of whether workers are either satisfied or very satisfied with their jobs (Figure 2.3). What is most surprising perhaps is that so many employees are satisfied even in those countries with low levels of job satisfaction; Romania, for example is the worst performer in the EU 27 on the job satisfaction measure, but 60 percent of Romanians report that they are either satisfied or very satisfied with their jobs.

Once again the Danes are the most satisfied of any workers in the EU and the British are the second most satisfied. There are two observations to be made about these findings. First, they may be shaped by cultural expectations or indeed by other factors in the wider economic and social environment. Second, the level of satisfaction may, to a degree, reflect adaptive behaviour. People can get used to anything; unless they have good cause to

Figure 2.3   Job satisfaction in Europe (% of employees satisfied or very satisfied)

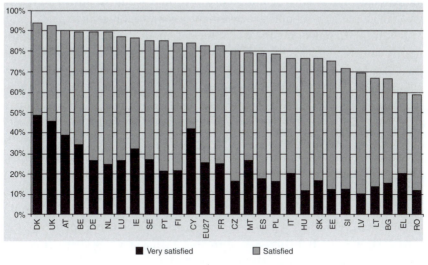

Source: Job Quality in Europe and the UK, DTI, March 2007.

believe that their situation can and should be better employees may take the view that their position is about the best that it can be. This certainly helps to explain why the UK appears to perform so well on this measure but falls short on the 'objective' measures of job quality.

'Good Work' in the UK and the EU

The job quality paradox in the UK is illuminated by the fact that both job satisfaction levels are high and that, according to the Workplace Employment Relations Survey (WERS), employment security improved over the period 1998–2004. On the other hand, there is evidence to show that work got harder over the course of the 1990s, with work intensification reported for all occupational groups (Green, 2003). The phenomenon seemed to come to an end in 1997 (although there was no *reduction* in work intensity after that time) and this may be partly attributable to the fact that workers learned how to manage the technologies that had become ubiquitous by the end of the decade. Initially at least, employees may have found it hard to cope with a raging torrent of emails, manage the endless requests for meetings or cope with endless computer crashes. But as time went by employees adapted to the new digital world and discovered how to use ICT most effectively. We might hypothesise that another wave of technology driven work intensification is about to break as a consequence of the Blackberry syndrome, where workers are never out of touch with the office (or their manager) so that the distinction between work and the rest of life has become increasingly blurred and the notion of 'downtime' – time to think and reflect on a rail journey for example – increasingly becomes a thing of the past.

Returning to one of my initial comments about the importance of autonomy, control and task discretion, there is also evidence to suggest that, in the UK at least, all these factors were in decline at a time when the HR profession increased the rhetorical volume about the importance of empowerment (Gallie, 2004). WERS 2004 revealed widespread dissatisfaction with pay (suggesting widespread effort-reward imbalances) and with job influence, while the Working in Britain Survey suggested rising dissatisfaction with excessive working hours and working life more generally (Taylor, 2002). Moreover, there was evidence too that the rhetoric of empowerment was often just that, with employers saying that employees had the freedom to decide how to meet their targets, but that adverse consequences would follow if targets were not met. Far from being a liberating experience, the introduction of such intrusive performance management systems often left employees feeling powerless (White *et al.*, 2004).

Research commissioned by the Chartered Institute of Personnel and Development, the professional body of HR managers in the UK, confirmed that 15 years of strong growth and a shift in employment towards higher level occupations had not necessarily led to an improvement in people management (CIPD, 2007). They began by reporting that 'people are generally unhappy with how they are managed' and went on to record that a third of employees never received feedback from their managers, only half believed that they would be dealt with fairly if they had a problem at work, two in five said they were not informed about what was happening in their organisation, just a third believed that their views were taken seriously by managers, only a third trusted senior managers and a third were 'engaged' – in the sense that their values and aspirations were aligned with the goals of the business.

One might say that this was an effort by the official representatives of the HR profession to make the case that they should be taken more seriously. But another and more convincing interpretation is that these findings are a damning indictment of 'enlightened' HRM. The last two decades have witnessed a reassertion of employer prerogative in the UK, especially in the private sector with the retreat of trade unionism. Progressive HR policies were meant to be a superior substitute for a more conventional approach to industrial relations, creating a better workplace climate, higher levels of employee motivation and higher performance. Yet the CIPD's own research tells us that the UK looks more like Bleak House than the sunlit uplands. Whatever one might think of the principles of enlightened HRM, it has clearly failed to deliver its promise.

A reader with a sense of history and a sophisticated understanding of workplace realities may find this conclusion unsurprising, simply because the HR profession has sold itself a false prospectus over the last two decades. At the heart of the commonsense of HRM is the view that there is no problem that cannot be solved through the application of the right policy, practice or procedure. It is possible (indeed essential) to achieve alignment between individuals' goals and business objectives. There is no reason why, with the right policies in place, conflict cannot be eliminated from the workplace and no reason why 'employee engagement' cannot be achieved through effective communication and involvement strategies focused on individual workers.

These may sound like laudable aspirations but they are out of kilter with workplace realities. It may be unpopular to say so, but sometimes conflict between employees and their employer is both inevitable and legitimate – although it is also true to say that cooperation to solve shared problems is essential. Perhaps we still have something to learn from earlier commentators who had a keener appreciation of the nature of the employment relationship than many HR professionals today. Otto Kahn-Freund, the intellectual architect of the academic discipline of labour law in the UK offered the following characterisation of the employment relationship:

> [T]he relation between an employer and an isolated employee is typically a relation between a bearer of power and one who is not a bearer of power. In its inception it is an act of submission, in its operation it is a condition of subordination, however much that submission and subordination may be concealed by that indispensable figment of the legal mind known as 'the contract of employment' (Kahn-Freund 1983, p. 18).

Of course, this is at some distance from the commonplace HR perspective that the objective must be to achieve shared goals and shared values – reinforced by the idea that 'we're all in this together and sink or swim together'. Another commentator, reviewing similar rhetorical tropes more than 40 years ago, described such language as an 'orgy of avuncular pontification' (McClelland, 1963, quoted in Fox, 1966). There is no malign intent here, but employees might reasonably feel that they are being patronised or being misled when, from their standpoint 'we are definitely not all in this together'.

To summarise, employers may find that the best route to high trust employment relations (a more realistic approach to the notion of employee engagement) is that identified by Alan Fox in his classic paper for the UK's Royal Commission on Trade Unions and Employers Associations (the Donovan Commission):

> It is a necessary – though not sufficient – basis for recognising that co-operation is unlikely to be achieved in modern industry through the

attempted manipulation of 'team spirit', 'high morale' and 'loyalty', but needs to be engineered by structural adaptations in work organisation, work rules and work practices, and that direct negotiation with work groups is an essential part of this process (Fox, 1966, p.4).

No doubt some HR professionals will say that this material is of historical interest only and has nothing to offer in a more complex, knowledge driven economy where trade unions are conspicuous by their absence. But my case is not that there should be any attempt to recreate a world that has passed. Instead I am arguing that HR professionals should be a little more self-critical and ask themselves why their prescriptions have yet to deliver, despite the fact that the profession has had a largely free hand for the last quarter century, and why they have ignored the research findings suggesting that the appropriate mix of individual and collective employee involvement is most likely to drive high productivity and performance? There is more to be gained from a careful evaluation of power relationships in the workplace than from attempting to implement the most recent employee engagement fad being promoted in the professional press.

We can also look beyond the job satisfaction data and the evidence gathered by the HR profession to some of the more 'objective' indicators of job quality identified in the 2005 European Working Conditions Survey (Fitzner *et al.*, 2007). For example, more than half of all British workers say that their work involves a lack of variety or monotonous tasks. One might say that this is entirely predictable, since all work involves elements that are routine or unrewarding. But the surprise is that the levels of 'boredom' reported in The Netherlands, Sweden, Austria and Denmark are less than half those in the UK. Moreover, it seems that workers in the UK are less likely to learn new things in their jobs than in Finland, Sweden, Denmark and The Netherlands. And more generally the UK seems to have a job content problem if a number of factors are combined to produce a generic measure of job quality (monotonous tasks, learning new things, problem solving and task complexity). On this measure the UK is below the EU average, its near neighbours are Romania and Bulgaria and other countries – Sweden, The Netherlands, Austria, Denmark and Finland – do significantly better.

Once again, a critic might say that these differences are explained by cultural factors, but it cannot be the case that a representative sample of employees across the EU 27 produces no useful comparative data when common questions have been asked using identical language. There is something interesting happening here, which suggests that the quality of employment available to workers is shaped (if not determined) by national policy choices and institutions.

Explaining the differences in job quality

This rapid review of the evidence should have made one thing clear; there are significant variations in job quality across the EU 27. An obvious conclusion therefore is that there is no irresistible pressure from 'globalisation' forcing convergence on a lowest common denominator of poor pay and conditions of employment. These countries are characterised by a wide variety of policies, diverse institutions, a huge variation in the extent of regulation, both strong and weak trade unions, low taxes as well as high taxes and weak or strong welfare states. Far from there being a process of convergence, there appears to be no reduction in the diversity of either policies or outcomes.

But if this is right then we are still left with something to explain. It is insufficient to say that different policies lead to different results, or that all countries are different and that there are no generalisable lessons. One possibility is to return to the 'varieties of capitalism' story developed by Peter Hall and David Soskice at the end of the 1990s (Hall and Soskice, 2001). Although critics have reasonably pointed out that the sharp distinctions drawn here between groups of countries are based on very broad and slightly misleading categories. Central to their analysis is the distinction between 'liberal market economies' (USA, UK, Australia) and 'coordinated market economies' (Germany, France the Nordic Countries). In the former, institutions are weak and most of the work of economic coordination is achieved through the market. In the latter, institutions are strong and mutually reinforcing: capital markets, corporate governance regimes, collective bargaining and the training system are all geared to delivering incremental innovation over the long term in product markets where quality rather than price is what counts. The skills system supplies well-qualified employees with a capacity for problem solving. Capital markets are characterised by long-term thinking rather than a demand for high returns over the short term. Companies also make long-term commitments to their employees; their production strategies rely on a highly skilled labour force, which is given extensive autonomy 'to generate continuous improvement in product lines and production processes' (Hall and Soskice, 2001, p. 24). Employees are a source of innovation and have to be treated well.

The hypothesis for our purposes is clear. Coordinated market economies ought to have higher job quality than liberal market economies. Unfortunately, more recent work suggests that the 'varieties of capitalism' approach, whilst retaining some explanatory power, fails to account for the differences in job quality *between* coordinated market economies. According to Duncan Gallie and his colleagues, jobs in Germany are not very different (or not as different as you might expect) from jobs in the UK (Gallie, 2007). Jobs in Sweden and Denmark are less like jobs in Germany than you might expect too. A subtler analysis is needed to understand why these variations exist.

A better approach perhaps is to look at the *employment* regime in each of these countries rather than the *production* regime (which is what the varieties of capitalism story amounts to) as the source of the differences in job quality. The employment regime focuses on the nature and quality of workplace relationships, on the balance or power between employers and employees (and therefore the strength of trade unions), on the commitment to creating quality employment for all and on the extent to which a focus on the quality of working life at the enterprise level translates into a national political conversation about the quality of work – often as part of a wider politics of the quality of life. In Sweden, for example, trade unions are both strong and responsible, placing a high value on job quality and making a determined effort to keep these issues on the agenda with employers. Perhaps we should add that the consequence of union power is that employers have understood the importance of quality of working life issues too. And the strong views of these social actors influence the behaviour of the major political parties; even though Sweden has a centre-right government today it is inconceivable that they would implement a programme of extensive labour market deregulation or a determined assault on the bastions of union power, unless of course they wished to commit political suicide.

The differences in job quality across countries are therefore not best understood as determined by whether a country is a liberal market or a co-ordinated market economy. Instead, we should direct our attention to whether the employment regime is liberal (the UK and the USA), corporatist (Germany and the Rhenish countries) or inclusive (the Nordic countries). It would be absurd to suggest that any other country could suddenly decide to adopt the Swedish or Danish models and witness a sudden improvement in job quality. On the other hand, there are some elements in the model from which we can all learn. Most obviously, perhaps, the role of trade unions as legitimate institutions is not in question; but the corollary here is that unions are committed to the success of the enterprise *and* recognise their responsibility to protect their members and contribute to productivity enhancing innovations. The workplace agenda is not just about distribution or cutting the cake, but also about making the cake bigger *and* ensuring a fair distribution. The contrast with Germany is striking in that while German unions, despite the institutional architecture of works councils and board level codetermination, now represent fewer than one in five workers, the Swedish unions are holding their position in a challenging political environment. It seems, therefore, that an apparently worker friendly legal regime is no guarantee of trade union success; otherwise German unions would be in a much happier position than they are today.

Another important observation is that public policy can help to shape an inclusive employment regime. France is a case in point because trade unions appear to be relatively weak but job quality is higher than one might expect given the apparent imbalance of power between capital and organised labour. Gallie explains this phenomenon as a consequence of the architecture of workplace institutions in France. The debates about *autogestion* (industrial democracy) in the 1970s led to the Lois Auroux in 1982, which gave works councils a clear locus to put quality of work issues onto the agenda with employers. Even in an environment where trade union membership is low, the presence of workplace institutions with such guaranteed rights means that quality of work and working life is a mainstream issue. The generalisable principle ought to be clear: different countries can choose different institutional paths to progress a quality of work agenda, but the common element is that the parties are able to engage in these discussions at the workplace as well as at national level.

Implications

Whether we find ourselves on the sunlit uplands or in Bleak House depends more than anything else on social, economic and political choices. We have seen that outcomes vary widely across the EU and that both public policy and institutional arrangements are important factors shaping the quality of employment and the experience of work. That there is considerable national room for manoeuvre is perhaps *the* critical conclusion since it undermines the 'globalisation = labour market convergence' thesis – the belief that all nations are now involved in some race to the bottom because multi-national firms are engaging in regulatory arbitrage. Indeed, the Nordic countries are more open to international trade than the USA, have generally higher labour standards and have liberalised their markets more aggressively over the last decade, yet it is in the United States that we see the greatest concern about downward pressure on wages and conditions as a result of international competition.

Perhaps the best explanation for this phenomenon is that the Nordics have strong welfare states to protect the unemployed when they lose their jobs. Most importantly, this is an enabling welfare state that equips people with the skills they need to succeed in a changing world of work – a springboard as well as a safety net. In the United States, in contrast, unemployment benefits are low and the unemployed are left to their own devices: whether you sink or swim is a matter of luck. American workers therefore have much more to lose than their Nordic counterparts when they lose their jobs, including their healthcare benefits. We might conclude that social democratic policies are better oriented to success in a more integrated world economy than the laissez-faire of the market fundamentalists.

In other words, there is no reason to succumb to global pessimism and every reason for intellectual self-confidence. There are no irresistible forces preventing developed countries from creating more high quality jobs or better workplaces. We can identify the ingredients of good policy and we can describe the elements of an inclusive employment regime. Any developed country can choose this destination even if they use different route maps for the journey.

REFERENCES

Budd, J. (2004) *Employment with a Human Face: Balancing Efficiency, Equity and Voice,* Ithaca: Cornell University Press.

Bolton, S. C. and Houlihan, M. (2007) *Searching for the Human in Human Resource Management: Theory, Practice and Workplace Contexts,* London: Palgrave Macmillan.

Chartered Institute of Personnel and Development (CIPD) (2007) *Employee Engagement Survey 2006.*

Eurofound (2005) European Working Conditions Survey 2005, European Foundation for the Improvement of Living and Working Conditions, www.eurofound.europa.eu, accessed July 2008.

Fox, A. (1966) *Industrial Sociology and Industrial Relations,* Research Paper 3, Royal Commission on Trade Unions and Employers' Associations, London: HMSO.

Fitzner, G. (2006) 'How have employees fared? Recent UK trends', *Employment Relations Research Trends,* 56. UK: Department of Trade and Industry.

Fitzner, G., Williams, N. and Grainger, H. (2007) Job Quality in Europe and the UK: Results from the 2005 European Working Conditions Survey, UK: Department of Trade and Industry.

Gallie, D., Felstead, A. and Green, F. (2004) 'Changing Patterns of Task Discretion in Britain', *Work, Employment and Society,* 18(2): 243–378.

Gallie, D. (ed.) (2007) *Employment Regimes and the Quality of Work,* London: Oxford University Press.

Goos, M. and Manning, A. (2003) 'McJobs and MacJobs', in Dickens, R., P. Gregg and J. Wadsworth (eds) *The Labour Market Under New Labour: The State of Working Britain,* London: Palgrave Macmillan.

Green, F. (2003) *The Demands of Work* in Dickens, R., P. Gregg and J. Wadsworth (eds) *The Labour Market Under New Labour: The State of Working Britain,* London: Palgrave Macmillan.

Hall, P. and Soskice, D. (2001) *Varieties of Capitalism: The Institutional Foundations of Comparative Advantage,* Oxford: Oxford University Press.

Kahn-Freund, O. (1983) *Labour and the Law,* London: Stevens and Sons.

Kivimaki, M., Vahtera, J., Elovainio, M., Virtanen, M. and Siegrist, J. (2007) 'Effort reward imbalance, procedural injustice and relational injustice as psychosocial predictors of health: complementary or redundant models?', *Occupational and Environmental Medicine,* 64(10): 659–65.

▶

▶

Marmot, M. (2004) *Status Syndrome*, London: Bloomsbury Press.

OECD (2004) *Employment Outlook*, Geneva: Organisation for Economic Co-operation and Development.

Paugam, S. and Zhou, Y. (2007) 'Job Insecurity', in Gallie, D. (ed.) *Employment Regimes and the Quality of Work*, Oxford: Oxford University Press.

Putnam, R. (2000) *Bowling Alone: The Collapse and Revival of American Community*, New York: Simon and Schuster.

Sisson, K. (1997) *New Forms of Work Organisation: Can Europe Realise its Potential?*, European Foundation for the Improvement of Living and Working Conditions, Luxembourg: Office for Official Publications of the European Communities.

Taylor, R. (2002) *Britain's World of Work: Myths and Realities*, UK: Economic and Social Research Council.

UK Labour Force Survey, 1986–2006, Economic and Social Data Services, www.esds.ac.uk/government/lfs/, accessed July 2008.

White, M., Hill, S., Mills, C. and Smeaton, D. (2004) *Managing to Change? British Workplaces and the Future of Work*, London: Palgrave Macmillan.

Zartouloudis, S. (2007) *Equality – A Political Choice*, London: Policy Network.

Working But Poor: Experiences in the U.S. Low-Wage Labour Market

3

Marcia Bok and Louise Simmons

Introduction

What is it like to be working but poor? If work matters, how and why does it matter, and what matters about it; and how does change affect different groups of low wage workers?

Being part of the working class in the US has never been easy; and workers have struggled to achieve gains in the workplace. But in the past these struggles have usually paid off in higher wages, better benefits, and more job security. Today, it continues to be difficult to be part of the working class and workers continue to struggle, often facing intimidation, harassment, and lost jobs while simultaneously experiencing declining wages, fewer benefits, and greater job insecurity. All of this is occurring in the context of major changes in the political economy in the US and on a global level.

Previously generations of workers grew up in a town, worked in its factories, and experienced pride and loyalty to the job. All of this has changed. Today, communities and lives are disrupted as workers move horizontally from job to job, as plants close, and as workers look for better opportunities. Work has mattered not only because people lived and worked together, they formed communities around their unions and their work, and they socialised together after work. But as the workforce has fractured, now there are many different groups of workers with different experiences; and with short tenures on the job and without unionisation, there is little that binds these workers together. Not enough has been written about the different categories of the working poor that have been created, as well as other changes that have occurred for working class and middle income people.

We hear repeatedly that the US has reneged on its promise that if you work hard, you will prosper. To understand working but poor, we now must consider the problems faced by the very poor, the working poor, the near poor, those in mid-level skill jobs, and the 'disposable' American. There are part-time jobs, temp work, contract work and the informal economy. There is lower-paid 'women's work' and there is work consigned to immigrant workers that ostensibly 'no one else wants to do'. The need to enhance the upward mobility of workers of colour remains. This diversity of issues faced by the working class suggests a need to understand the specific characteristics of different individuals and groups of working people in order to develop effective strategies that can produce an improved standard of living.

Background

The poverty level for a family of four in the US in 2008 is $21,200. (This national figure is computed annually by the US government). It is often noted, however, that this standard grossly underestimates the actual living expenses of US families. A 'self-sufficiency' measure that has been developed as a more realistic alternative has been applied in some situations but does not have national authority (see Pearce and Brooks, 1999). An organisation that works on issues of low wage workers in the authors' home state of Connecticut, the Connecticut Centre for a New Economy (2001), notes that working families cannot maintain self-sufficiency on wages paid by most service sector jobs. As they frankly state: 'The entry-level wage for a nurse's aide provides only 60 percent of the income needed to maintain self-sufficiency for a single parent and one pre-school and one school age child in the Hartford, Connecticut area' (2001, p. 1) Individuals earning the current national minimum wage of $5.85, working full-time, year-round earn $12,168 annually. (This will increase to $7.25 an hour in 2009 or $15,080 annually). In Connecticut, the minimum wage is increasing to $8.00 in 2009 so that these same individuals would earn $16,640 annually. For a family of three in Connecticut receiving benefits in the state's Temporary Assistance to Needy Families (TANF) programme or what is commonly known as 'welfare', their monthly cash benefit is $560 or $6,720. These families might also receive food stamps, medical assistance, housing assistance, but this is by no means assured. It is within this context that it is helpful to understand the situation of low-wage workers in the US, and to consider whether and how such patterns are emerging worldwide.

Since 2000, the US has lost 3.5 million jobs in manufacturing – jobs that were once considered a stepping stone to the middle-class (Greenhouse, 2008a). Reflecting this trend, in our state of Connecticut, as is the pattern elsewhere within the US, thousands of manufacturing jobs have been replaced by service sector jobs; and currently, the income distribution of Connecticut residents is among the most unequal in the nation. Recent projections through 2008, prepared by the Connecticut Department of Labour, describe an economy that will continue to fracture, producing greater inequality, instability, and insecurity in the workforce. While manufacturing employment is historically associated with good jobs, with good wages, benefits, and job security, service sector employment is generally associated with poor jobs with low wages and few benefits. But as the Connecticut Centre for a New Economy (2001) points out, there is nothing inherent in these jobs that presupposes high or low pay – these 'good jobs' are the result of collective action and workers organising to better their conditions. In this chapter we present an overview of the different components of the low-wage workforce (the very poor, the working poor, the near-poor and middle-skilled jobs, and the 'disposable American') and the experiences of individuals working in these jobs. We also comment on the political economy that has created the current situation and future prospects for change.

Low wage workers

The very poor

There are now 37 million people in the US living in poverty and half of all families living in poverty are single mothers with children. US Census data from 2005 documents that minority communities (especially African-Americans and Latinos) are disproportionately poor; and women and their children are disproportionately poor. Single mothers are more likely to be very poor than other families with children; and households with children maintained by women of colour alone have the highest rates of income inadequacy (i.e. unable to meet basic needs) (IWPR, 2007). Poverty rates have been rising since 1999 and are now above where they stood in 1973. Education reduces the rate of income inadequacy, especially for people of colour and/or women. As Pearce argues, 'families are not poor because they lack workers or work hours... but because their wages within their occupations are inadequate to meet basic expenses' (2007, p. 3).

The very poor, mainly female-headed households, are affected by neo-liberal public policies that limit welfare and other government safety-net programmes which have often been necessary for survival. These very low-income women are likely to be precariously attached to the labour market and their work experience is generally unstable, with low wages, without benefits, and without worker rights. Working in minimum wage jobs, we have noted above how low their income is.

Unfortunately, since welfare reform was enacted in 1996, there is little attention paid to the very poor since the 'conventional wisdom' is that most were on welfare (previously known as Aid to Families with Dependent Children [AFDC]) and, moreover, that most of these former welfare recipients are now working. In the US we are used to thinking of poverty as a consequence of unemployment (Ehrenreich, 2001). However, the current recession within the US brings home once again the threat of poverty as a reality for many Americans. The problems these individuals face need to be highlighted if improvement in their economic situation is to occur. Integration into the workforce is needed, but work conditions also need to improve. Currently, very low-income women may need two or three jobs to make ends meet, and without good pay, health benefits, paid sick days, and adequate and affordable childcare and transportation, self-sufficiency may be a daunting goal. In addition to limited education and work experience, very poor women may have other barriers to employment such as homelessness, and physical and mental disabilities. Thus, a variety of public policies supportive of very low income groups are urgently needed to enhance the standard of living of the very poor. These policies need to balance work imperatives with realistic supports that include health, mental health and housing consider-ations, as well as employment, childcare and transportation opportunities.

With emphasis on work and personal responsibility, the Temporary Assist-ance to Needy Families (TANF) Programme, AFDC's successor, welfare case-loads have been reduced by 60 percent or more (DeParle, 2004) primarily through strict time limits for receiving cash assistance and sanctions for non-compliance. The result has been a characterisation of TANF as successful and, most profoundly, the simultaneous escalating invisibility of the very poor. Advocates for poor women note that the goal of the programme was never about poverty reduction and, in fact, poverty reduction has not necessarily occurred.

Consider the example of Carletta Connor, a single mother in a rural area, discussed by Friedlin (2004) cited in Neubeck (2006):

> In 2002, Carletta Connor lost her ride to her job as a medical technician several miles from her home in rural Mexico, Missouri. A few days later her babysitter announced she was moving. With no available public transport-ation and no one to take care of her four children, all under the age of 13, Connor, 44, could not keep her job. With no reliable child support to rely on, Connor had cycled on and off welfare for years and now found herself again turning to the government for assistance... this time, however, after a year, she hit the federally mandated five-year lifetime limit for receiving cash benefits... Connor and her kids now subsist on food stamps and sporadic child support payments... 'It's a struggle every day,' said Connor with a sigh. 'When you get up you're looking forward to really nothing' (Neubeck, p. 79).

In a 2003 report, the Institute for Women's Policy Research notes that although more low-income single parents are working in the wake of welfare reform, well over three-fourths (78 percent) are concentrated in four typically low-wage occupations in the service sector including food services, personal household services, janitorial/maintenance and building services, and health services. Yet despite increased work participation, no significant increase was found in those who received health insurance through employment – 'a key barometer of job quality'. In fact, employed welfare recipients actually experienced a decline in access to employer provided health insurance (from 21 to 14 percent) after welfare. The report goes on to say that following welfare reform, poor single parent families not receiving TANF were more likely to live in dire poverty.

Throughout his book, DeParle (2004) questions why we view work as so rewarding and welfare as so negative. His answer is:

> The welfare revolution grew from the fear that the poor were mired in a culture of entitlement – stuck in a swamp of excessive demands, legal prerogative, social due. There certainly was a culture of entitlement in American life, but it was scarcely concentrated at the bottom (as anyone following the wave of corporate scandals now knows). What really stands out about Angie and Jewell (two individuals whose lives he describes) is how little they felt they were owed. They went through life acting entitled to nothing. Not heat or lights. Not medical care. Not even three daily meals. And they scarcely complained. When welfare was there for the taking, they got on the bus and took it; when it wasn't they made other plans. In ending welfare, the country took away their single largest source of income. They didn't lobby or sue. They didn't march or riot. They made their way against the odds into wearying, underpaid jobs. And that does now entitle them to something – to 'a shot at the American Dream' more promising than the one they've received (p. 330).

Of the individuals and families he studied, DeParle notes that the standard of living and quality of life of individuals transitioning from welfare to work barely changed as they became employed. As to the notion suggested by conservative writers that their children would have more pride in them because they were working: 'I don't think the kids think about that... They'd like it if I'd just sit around with them all day' (p. 321).

The working poor

While the very poor and the working poor may be somewhat overlapping categories, the working poor, as described by Shipler (2004) are living in the twilight between extreme poverty and wellbeing. He states: 'many people tread just above the official poverty level, dangerously close to the edge of destitution' (p. 4). These individuals work as fast food workers, cashiers, child care workers, hotel maids, and nurses' aides. They generally move horizontally within the workforce, but with little upward mobility. A worker at Wal-Mart tells Ehrenreich (2001) that she is thinking of quitting her job because $7 an hour isn't enough for how hard she works: 'She's going to apply at a plastics factory where she hopes she can get $9' (p. 190). According to Boushey, *et al.* (2007):

> Inequality in the U.S. is complicated by limited economic mobility. A review of the evidence on economic mobility over time in the U.S. shows that most low-wage workers do not usually move up ... It turns out in the U.S. labour market, it is not possible for everyone to be middle-class, no matter how hard they work. Moreover, it has been getting harder to do over time (p. 17).

Low-income workers are affected by changes in the labour market as more skilled individuals become unemployed and compete for low-wage jobs, but it is generally believed, as noted by Card and Blank (2000), that fluctuating labour market conditions play a limited role in the labour market experiences of the working poor (and the welfare poor, as well). Shipler (2004) says, 'The rising and falling fortunes of the nation's economy have not had much impact on these folks. They suffer in good and bad times' (preface, p. x).

In describing the rural poor in Appalachia, Duncan (1999) discusses how isolation, low education, high unemployment and corrupt, undemocratic politics reinforce disempowerment and a two-class system. She presents the following example:

> Gwen and Billy live right on the edge, with no security and no cushion. They are surviving, but they are not getting ahead. They both dropped out of school, and their limited education and their parents' low status and lack of connections have limited their job prospects. Local institutions fail them – the schools, the health care system... national safety-net policies also fail them. The Boggses are the working poor – uninsured, unprotected, and struggling to keep a marriage together against the odds (p. 45).

Duncan firmly believes that education can produce upward mobility, but she recognises the importance of other factors that keep people down or help them to progress. She says 'study after study shows that educated people are not chronically poor' (p. 207), but she also notes that 'those who study the structural underpinnings of social change consistently find a relationship between greater equality, democracy, and economic development' (p. 198).

Ehrenreich (2001) emphasises the many indignities and violations of human and civil rights that occur in the low-wage workplace. Workers are often not permitted to take bathroom breaks or sit down to rest. Video cameras provide constant surveillance of workers (not just customers). Many workers earn $6.00 an hour at jobs where they are often expected to work more hours than they are paid for, fewer hours than necessary to support their families, or 12 hours a day, six days a week. She notes that affordable housing is a major problem for low-wage workers, and rents constituting more than 50 percent of income are not uncommon.

Greenhouse (2008a) describes the experiences of Michael Johnson:

...a father of five who worked for 17 years as a security guard in downtown Los Angeles. His job paid him $10 an hour. His rent was $975 a month. To make ends meet, Johnson took a second full-time job guarding a construction site. His wife was unable to work because of an injury sustained as a nursing home aide. When Johnson took his second job, the family lost its food stamps. His long hours took him away from his children. 'I'm missing them grow up... I can't do this forever' (p. xiii).

So what can be done to address these issues? One solution is what Fine (2006) describes as an emerging phenomenon of community-based and community-led worker centres that provide support primarily (but not exclusively) for low-wage immigrant populations. These supports include services such as help with filing unpaid wage claims; accessing healthcare and learning English; advocacy, including exposing problematic individual employers and industry-wide practices and needed policy change; and organising, i.e. pressing a set of demands on a specific employer, hiring agency, or industry-wide coordinating body. While other immigrant service organisations generally engage in service provisions, it is the addition of organising and advocacy that sets worker centres apart. Organising day labourers is an example of direct economic action. Many worker centres place emphasis on leadership development and democratic decision-making, and education is considered integral to organising. Workshops, courses, and training sessions are structured to emphasise the development of critical thinking skills that workers can apply to all aspects of their public lives, including work, education, neighbourhood interaction, and healthcare. On the policy level, worker centres have had their greatest impact on improving working conditions and raising wages by pressuring government to take action and advocating for other local and state public policy initiatives. In cooperation with labour unions they can increase the scope and effectiveness of their efforts in specific industries and also increase union density. This is a slowly evolving process, however it is clear that such initiatives have a vital role to play in influencing from the ground up.

The near poor and middle-skill jobs

Newman and Chen (2007) write about the 'missing class' or the near poor in America. They note that while 37 million Americans live below the poverty level, there are 57 million Americans – one-fifth of the population, including 21 percent of the nation's children – who live above the poverty line but well below a secure economic situation. They describe this missing class as 'composed of households earning roughly between $20,000 and $40,000 for a family of four' (p. 3).

These individuals earn less money, have fewer savings, and are less likely to be home-owners than middle-class families. They live in inner-ring suburbs on the fringe of poor urban areas and send their kids to schools that are under-funded and crowded. Sometimes they live in large cities with changing neighbourhoods of decline and rejuvenation as different ethnic and racial groups arrive and depart; some of the neighbourhoods are dangerous and some are prosperous. It is not uncommon for these families to have financial obligations to their extended families in the US and transnationally. Sending their children to college is a challenge. And while somewhat upwardly mobile, 'they experience an odd fusion of optimism and insecurity: the former from their upward mobility, the latter from the nagging concern that it could all disappear if just one thing goes wrong: One uninsured child sick enough to pull a parent off the job; one marriage spiralling into divorce; one layoff that shuts off the money spigot' (Newman and Chen, 2007, p. 6). They have high credit bills and debts, few health and retirement benefits, they pay high prices for goods in local stores, and they live in poorly maintained apartments with health hazards. They have many health problems, similar to poorer families. Their lives are characterised by economic insecurity, particularly in a volatile economy.

Greenhouse (2008a) notes that for men with just a high school diploma, 87 percent of new jobs pay less than $25,000 a year. He chronicles such situations as sexual harassment, dangerous working conditions, workers locked in warehouses overnight, off-the-clock work, lack of any time at home, strike breaking, and fear of retaliation if a worker lodges a complaint. These conditions exist in many work settings, as diverse as retail jobs (even on the management level in such companies as Wal-Mart where district managers may earn around $26,000 and supervise workers earning $10.50 an hour), meat-packing plants, gas station attendants, and call centres.

Regarding education and training as a pathway to better jobs, Newman and Chen (2007) note a recent initiative for the near poor.

The Workforce Alliance has recently launched a national Skills2Compete campaign. Holzer and Lerman (2007), in a report released as part of this campaign, indicate 'that for every job in the U.S. requiring a four-year degree, significantly more require some training past high school, but not necessarily a bachelors or graduate degree'. These middle-skill jobs make up nearly half of all jobs today. Yet national policies are doing little to build out this crucial part of America's workforce team. Middle-skill jobs experiencing shortages include construction workers and inspectors, medical technicians and emergency medical technicians, nurses, fire-fighters and other positions that cannot be outsourced but which are crucial to the U.S. infrastructure, health, quality of life and standard of living. Community colleges can play a critical role in providing the education and training that are needed. The near poor, working in mid-skill jobs, need vocational training, post-secondary education that is family-friendly, with financial aid, flexible programs and scheduling, and career ladders that enhance career opportunities and upward economic mobility. Non-traditional students – i.e. students older than 24 years or enrolled on a part-time basis – are the majority of all students needing assistance (p. 276).

Newman and Chen (2007) also describe the importance of asset building for the near poor, such as home ownership, '(t)oo poor to buy a townhouse or apartment but too rich to qualify for traditional affordable-housing programmes, they feel cheated out of the American dream's promise of home ownership' (p. 76).

For those who do fulfil this dream, considering the precariousness of their work experiences, it is predicted that the sub-prime mortgage crisis will result in two million foreclosures by the end of 2008, with particularly harsh impacts on near poor families. Kuttner (2007) notes that this could not happen in France, for example, because it is illegal for banks to foist deceptive loans on borrowers and because there are no unregulated storefront mortgage companies.

Disposable Americans

There is probably most visible concern in the U.S. about the declining middle-class since this segment of the population generally represents individuals and families who have fulfilled the legendary 'American Dream' – i.e. the group that had achieved job security, upward mobility and a higher standard of living than their parents. Uchitelle (April 20, 2008) quotes University of California-Berkeley labour economist Harley Shaiken who states that 'the most important model that rolled off the Detroit assembly lines in the 20th century was the middle class for blue-collar workers'. Uchitelle goes on to say that 'the $20 hourly wage, introduced on a large scale in the middle of the last century, allowed masses of Americans with no more than a high school education to rise to the middle class. It was a marker, of sorts. And it is on its way to extinction' (p. 3). This threshold of $41,600 annually is considered by many experts the minimum income necessary to put a family of four into the middle-class. Currently, this is the population generally included in the description of 'disposable Americans'.

Thousands of Americans have lost their jobs or are downwardly mobile as a result of globalisation, outsourcing, productivity increases resulting in downsizing, and lack of public policies that protect worker rights. Uchitelle (2006) provides an historical review of job security in the US. He notes that from 1945–1970 job security was affordable as long as economic growth surged and American companies dominated not only their home market but those abroad as well. 'When that domination began to come apart in the 1970s so did job security' (p. 46). He details how President Carter initiated deregulation that accelerated in the Republican Reagan years:

> Starting in 1979 the manufacturing labour force steadily declined, mainly through lay-offs... as more and more efficiencies kicked in and more and more merchandise once made in America came from abroad. ...Raising shareholder value became the great justification for mergers and acquisition activity (p. 139).

Free trade agreements exacerbated the problem: after the passage of NAFTA formerly unionised steel and auto workers were left to compete for minimum wage jobs in service industries. A worker interviewed by Greenhouse (2008a) says 'I don't consider any job a lousy job. I will do whatever I have to do to make money' (p. 17)

In addition to manufacturing jobs, globalisation threatens the jobs of between 11 million and 42 million white-collar workers in the US. It is estimated by Forester Research that 3.4 million white collar jobs – some 260,000 a year – will be sent overseas between 2003 and 2015 (Greenhouse, 2008a).

One aspect of major changes in employment has been the growth of temp work, contract work, and part-time work with few (if any) benefits or security, as well as growth in the informal sector. Massachusetts Institute of Technology economist Paul Osterman describes these workers as 'America's new migrant labourers, moving from job to job without security and without benefits' (Greenhouse, 2008a). Mehta and Theodore (2004) note that the temporary staffing industry has experienced major growth since the 1990s, and that the temp industry is so beneficial to employers that there is little motivation to hire permanent workers, especially in a fluctuating labour market. One of the key benefits to employers is that temporary staffing agencies relieve business clients of the responsibility for contributing unemployment taxes for temporary workers. As they note: 'Worksite employers ... are free to adjust the size of their workforce without necessarily incurring rising UI (unemployment insurance) costs' (p. 92). And further, '...agency-supplied temps experience the lowest UI recipiency rates compared to other contingent workers (independent contractors, part-time workers, and on-call workers) of all adult workers regardless of type of employment' (p. 98). Mehta and Theodore conclude that temporary work continues to be associated with low wages and pronounced job insecurity, without much relief in sight.

Another employer initiative in the workplace is the development of a two-tiered pay-scale where younger and older workers, performing the same job functions, receive drastically different wages. In a Caterpillar facility near Peoria, Illinois, this situation exists:

> Twenty-eight year old John Arnold works in the same Caterpillar factory in Illinois as his father, but under the plant's two-tier contract, the maximum he can ever earn is $14.90 an hour, far less than the $25 earned by his father... 'A few people I work with are living at home with their parents,' Arnold said. 'Some are even on food stamps'.

> Scott Wilcoxon, a twenty-six year old navy veteran who not long ago served as an electrician on a nuclear submarine, operates five computer-controlled metal-cutting machines at Caterpillar. The maximum he can earn is $19.84 an hour, 21 percent below the maximum for the fifty year olds working next to him... (Greenhouse, 2008a, p. 262).

Greenhouse (2008b) notes that John Arnold and Scott Wilcoxon represent the type of workers on whom America's industrial success was built: 'diligent, dedicated, and determined. But because their wages are lower than those of the previous generation, they are part of a reverse economic evolution unfolding at workplaces across the country...' (p. 22).

The CEO of Caterpillar argues that the company's competitive wage strategy isn't destroying middle-class jobs as much as it is preserving jobs in America. The strategy helped the company expand its workforce in 2005. However, with record earnings and executive salaries at an all-time high, these cost savings have generated huge resentments.

While younger workers are experiencing these changes in the economy, older workers are also losing their pensions and healthcare which constitute major erosions of retirement security. Younger workers generally do not have health insurance from any source, by far the highest rate of any age group, nor do they participate in employer-sponsored retirement plans. All workers are affected by pension and health insurance inadequacy. Unpaid debt and the home foreclosure crisis reflect the hardships experienced by this population.

Workers are also given the option to accept 'buy-outs' rather than return to the assembly line and forfeit the higher rank they had worked years to secure. With a union contract negotiated with General Motors, in 2007 more than 30,000 'Big Three' employees (Ford, General Motors and Chrysler) joined the largest exodus of workers from a single American industry in decades.

> As the workers depart in greater numbers than either their union or their employers anticipated, the exodus becomes more than a long ledger of altered lives. It is an accounting, of course, but an accounting of the most personal and poignant sort. Communities are fragmenting, families are relocating, and years of individual choices tethered to the notion of a certain kind of job in a certain kind of place are giving way to uncertainty, regret, and loss of control.

> The question is, Are we seeing a final end to what we have called blue-collar aristocracy? (quoting Sheldon Danziger from the University of Michigan) Big steel is gone, coal is gone, ship-building is gone – all the big industrial unions are gone or going, except the auto workers. These are the people who had the strongest ability to fight and now they seem to be giving up the struggle (Uchitelle, May 1, 2007).

Worthen (2004) argues for the importance of educating individuals on their rights as workers in these settings, as well as skill-training. Shipler (2004) also notes that job training programmes rarely train workers on their rights. 'The entire burden rests on the trainee to be good enough to get a job, not on the employer to be good enough to provide decent pay and working conditions' (p. 263).

While a college degree is always an important route to economic mobility, Uchitelle (2006) questions the availability of jobs that require even the skill levels that exist in the workforce today:

> Rather than a skills shortage, millions of American workers have more skills than their jobs require. That is particularly true of the college educated, who make up 30 percent of the population today, up from 10 percent in the 1960s ... Most of the unfilled jobs pay low wages and require relatively little skill, often less than the jobholder has (p. 66)... More than 45 percent of the nation's workers, whatever their skills, earned less than $13.45 an hour in 2004, or $27,600 a year for a full-time worker... Surely lack of skill and education does not

hold down the wages of nearly half the workforce... The oversupply of skilled workers is driving people into jobs beneath their skills and driving down the pay of jobs equal to their skills... (pp. 66–7).

Uchitelle therefore contends that simply focusing on training is misguided, based on 'the mistaken assumption ...that the wages workers earn are primarily determined by the skills they bring to a job' (Uchitelle, 2006 p. 65). And Ehrenreich (2001) asserts that 'no job, no matter how lowly, is truly "unskilled"' (p. 193).

Thus, we see that despite differences in income, education, and work experiences, the workers described in this chapter are representative of the current labour market for low-wage workers in the US and it is not an uplifting picture. The problem is global and complex but it is not beyond solutions.

Strategies for change

Unionisation

Perhaps one of the most important strategies to address low-wage and vulnerable workers is unionisation. Particularly for workers in occupations that are insecure, lack benefits and are low paid, the benefits of unionisation can be considerable. The U.S. Bureau of Labour Statistics issues a yearly report on unions that details the differences in weekly wages between union workers and non-union workers. The data are presented by demographic groups and occupation. Several categories are summarised in the tables below (Table 3.1), first by demographic group and then by selected occupations.

For the majority of workers in most demographic groups and in most occupations and industries in the US, the 'union premium', that is, the difference in wages between those represented by unions versus non-union status, translates into thousands of dollars per year. Several reports by the Centre for Economic and Policy Research (CEPR) on low wage and African American workers also demonstrate this effect. As we see in Table 3.1, African American workers who are unionised earn more than non-unionised African-American workers, but Schmitt (2008a) of CEPR also reports that unionised African-American workers are more likely to have health insurance than non-unionised counterparts (75.3 percent versus 51.1 percent) and pensions (65.6 percent versus 39.6 percent). Additionally, black workers in 15 low wage occupations earned much higher wages if they were unionised, close to $3 more per hour on average, and were more likely to have health insurance (54.3 percent versus 32.5 percent for non-union black workers in the same occupations) or a pension (56.8 percent to 23.4).

Table 3.1 Median weekly earnings of full-time wage and salary workers by union affiliation and selected characteristics (full-time workers)

Characteristic	Median weekly earnings 16 years and over	Union members	Non-union workers
All Workers	$695	$863	$663
White Men	$788	$937	$757
White Women	$626	$814	$603
Black or African American Men	$600	$768	$573
Black or African American Women	$533	$697	$513
Hispanic or Latino ethnicity, Men	$520	$793	$505
Hispanic or Latino ethnicity, Women	$473	$675	$446
Asian Men	$936	$867	$940
Asian Women	$731	$842	$712

Source: BLS, Union Members in 2007, January 25, 2008.

Table 3.2 Median weekly earnings of full-time wage and salary workers by union affiliation, occupation, and industry (Amount in U.S. Dollars)

Occupation and industry	All workers	Union members	Non-union workers
Service occupations	454	666	421
Healthcare support occupations	454	502	446
Food preparation & serving occupations	385	502	379
Building & grounds, cleaning & maintenance occupations	422	551	407
Personal care and service occupations	434	585	420
Sales and office occupations	598	717	587
Healthcare and social assistance	644	752	632
Leisure & hospitality	440	580	431
Accommodation and food services	413	534	410

Source: BLS, Union Members in 2007, January 25, 2008.

In Table 3.2 we see that unions can make a large difference in wages, particularly for low wage workers. The average annual wage for non-union hotel housekeepers in the U.S., for example, is $17,340, compared to $26,000 for unionised workers, according to the leading hotel workers union in the U.S., UNITE-HERE (Hotel Workers Rising! Fact Sheet, n.d.). CEPR estimates that the union premium for the lowest 10 percent of hourly wage earners is 20.6 percent; for the lowest 20 percent the union premium is 18.9 percent and for the 50 percent percentile of earners, it is 13.7 percent. Thus, lowest wage workers tend to reap the greatest benefits from unionisation (Schmitt, 2008b).

Given these data, one might wonder why large masses of low wage workers are not organising into unions in the US. The answer lies in the ineffective protections afforded workers who try to unionise within the system of US labour law and the roadblocks put in the way of workers and unions who attempt to organise the unorganised. Fierce employer resistance, often using illegal tactics such as firing workers who lead organising drives, is met with weak penalties and a National Labour Relations Board (NLRB) (to some extent an equivalent to a labour court) stacked with conservative appointees who rarely take strong action to secure workers' rights.

Consider one case highlighted by the non-governmental organisation, American Rights at Work. Verna Bader (a widow who helped her extended family support itself) and six other workers at Taylor Machine Products in Detroit waited over 12 years for a backpay award after being illegally fired for union activity.

> In 1989, Verna began work as a machine operator for Taylor Machine Products... In 1991, she joined her co-workers in their attempts to form a union in order to win better wages and improve health and safety on the job. She was earning only $5 an hour, and machinists with more seniority were barely making over $6 an hour... Soon after the workers began organising with the Machinists union... an inspector from the Occupational Safety and Health Administration (OSHA) visited the plant. The inspector immediately shut down a machine Verna was working on that had exposed wires, which threatened to electrocute her... Once Verna and other union supporters were identified, harassment by the foreman and anti-union co-workers plagued their final months at the company. Verna described instances where the foreman would stand behind her machine for hours, watching her every move. She recalled him threatening her, 'If you do get a union in here, you're gonna find out that you aren't gonna have a job, because it's by the grace of me that you're here.' ...After Taylor employees voted to form a union on March 25, 1992, the escalating harassment became unbearable for Verna: 'There's days that I literally went out of there crying.'

On August 6, 1992, Taylor shut down the entire department where the pro-union women worked. Their workers were told to get their belongings and to not come back (American Rights at Work, 2004).

Three years later, the NLRB ruled that Verna and the others were terminated due to union activity and ordered the company to reinstate them and compensate them with back-pay and interest. Appeals and hearings followed for years. It took over 12 years for them to finally receive any of the back-pay. Every union organiser in the US could recount such stories, many of which don't end in restitution. Thus, the goal of organising workers is an immensely difficult project in the US. Union density has been in a trajectory of decline for several decades, although there was a slight increase (0.2 percent) in 2007.

Several non-governmental organisations, including Human Rights Watch and American Rights at Work, issued reports on how labour laws in the US undermine workers' rights to organise (Human Rights Watch, 2000; Lafer, 2007). This is a quandary for the entire labour movement in the US and some unions have been particularly innovative in responding to these challenges. However, the percentage of the US workforce that is unionised is still precipitously low. A variety of new methods are being attempted, many of which involve community organising initiatives and labour-community partnerships, as will be discussed below. However, with the cumulative effect of conservative NLRB appointments and a conservative Congress, labour organising is one of the most difficult social change tasks in the contemporary US.

A low rate of unionisation means, for example, that it is exceedingly difficult for low-wage workers to afford decent housing or to send their children to college. Moreover, there are vast inequalities between the highest and lowest paid workers in society. Greenhouse (2008a) notes that income inequality in the US is so great that it more closely resembles the inequality in a third world country than that of an advanced industrial nation. Unionisation, which would begin to tackle such disparities, has not been successful in many of the industries in which these inequities exist.

Education and training

Despite the issues outlined earlier, training and education remain important avenues for achieving some measure of economic security. Yet, training must be tailored to the needs of workers, as well as corporations, and must offer realistic options within the global labour market. Better segmented and individualised education and training is one suggestion, including more effective up-front assessment of worker needs, from literacy through basic education, English language training, vocational training and post-secondary opportunities. All of this needs to be accompanied by follow-up supports on the job and in the community. Quality child care and success on the job are highly related and children benefit from early pre-school experiences (Boushey and Gundersen, 2001). Additionally, the development of career ladders on the job and through education and training would break through the pattern of horizontal mobility that so many low-wage workers experience and enhance upward economic mobility. Insufficient financial aid and welfare policies that discourage and impede educational and training opportunities are additional problems to be addressed.

Family-friendly policies

More and more attention is being given to 'family-friendly' policies in the US. A labour-sponsored organisation, the Labour Project for Working Families, advocates for extension of paid family and medical leave provisions, as well as paid sick days for all workers, expanded childcare options, elder care, more control over work time and arrangements (e.g. job sharing, flex time and other arrangements), benefits for part-time workers and more. The project also highlights additional family-friendly measures that have been successfully incorporated into collective bargaining agreements such as adoption benefits, an expanded definition of family, AIDS benefits, tuition assistance, and even a homework hotline to assist children (www.working-families.org, n.d.). On the organisation's website are suggestions for contract language and organising strategies to advance family-friendly policies.

The project also advocates for legislative action to achieve family-friendly policies for all workers, given that low union density in the US translates into a small percentage of workers being able to achieve these policies through collective bargaining. Broad adoption of these policies would help all workers, particularly working parents, more fully participate in the labour force, would signify a recognition of the issues that modern families face, and would demonstrate an attempt to find potential solutions. In comparison to public policy in many European countries, the US lags far behind in relation to programmes and policies to address family needs.

Greenhouse (2008a) describes a worker whose great pleasure was coaching his children's soccer and baseball teams. However, the expectation of more than a 60 hour work week (often with time-off-the-clock) was one of the many acutely frustrating experiences on the job. When women have to take time off from work without pay for childcare and eldercare, and then sometimes lose their jobs in the process, job demands serve to undermine rather than support a positive quality of life for working people.

These issues relate to an emphasis on profits to the exclusion of job satisfaction or job security for workers in many firms. There are exceptions, however, as some firms believe that work productivity and company profitability are, in fact, related to worker satisfaction on the job. The accounting firm Ernst and Young has had a family-friendly work environment since 1996. The company offers flexible work arrangements, full benefits to part-time workers, and grants partnerships to more women. A manager says, 'We want people to stay. We want people to make a career at E and Y' (Greenhouse, 2008a, p. 198). It is noteworthy, however, that this is a high skills, not a low-wage employer.

Other strategies

An additional set of strategies to lift earnings of workers involves community and labour involvement in economic development so that provisions for living wages, community benefit agreements, employer neutrality in union organising drives and other terms are included in local economic development projects. These strategies generally require intensive local organising and coalition building when large development projects are announced in specific cities. There have been some highly successful campaigns in California and other states (see The Partnership for Working Families' website, www.communitybenefits.org for information on campaigns and achievements). Generally, the organising goal is for these development projects to include family-sustaining wages, local hiring and training, and community benefits such as housing, recreation, 'smart growth' techniques, environmental considerations and other local needs. The growing interest in 'green' industries and reclamation of brownfields (older polluted industrial sites) are also now reflected in economic development initiatives. Another related example within the US has been campaigns against 'big box' stores, particularly Wal-Mart, whose wage levels and benefit levels have not provided equitable wage levels and adequate healthcare plans for employees.

Briefly, there are several more areas that need to be mentioned but will not be discussed in detail. One of the most critical needs in the US that would make a huge difference to workers' wellbeing is that of healthcare access and quality. This is a huge topic and is the subject of entire conferences, national and state-level organising campaigns, legislative initiatives, presidential candidates' debates, academic analysis and more. Any discussion of the needs of all strata of workers in the US has to encompass the broken healthcare system in the US.

Additionally, it has been decades since policy goals of job creation and full employment have been on the public agenda within the US. Since the Reagan era of the 1980s, an ethos of less government intervention on behalf of vulnerable individuals and families has been a mantra of politicians in both major parties. However, government action on behalf of corporate interests and the wealthiest segments of society play a major role in political and economic policies. A resurrection of the goals of full employment and job creation could help reverse the rising levels of inequality within the US workforce and population. Bob Herbert (2008), a New York Times columnist, writes that 'If we can't achieve something close to full employment for the wider society, there is very little hope for those mired at the bottom' (p. A19).

Can our European friends help show us how to reclaim some of the lost power of the working class in the U.S.? While the European Union was formed to strengthen European countries through cooperation and uniform economic policies, Kuttner (2008) notes that there is hardly unity within the European Union today:

> The European constitution is looking more American. It has more fragmentation, more federalism, and more centres of veto power... Since it takes a strong state to develop policies to balance powerful business elites, the EU has become a net conservative force.

> With national centre-right governments now dominant, most commissioners of the EU are less interested in advancing social counterweights than in accelerating free capital movements (p. 25).

But Kuttner (2008) does not end on a totally dismal note. He thinks that Europe remains far more of a mixed economy than the US and he concludes that the ideal of social partnership remains strong. He believes the strength of labour unions is paramount and 'good ideas to restore a more balanced economic system are plentiful' (p. 27). The US, with its power and influence, can help to tip the balance away from 'toxic financial products and market-fundamentalist ideology' (Kuttner, 2008) to a more humane, more egalitarian, more just, economic and political system.

Summary and conclusions

Mishel and Rothstein (2007) argue that a progressive economic agenda for the 21st century in the US requires a commitment to equality. The Economic

Policy Institute has developed an economic agenda that is designed to 'spur growth, reduce insecurity and provide broadly shared prosperity'. This 'Agenda for Shared Prosperity' is a response to 'the growing gap between America's promise and its problems'. With an emphasis on addressing economic insecurity and inequality, and stimulating economic growth as primary goals, the Agenda proposes a broad range of progressive proposals for health and retirement security, fair trade, rewarding work, building infrastructure and jobs through production of renewable energy, and providing opportunity for all:

> This agenda challenges the superficial assertion that global forces, technology, and competition have rendered Americans helpless to do anything but adjust individually to the outcomes of an unregulated market. Despite the assertions of pundits and policy makers who preach that we're all on our own, there had never been a single reason for Americans to despair of our own capacity to improve our condition (Economic Policy Institute, 2008).

Uchitelle (2006) believes that under President Clinton, conservative populism replaced progressive populism as the dominant political force and 'as much as anyone, Clinton disconnected the Democratic Party from its past, specifically its New Deal concern for job security and full employment' (p. 150). Layoffs began to disappear as a political issue. According to Uchitelle, for the first time, a Democratic administration distanced itself from job security through government intervention and strong unions that the party had for so long represented.

To return to the departure point of this chapter, the problems facing US workers require a variety of strategies and policies to reverse the social and economic polarisation taking place currently in the US. We have discussed the characteristics and problems of the very poor, the working poor, the near poor, and the 'disposable' Americans. We have argued that there is a need to move beyond current educational policies and toward a much more individualised education and training system. We have discussed the need for family policies, unionisation, economic development, healthcare, job creation and full employment policies. After more than 30 years of deindustrialisation, neoliberal policies, decline in union density, increased inequality and economic insecurity, conservative tax and trade policies, there is a very full agenda ahead in the United States for those who take these problems seriously. Michael Johnson, the Boggs, Angie and Jewell, John Arnold, Carletta Connor, Scott Wilcoxon and Verna Bader deserve nothing less.

REFERENCES

American Rights at Work (2004) Workers Wait and Wait for the NLRB to Enforce the Law. http://www.americanrightsatwork.org/workers-voices/stories/workers-wait-and-wait-for-the-nlrb-to-enforce-the-law-20040422–257–155.html, date accessed 14 July 2008.

Boushey, H. and Gundersen, B. (2001) *When Work Just Isn't Enough: Measuring Hardships Faced By Families After Moving from Welfare to Work*, Washington, DC: Economic Policy Institute.

Boushey, H., Fremstad, S., Gregg, R. and Waller, M. (2007) *Understanding Low-Wage Work in the U.S.*, Washington, DC: Centre for Economic Policy and Research.

Card, D. and Blank, R. (2000) (eds) *Finding Jobs: Work and Welfare Reform*, NY: Russell Sage Foundation.

DeParle, J. (2004) *American Dream: Three Women, Ten Kids, and a Nation's Drive to End Welfare*, NY: Viking.

Duncan, C. (1999) *World's Apart: Why Poverty Persists in Rural America*, New Haven: Yale University Press.

Economic Policy Institute (2008) 'Agenda For Shared Prosperity', http://www.sharedprosperity.org date accessed 30 July 2008.

Ehrenreich, B. (2001) *Nickel and Dimed: On (Not) Getting By in America*, New York: Metropolitan Books, Holt and Co.

Fine, J. (2006) *Worker Centres: Organising Communities at the Edge of the Dream*, Ithaca, NY: ILR Press, Cornell University Press.

Friedlin, J. (2004) Welfare Series: Services for Abused Women Scarce. Women's eNews, 27 August. http://www.womensenews.org/article.cfm/dyn/aid/1964/context/archive date accessed 31 July 2008.

Connecticut Centre for a New Economy (2001) *Good Jobs Strong Communities*, New Haven, CT: Connecticut Centre for a New Economy.

Greenhouse, S. (2008a) *The Big Squeeze: Tough Times for the American Worker*, NY: Knopf.

Greenhouse, S. (2008b) 'Starting Out Means a Steeper Climb', *The Nation*, 12 May, 22–4.

Herbert, B. (2008) 'A Dubious Milestone', *New York Times*, 21 June, A19.

Holzer, H. and Lerman, R. (2007) *America's Forgotten Middle-Skill Jobs*, Washington, DC: The Workforce Alliance.

Hotel Workers Rising! (n.d.) Fact Sheet: U.S. Hotel Industry & Record Profits. http://www.hotelworkersrising.org/media/RecordProfitsFactSheet.pdf date accessed 17 June, 2008.

Human Rights Watch (2000) *Unfair Advantage: Workers' Freedom of Association in the United States under International Human Rights Standards*, New York: Human Rights Watch.

Institute for Women's Policy Research (IWPR) (2003) *Before and After Welfare Reform: The Work and Well-Being of Low-Income Single Parent Families*, Washington, DC.

Institute for Women's Policy Research (2007) *Quarterly Newsletter* Spring/Summer, 2007 Washington, DC.

▶

▶

Kuttner, R. (2007) *The Squandering of America: How the Failure of Our Politics Undermines Our Prosperity*, New York: Knopf Press.

Kuttner, R. (2008) 'Continental Drift', *The American Prospect*, July/August, 23–7.

Labour Project for Working Families (n.d.). www.working-families.org. date accessed 9 February 2008.

Lafer, G. (2007) *Neither Free Nor Fair: The Subversion of Democracy Under National Labour Relations Board Elections*, Washington, DC: American Rights at Work.

Mehta, C. and Theodore, N. (2004) 'Revolving Doors: Temp Agencies as Accelerators of Churning in Low-Wage Labour Markets', in L. Simmons (ed.) *Welfare, The Working Poor and Labour*, Armonk, NY: M.E. Sharpe.

Mishel, L. and Rothstein, R. (2007) 'Schools as Scapegoats', *The American Prospect*, October, 44–7.

Neubeck, K. (2006) *When Welfare Disappears: The Case for Economic Human Rights*, New York: Routledge/Taylor & Francis.

Newman, C. and Chen, V. (2007) *The Missing Class: Portraits of the Near Poor in America*, Boston: Beacon Press.

Pearce, D. and Brooks, J. (1999) *A Self-Sufficiency Standard for Pennsylvania*, University of Washington School of Social Work, Wider Opportunities for Women.

Pearce, D. (2007) *Overlooked and Undercounted: Where Connecticut Stands*, University of Washington School of Social Work, http://www.cga.ct.gov/pcsw/Publication percent20PDFs/2007/Where percent20CT percent20Stands percent20Exec percent20Sum.pdf date accessed 31 July 2008.

Schmitt, J. (2008a) 'Unions and Upward Mobility for African-American Workers' Centre for Economic Policy and Research, April, http://www.cepr.net/documents/publications/unions_2008_04.pdf date accessed 17 June 2008.

Schmitt, J. (2008b) 'The Union Wage Advantage for Low Wage Workers' Centre for Economic Policy and Research, May, http://www.cepr.net/documents/publications/quantile_2008_05.pdf date accessed 17 June 2008.

Shipler, D. (2004) *The Working Poor: Invisible in America*, New York: Knopf.

Uchitelle, L. (2006) *The Disposable American: Lay-Offs and Their Consequences*, New York: Knopf.

Uchitelle, L. (2007) 'The End of the Line as They Know It', *The New York Times*, 1 April, Section 3:1.

Uchitelle, L. (2008) 'The Wage That Meant Middle Class', *The New York Times*, 20 April, 3.

Worthen, H. (2004) 'The Workforce Investment Act and the Labour Movement', in L. Simmons (ed.) *Welfare, The Working Poor and Labour*, Armonk, NY: M.E. Sharpe.

The Reality of Vulnerability Among Britain's Non-Unionised Workers with Problems at Work

Anna Pollert

Introduction

There has been a steady decline in trade union membership in Britain since the 1970s, so that today, the vast majority of employees – over 70 percent – are non-unionised. In 2006, only 28.4 percent of employees were union members, down 0.6 percentage points from 2005 and in the private sector, it fell by the same amount to just 16.6 percent (DTI, 2007a: 1). For the past decade, only approximately a third of UK employees have been covered by collective agreements on pay, and in the private sector, which comprises 80 percent of employment (Labour Market Trends, 2006), only 19.6 percent (DTI, 2007a: 37). The lower paid among the non-unionised are, arguably, the most vulnerable among them. Yet, while the government is now alluding to 'vulnerable' workers, its definition is narrow, since it is only considered problematic if employers 'exploit' it (DTI, 2006: 25) and little systematic evidence exists on the experience of non-unionised workers earning below the median – 40 percent of the workforce, according to the Labour Force Survey – and how they deal with problems at work. This chapter, based on 50 in-depth interviews with a sample of workers who sought help on employment problems with the Citizens Advice Bureaux (CAB) and contextualised in a regionally representative survey of 501 low paid, non-unionised workers with problems at work in Britain (the Unrepresented Worker Survey, or URWS) sheds light on this under researched issue.[1]

The unrepresented worker survey

Problems experienced

The URWS first asked respondents about problems experienced in any job in the previous three years, then on all problems in one job, and finally on the main problem they 'pushed hardest' to resolve. The most frequent *categories of problems* among vulnerable workers in the three years prior to interview were over pay (primarily pay being less than others in similar jobs or pay being incorrect), work relations (overwhelmingly stress, followed by management bullying), workload, job security (primarily a worry that they would lose their job), working hours (mainly unpredictability and working more than agreed), contract or job description (mainly lack of a written job description and being asked to do things not specified if there was one), health and safety, job opportunities, taking time off and discrimination (Table 4.1). In most of these areas, around half felt their problem an infringement of their rights. All suffered multiple problems over several years, but focusing on the *one* screened job with the main problems, two-fifths of the sample had *one* problem, a fifth had two problems and fewer had three or four problems.

When *details of problems* are examined, aspects of work intensification emerge as the main ones: stress, being given too much work without enough time and management taking advantage or bullying.

Table 4.1 The nature of problems identified by the Unrepresented Workers Survey

	All problems experienced in all jobs in past three years		All problems experienced in screened job	
	Number	Percent	Number	Percent
1. Pay[1]	191	38.1	181	36.1
2. Work relations, such as stress or bullying	184	36.7	172	34.3
3. Workload	160	31.9	143	28.5
4. Job Security	152	30.3	124	24.8
5. Working hours	143	28.5	127	25.3
6. Contract or job description	133	26.5	115	22.8
7. Health and Safety	122	24.4	109	21.8
8. Opportunities	121	24.2	102	20.4
9. Taking time-off	120	24.0	109	21.8
10. Discrimination[2]	89	17.8	76	15.2

Notes: Results rounded to one decimal place.

[1] Such as not being paid the correct amount, not being paid regularly, or not receiving pay for holidays or overtime etc.

[2] Towards yourself.

Seeking advice

Sixty one percent of the URWS sample sought advice about the problem that they pushed hardest to do something about. Overall, about one in five of those who sought advice (i.e. 12 percent of all vulnerable workers with problems) went to an independent, external source of advice, such as a trade union, ACAS, a CAB, solicitor or Law Centre, professional body, but the single most important external recourse was the CAB (12.8 percent of those who sought advice went to a CAB, and 4.7 percent rated this as the most influential advice they received).

The majority (over half) were advised to approach their line managers and senior managers informally, a fifth to use the formal grievance procedure and 11 percent to seek support from a CAB. Those most likely to seek advice from CABx include workers who felt that their rights were violated, and those whose problems concerned discrimination, pay, job security, taking time off and working hours.

Action taken

The vast majority of workers – 86 percent – attempted to do something to overcome their problem. Those in semi-skilled manual occupations and with less than a year's tenure in the 'problem' job were more likely to have done nothing than the average 14 percent of the sample. The most common forms of action were an informal approach to line managers (81 percent of those taking action) or to senior managers (50 percent). A surprisingly large 28 percent of actors took informal joint action with other workers with a shared problem.

While the government introduced legislation barring ET application until all 'internal procedures' were exhausted (DTI, 2001: 21) the finding that only 14 percent of those trying to resolve matters used the formal grievance procedures raises serious questions about their adequacy. It can be seen in the context of is the Workplace Employment Relations Survey (WERS) evidence of a disjuncture between formal procedures and their actual use: 91 percent of workplaces had them in 1998, but only 30 percent used them (Cully *et al.*, 1999: 74).[2] The interviews with CAB clients (below) illustrate how formal procedures can be pursued in name, but subverted in content by managers.

Seeking external support was rare: 11 percent went to a CAB and 9 percent to a union. Recourse to CABx was less likely if respondents reported a formal grievance procedure at their workplace and if they were educated to degree level. A larger sample would be needed to test for significance in the findings of higher proportions seeking the CAB who had problems with discrimination, job security (dismissal, redundancy), pay and working hours, although these findings corroborate other research on the types of problems dealt with by CABx (below and Pollert, 2007a).

Only 2 percent began an application to an Employment Tribunal (ET), which is similar to other survey findings. According to WERS, in 2004 only 2.2 ET claims were brought per 1,000 employees across all workplaces (1.7 in 1998) although this varied considerably by industry (Kersley *et al.*, 2006: 227; Cully *et al.*, 1999: 129). A DTI survey found only 3 percent of those with employment problems applied to an ET (Casebourne *et al.*, 2006: 118). More anecdotally, the CAB reports large numbers of aggrieved workers who, even when advised of their rights, fail to take them further (Citizens Advice, 2001a, 2001b).

Outcomes to problems

Did the workers who participated in our survey manage to bring the problem that they pushed hardest to solve to a conclusion and if so, was this successful? The 2002 Employment Act, which introduced the Statutory Dismissal and Disciplinary and Statutory Grievance Procedures in October 2004, was designed to reduce ET applications and confine dispute resolution to the workplace. Although this legislation is to be repealed in 2009 (House of Lords, 2007; DTI, 2007b), the government retains its commitment to 'seeking to resolve more disputes in the workplace' (DTI, 2006: 39). The URWS, however, demonstrates how poorly this system operates. Almost half our respondents had no result at all. Of the 429 respondents who took action about their problem, 47 percent had no outcome.[3] Just 38 percent reported that their problem was brought to a conclusion and while half of these were satisfied with it, this amounted to only 16 percent of workers who experienced problems and 18.6 percent of workers who took some action.

A significant finding was that the probability of achieving a satisfactory resolution was double for respondents still in their job compared to those who had quit: 29 percent of those who had achieved a satisfactory resolution had quit, compared to 44 percent of those who had not. The low levels of satisfactory resolution in the URWS confirm other research findings. Genn (1999: 157) found that 52 percent of those who took action on an employment problem reached no agreement and no resolution. Similarly, just under half of respondents to a survey of users of a West Midlands employment advice line resolved their problem (Russell and Eyers, 2002: 2).

The qualitative study of CAB clients with employment problems

The work of the CAB

Citizens Advice is a generalist, volunteer-led service providing free advice on a range of issues, including employment problems, across England, Wales

and Northern Ireland.[4] Its general approach is to 'empower' clients by providing information, help in writing letters and referring them to experts
(Abbott, 1998). In 2006/2007 144 out of 433 bureaux had an adviser with
specific knowledge of employment law (paid and/or voluntary) – just 33 percent. Thus, the majority of CABx do not have advisers with more than a
general knowledge of employment rights (Citizens Advice, 2007).

As a charity, the CAB has always been under-funded and under-resourced
(Citron, 1989; Richard, 1989; Pollert, 2005, 2007b: 124; Genn, 1999: 76, 89).
In recent research for the TUC Commission on Vulnerable Employment
(hence referred to as 'the CoVE research'), 70 percent of CAB advisers felt
they had too few or far to few advisers, around two-thirds had experienced
cuts in real terms in the previous three years and for 81 percent, time spent
on fund-raising had increased or greatly increased over the same period
(Pollert *et al.*, 2008: 39–51). State funding to Citizens Advice headquarters
– the provider of legal information and training to bureaux – was cut by 10 percent in 2006/07, forcing a £4 million (20 percent) savings programme and
an inevitable 'impact on the levels of service' (Citizens Advice, 2006: 4).
Contractual changes to state funding for free 'legal-aid' has reduced the con-
stituency of solicitors providing free employment advice to whom the CAB
can refer clients (Citizens Advice, 2004a; Pollert, 2005: 225, 2007b: 121).
Most referrals are now to 'no-win, no-fee' lawyers, the system extended from
personal injury to other areas of law since 1998, but while no fees are charged
if a case is lost, a higher fee than 'normal' is charged if it is won (Lord
Chancellor's Department, 1998: 24). Growing concerns about the quality of
the 'no-win, no-fee' arrangements, reflected in interviewees' experiences
here, prompted the government to commission a major research review into
its operation (Ministry of Justice, 2008).

The CAB study

The telephone interviews with 50 workers who approached a CAB for help
does not claim to be representative, since its aim is to provide qualitative
insights into the types of problems experienced by those approaching a CAB
– the most common source of external advice (Pollert, 2005: 223).[5] The
majority of participants came from sectors identified as those at risk of vulnerability (Citizens Advice, 1997, 2000), and by surveys of ET applications
and those facing breaches of Minimum Wage regulations (DTI, 2006: 25):
pubs, hotels, restaurants, care-homes, cleaners, security companies, small
shops, hairdressers and small factories. However, many also came from large
organisations in both the public and private sectors, including multinational
companies with Human Resources (HR) departments. The problems that
drove workers to a CAB included summary dismissal, forced redundancy and

resignation, prolonged bullying and victimisation, unpaid wages, no paid holidays, sexual and racial discrimination, dismissal during sickness, unlawful contract change and dismissal during takeover. Experiences ranged from crude employer abuse of rights to protracted harassment and sophisticated evasion of legal challenges to malpractice (Table 4.2, Appendix, summarises 28 interviews focused upon).

Problems in small establishments: dismissal and unpaid wages

Dismissals and unpaid wages were embedded in wider intimidation and unfair practice. Workers were often sacked as they approached one year's service, because they requested an employment right, were pregnant (Citizens Advice, 2001c), or because they were no longer wanted (possibly because of age) – often on fabricated charges and on provocation. *Tina*, an 18 year old hair-stylist, paid as a 'helper' at £1.57 per hour (in 2004), and having no paid holidays or lunch breaks, merely asked for a rise when she discovered the legal minimum wage. Her employer, who also resented Tina attracting her clients, had been harassing her by forcing her to manage the salon alone, making her work while ill and undermining her in front of customers. She sacked her as she was about to complete her first year. The CAB obtained unpaid wages and holiday-pay for Tina, but did not challenge other negligence. The only penalty for the salon was that the local college stopped providing trainees. *Christine* worked part-time for almost a year at a holiday camp. When she informed her manager that she was pregnant, she was told to take two weeks off and on her return, found her P45 end-of-employment form, but no manager. The CAB prepared an ET application for unfair dismissal and sex discrimination, but the hearing was twice postponed, and at nine months pregnancy she accepted £200 in compensation. She had hoped for between £500 and £1,000, was left with no job or support, lost her home and lived on income support. *Tony*, a 24 year old with two years' service in an animal shelter charity, was unaware that he was earning below the minimum wage and when he queried this, was accused of smoking drugs and dismissed. The CAB successfully challenged the unfair dismissal, but although Tony was re-engaged, management bullying ensued and he was finally provoked to walk out. The CAB now told him 'not to bother with a constructive dismissal case', because it was 'your word against theirs' – a recurrent refrain.

In each of these narratives, the interviews presented a cluster of problems. To resolve, or prevent the problem, the entire ensemble of working conditions required intervention to exert workplace and/or external pressure. But the CAB advisers generally managed to challenge simple legal breaches, such as unpaid wages, or dismissals which were clearly unfair on procedural grounds, but could not take on the full ensemble of malpractice, including bullying. The reluctance of advisers, particularly non-specialists in employment law, to pursue complex constructive dismissal cases, may also have increased following the 2001 Tribunal Regulations, which raised the maximum which could be awarded against an ET applicant from £500 to £10,000 and the 2004 Tribunal Regulations, which extended this risk to advisers (Pollert, 2005: 230, 234).

Two cases of unpaid wages in security companies illustrate the ease with which employers escaped detection and highlight the problems of enforcing rights. Non-payment of successful ET awards was found to be common by 28 percent of advisers in the CoVE research (Pollert *et al.*, 2008: 134) and illustrated for *Jacque*, a young immigrant from Burundai, who was paid £100 instead of £380 for two weeks' work. The CAB entered an ET application for unlawful deduction of wages, but no respondent appeared at the hearing and although he won the case and was awarded £289, the employer refused to pay. Two months later, Jacque was still waiting to seek County Court enforcement and could not afford the £30 needed for an application form. His desperate straits were conveyed in his asking the research interviewer for money to help him. *Graham*, a Nigerian student, likewise had no success in obtaining unpaid wages in a large security company, but he did not even reach an ET application. The 'policy' at his workplace for grievances was a telephone, where workers could leave a message, and a manager would allegedly 'sort it out'. After repeated phone-calls about his pay, there was either no response, or a vague promise that it would be paid. Three months later, he left and approached three different CABx which merely informed him (according to Graham) that in Britain it was extremely easy for employers to avoid paying unpaid wages. His experience with the 'no-win, no-fee' solicitor, to whom he was referred, was poor: the latter failed to answer letters and asked Graham to do much of his work in pursuing the company. Graham abandoned these attempts and was grateful to find another job. Other respondents also reported a lack if interest by conditional fees lawyers in typical CAB clients: since their pay is low, compensation amounts for the common problem of unpaid wages are small and the solicitor's share therefore unprofitable.

In these cases of wrongful or unfair dismissal and unpaid wages in smaller establishments, the CAB sometimes succeeded in obtaining small compensation. Although ET claims increasingly cover multiple jurisdictions (ETS, 2006), the evidence among these vulnerable workers is that their advisers selected the simpler legal breaches and avoided more complex areas, such as constructive dismissal and bullying. Workers' experience fell into two groups. Where access to a CAB was easy (which was more likely for those already sacked since they were free to access the CAB during normal daytime opening hours) and a straightforward settlement reached, clients were satisfied with support, although often disappointed with the outcome. The other group was dissatisfied with poor access, discontinuity in advice, and lack of competence or unwillingness to deal with constructive dismissal. However satisfaction with 'no-win, no-fee solicitors' was no better. Here, lack of interest, rather than of expertise, was the primary objection.

Complex and prolonged problems in large organisations

While cases in the smaller establishment showed employers' casual disregard for or ignorance of the law, those in large organisations illustrated HR departments knowing the law, but although sometimes initially demonstrating conformity with 'good practice', finally failing to rectify employment abuse at lower managerial levels. Two narratives demonstrate blatant racism, and a common finding is of gendered, multiple discrimination – particularly by men against older, experienced women.

Pat was the only woman among six other managers in a large pub in Leeds. She was bullied into excessive hours, suffered verbal and physical harassment by the manager, took out a grievance after being refused a break, left, and approached a CAB, which (unusually) tried to pursue a constructive dismissal case, but failed to consider possible sex discrimination. The HR manager, knowing of the statutory right to be accompanied at a grievance meeting (1999 Employment Relations Act), arranged Pat's meeting for a Saturday, when none of her colleagues were working. Her 'accompanier' was picked from a management list and the grievance meeting was inconclusive, even though her former boss admitted to hitting her – claiming it was a joke – while denying the unreasonable hours. A tribunal hearing occurred a year later, but her ex-boss now rebuffed all allegations and claimed he 'couldn't remember the incident'. Pat felt too intimidated by the HR department and the tribunal process to continue and withdrew her case because she 'couldn't go through with it'.

Penny, an experienced 'Team Leader' in a large motorway service-station catering chain, was bullied by a new, young, inexperienced and unqualified male manager who was a friend of the site director. He sexually and verbally harassed women workers, introduced policies that demonstrated ignorance of the sector and persistently and publicly undermined Penny. She finally 'let rip' and informed the site director she could not continue working with him. The director told her to 'calm down' and return to work when she had 'had time to think about it'. Worn down, she walked out and was signed off sick for two weeks by her doctor: 'I had worked so many hours, I was so tired, I wasn't in the right state of mind to do anything'.

On resuming work, the site director, with whom Penny was to pursue the grievance, was on holiday. Meanwhile, the new manager had downgraded her post and changed her to three-hour shifts, which made travel unmanageable. She 'went back on the sick and eventually never went back again'. The CAB generalist advisor warned her against bringing a constructive dismissal case and Penny received nothing and was glad to find another job.

In two examples of racist harassment in large organisations, grievance procedures again proved spurious or non-existent. When *Alpay,* a Turkish employee in a leading luxury hotel chain was racially abused by another worker who was championed by his line-manager, he reported the incident to HR. Like Penny, he was told to take two weeks' leave to 'calm down'. On return, he faced further racist insults, complained again to HR, was again told to calm down and 'they would take care of it'. On the third occasion, he contacted the senior Director of HR, who appeared sympathetic and helpful, took details of the complaint and said she would resolve it. But when the formal grievance meeting was convened, she told him that he was a good employee but she did not accept there was a formal complaint. He was offered laundry work to avoid the racist colleague, which he refused. Suffering symptoms of stress, he contacted the CAB, which completed an ET application for racial discrimination. But nothing was successfully pursued and a year later, he had merely been moved to another department.

Lawrence, a wine waiter in a London hotel and the only black worker in this 'front of house' job was threatened by higher management:

> A member of staff (a head waiter) made very racist comments to me. I told the line manager and he did not do anything about it. I wanted an apology. Then I went to the personnel manager – but he was not prepared to take any actions. He told me to consider my position because I had not been there very long. Then they tried to find fault with my work – which they had never done before.

Lawrence left and accepted an Acas-conciliated settlement. No case of racial discrimination was recorded via a tribunal.

Each of these examples demonstrate that detailed, specialist evidence and cross-examination would have been needed to mount a serious challenge, particularly in racial and sex discrimination cases. In no instance did the CAB have the resources to provide this. And in each case, senior managers and HR departments either colluded from the start, or pacified the victim and failed to stop malpractice. Ritualistic and superficial compliance with the legal requirements of grievances procedures, if used at all, barely concealed open disregard in reality.

These dynamics are not confined to sectors notorious for exploitative practices, such as hospitality, but occurred in other large companies, including multinationals, where the victim was isolated at departmental level and then caught within a corporate machine which ultimately protected lower-level managers.

Chitra was a long-serving, middle-aged Indian employee in an international recruitment company with a respected reputation administering information technology (IT) orders. In 2004 she received a letter indicating her exclusion from a general pay rise, which was followed by her manager 'inviting' her to go to the pub to discuss this. She was alarmed. In the past, whenever he had taken anyone for a drink, he wanted to sack them, quipping there were two ways to get rid of people: the 'formal and informal'. He pressed her about the letter, forced her to concede she was surprised she did not get the bonus and told her the IT Director 'was not happy with her work'. Shocked and bewildered, she asked how she could improve her performance, but was told to leave. If not, he would make her life miserable and give her so many projects she would be unable to cope. She started crying, again asked what she should do and was told to resign within two weeks, with a month's salary and any holiday pay owing and to tell everyone she was resigning voluntarily.

Chitra discovered anecdotally that her managers intended a younger woman to replace her. If she resigned she would lose her share bonus in the company, but if she were redundant she would be entitled to it. Redundancy was refused. She was accused of 'telling bad stories', which she denied, pointing out that if others saw a worker voluntarily resigning crying, they must wonder what was happening. Taking a colleague's advice, she approached the HR manager, who assumed she was resigning because she was unhappy about the bonus. Chitra told her she had been dismissed and threatened and, as in the cases cited above, was assured 'she would see what she could do' and not to leave, since procedure had not been followed. Now suffering severe stress, Chitra was recalled by her manager and shouted at. He denied he had threatened or bullied her and, together with the HR manager, now set her 'objectives' and three monthly reviews. As in Alpay's case, HR's initial demonstration of 'good practice' was short-lived, since it failed to investigate her allegations of management threats or any grounds for alleged competence problems.

Henceforth, HR sent a series of contradictory messages, first asking why she did not return to work as it was willing to take her back, then suggesting redundancy. Thoroughly confused, Chitra approached the CAB and contacted Acas, which told her not to sign any agreement with the company. The CAB suggested she should apply for constructive dismissal. However, to apply for this, she was informed she had to resign first before completing an ET form, but she felt unable to do this, since she was off sick. She was too unwell to respond when HR phoned offering a 'compromise' agreement, but it subsequently switched to a redundancy offer of just £2,800, a bonus and 'the chance to discuss her shares'.

The CAB argued she should expect a settlement of around £10,000 (based on at least six months' pay). This the company rejected and again changed strategy, now stating it was happy to take her back. Chitra was too ill and frightened to return and was then sent an email threatening that if she did not return, she would be dismissed. She replied that she would return if her doctor agreed. Management sent her a medical form, which she completed, taking the precaution of photocopying it, and returned. Her caution was well grounded: HR claimed they did not receive it, so she sent the copied form.

Chitra's story continued for over a year. For three months, the HR department shifted its position, distorting information and colluding with the departmental manager. It now conceded that what had been said regarding her performance was upsetting, but strongly refuted the manager's bullying or dismissal threats. The CAB argued she could now apply to an ET for unfair dismissal while ill. But worried about delay Chitra was 'not very confident in the CAB'. A follow-up interview the following year revealed that she had been referred to a psychiatrist, was taking anti-depressants, regularly sent sick-notes to the employer, had left the CAB and resorted to a solicitor. She was advised she could no longer claim for unfair dismissal while ill, or constructive dismissal, since the company continued to claim it had received no sick-notes from her. HR told her they would terminate her contract on grounds of incapacity.

Her solicitor now changed the grounds for a tribunal application to general harassment, bullying and racial harassment and breach of contract. After a new grievance letter, the company responded that, 'as a favour, they would keep her on' and persisted in claiming it had not received her sick notes. When re-interviewed, she was still waiting for a grievance meeting, but could not find a colleague to accompany her, since they were all too frightened. She was not permitted to bring her legal advisor or a family member.

The end of Chitra's story was unclear. But it demonstrates how the existence of an HR department and formal grievance procedures can mask practices of legal evasion.[6] In her case, it appears that HR was determined to save a subordinate manager as well as its own costs, with a variety of tactics. While the solicitor may have been more successful than the CAB, the inequality of power between a vulnerable individual and a sophisticated management collective allowed the problem to become so protracted that the necessary evidence in her support had receded. Again, external remedy was too little and too late. Chitra ended with mental breakdown.

There were many other examples of workers intimidated by a management hierarchy colluding with or even initiating malpractice. These included a stylist in a major hairdressing chain, who, after 15 years' service, was downgraded after sickness leave with an occupational injury and found that

HR always deferred to the salon manager. She failed to obtain legal redress. There were also examples in the public sector. A non-unionised lecturer resigned after management refused to pay him an agreed grade and a senior university administrator left following downgrading, after HR forced her entire department to reapply for their jobs. The first could have claimed constructive dismissal, but ended unemployed and the second discovered, through her own legal research, that she should have been offered the opportunity of redundancy, or, in applying to remain, having her grade protected.

Changes in power relations as a result of company restructuring increased non-unionised workers' vulnerability, with women's harassment by men (as in many of the above cases) a frequent feature. After a large company acquired a small care-home, *Jean* was forced to resign after her job-sharer left and a new worker appropriated her hours and tasks. Delays and discontinuity at the CAB left her 'not very confident in the service', although she, like many interviewees, was no happier with conditional fees solicitors. She settled at £200 (a figure suggested by Acas), but this failed to protect her job. *Laura* had worked part-time for two years as a general office manager in a small manufacturing company. Her difficulties began after a takeover, when one of the new owners started 'getting nasty and made the job an absolute nightmare' in order to get rid of her. He sexually harassed her, cut her hours, narrowed her job and sacked her. She had a more satisfactory resolution than many: with CAB help she filed an unfair dismissal claim, was advised by Acas that she was entitled to between £1,200 and £1,500 and finally settled at £1,000.

Complications multiply in agency and subcontract relations. *Terry* had worked for eight years in a closed circuit television (CCTV) control room of 'X-Security', subcontracted to 'Midlands Trust', a partnership between a local council and a company responsible for the town's security. The 'Midlands Trust' manager accused him of stealing CCTV tapes, suspended and finally dismissed him, while X-Security tacitly supported this by failing to query the allegation. Terry's local CAB compiled an unfair dismissal ET application against 'X-Security', but 'X-Security's' solicitor stalled with demands for statements from Terry and 'Midlands Trust', and the CAB failed to pin-down the contractor and client for meetings. 'Midlands Trust' next ended the contract with 'X-Security' and its replacement, 'New Security', sacked Terry, so a transfer of undertakings element was added to the unfair dismissal claim. While the case dragged on, Terry's employment specialist adviser had retired and the CAB withdrew support, allegedly because it was part-funded by the subcontractor, the local council. He gave up. Isolation in the face of a complex, protracted grievance spelt defeat.

'X-Security' had also employed *Jenny* for several years. In her 40s, she was the only woman in a team of male CCTV operators and suffered a combination of sexual harassment, fear in dark night-time parking and unfair dismissal. She felt the client, 'Midlands Trust', manager had 'turned on her' after she complained and despite CAB support in a grievance letter to the subcontractor, 'X-Security', about 'disruptive communication' and poor safety, nothing was resolved. Jenny was forced to take eight weeks off with stress. After she returned she received a voicemail message from the 'Midlands Trust' solicitor 'not to report to work', with no explanation. 'X-Security' instructed her to work, but 'Midlands Trust' sent her home. On being told suspension was because she had asked to park in the police car park, Jenny 'could not believe this was what I was finished for'. She rang 'X-Security', was told that it would be 'sorted out', but nothing happened. 'X-Security' repeated she should report for duty; the CAB advised her likewise, but, like Terry, she was sacked when the contract moved to 'New Security'. 'Midlands Trust' had allegedly told the new company she 'did not want these three on site'. No reasons were given.

Jenny declared 'I haven't heard anything else. It's just been horrendous'. Her health had suffered after ten months of work-related stress and depression: 'I am forty-one years old – I sit and cry'. She wanted a voice: 'Tell the whole world, write to the papers. Nobody knows, you see'. A year later, her case was settled with £500 from 'X-Security'. The application for unfair dismissal had been withdrawn. She was grateful for CAB support – 'they have been fantastic' – but the outcome was poor. Terry and Jenny were silenced in a culture of intimidation and external CAB intervention failed to break the intransigence of both parties in the subcontract relationship.

Conclusions

The URWS demonstrates that most non-unionised workers with problems at work try to resolve them, but fail to get any result, let alone a successful resolution. The problems faced within the workplace are mainly concerned with pay, stress and bullying, workload and other aspects of work intensification. The same poor results are illustrated in qualitative research with CAB clients. Those who seek support with the CAB have experienced a range of problems similar to those identified in the URWS, but by the time they resort to external help, they have usually left their job or been dismissed. Among the CAB cases, sacking workers before the one year's qualifying period for employment rights, or for asking for minimal rights, were frequent abuses. Victimisation was often complex, yet while multiple discrimination (racial, sexual and age) and harassment often occurred, it was usually only final dismissal which was addressed by most CABx. Constructive dismissal was avoided because of insufficient resources for proper investigation and cross-examination, and therefore, problems of proof.

The CAB interviews reveal the ways in which employers frequently prolonged and disguised malpractice with more subtle processes, such as changing contracts, pseudo-appraisal, forced resignation, re-engagement, intimidating meetings, falsifying records and 'losing' employees' correspondence, including sick-notes. This occurred among larger organisations which had legal representation, and in addition to sophisticated evasive manoeuvres, used court cost threats to intimidate both workers and their representatives (Citizens Advice, 2004b). While a small study such as this cannot evaluate the general role of HR departments, these cases illustrated how higher-level HR managers may initially appear to uphold 'good practice', closing ranks with managerial subordinates was a common conclusion. These examples also demonstrate how lip-service to legal grievance procedures disguised continuing unfair practice. Those working within a subcontract or agency relationship suffered even more intractable attribution problems, caught in the web between a subcontractor or agency and its client. Many of these involved breaches of transfer of undertaking legislation, with workers dismissed or suffering pay cuts with ownership change.

A key problem for workers was access to bureaux, which was usually during daytime office hours; those trying to resolve problems while in their jobs were at a disadvantage compared to those already sacked. However, dismissed workers were then faced with the dilemma of pursuing their grievance with the CAB, or finding another job: time constraints meant these were irreconcilable goals. Although half the respondents were satisfied with CAB help, this includes those who were grateful for support but lost their jobs, suffered indignity and ended with paltry or no financial settlement (Table 4.2). Only two people received more than a few hundred pounds. Almost half of the respondents found the CAB inadequate and incapable of confronting the greater power and sophistication of the employer, particularly in constructive dismissal and more complex cases, however, satisfaction was no greater with 'no-win, no-fee' solicitors and many were deterred by cost.

All the CAB clients' stories were distressing. Workers experienced frustration and anger. They suffered financially, physically and psychologically. Many were forced to take time off work through stress-induced mental illness and were unable to pursue their grievance until well enough. The respondents in both the URWS and the CAB study testified to the crisis in support for the vulnerable, unorganised worker.

Notes

1 This research is based on ESRC Project R000 23 9679; 'The Unorganised Worker: Routes to Support and Views on Representation' (2003–2005).

The telephone survey of 501 workers was conducted by IFF in 2004. I would like to acknowledge joint work with Andy Charlwood in the analysis of the Unrepresented Worker Survey. I would like to thank Citizens Advice at both national and local levels for their help and support in providing information and access for the qualitative study of those seeking CAB help and the many people who gave of their time in reliving their experiences in the research interviews. Further Working Papers on this research can be found at the website of the Centre for Employment Studies Research, Bristol Business School, University of the West of England, http://www.uwe.ac.uk/bbs/research/cesr/workingpapers.shtml

2 WERS 2004 (Kersley *et al.*, 2006: 217) shows no change in the incidence of disciplinary procedures (91 percent of workplaces), while grievance procedures were present among 88 percent. However, the focus is on detailed procedural arrangements conforming to the 2004 statutory Dismissal and Disciplinary and Grievances procedures of the 2002 Employment Act and the survey took place too close to the start of legislation to ascertain its application in practice.

3 Respondents were asked: 'Did this action lead to any conclusion with your employer?' This question was framed so as to identify any conclusion at all, rather than a resolution to the problem.

4 Further details at http://www.citizensadvice.org.uk/index/aboutus/factsheets.htm

5 Research was conducted in 2004–2005. Thirty CABx managers agreed to participate and distributed to clients with employment problems a letter and a prepaid return-envelope inviting them to provide a contact number for telephone interview and offering a £10 gift voucher. A total of 50 people were interviewed, 35 women and 15 men with a mixture of ages. Twenty came from London and the South East, 17 from the Midlands and 13 from the North. The telephone interviews were tape recorded, after permission, and probed the problems experienced, the process of seeking redress, and the outcomes. They lasted from half an hour to over an hour and some were followed up a year later where there were ongoing problems. The names of all respondents have been changed and workplaces anonymised.

6 WERS 1998 noted the low *usage* (30 percent of workplaces) of formal grievance procedures where they existed (Cully *et al.*, 1999: 77). The 4 percent of workplaces (down to 1 percent in 2004) which did not allow a representative to accompany an employee at a grievance/disciplinary hearing were all non-union (Cully *et al.*, 1999: 98; Kersley *et al.*, 2006: 220).

REFERENCES

Abbott, B. (1998) 'The new shop stewards – the Citizens Advice Bureaux?', *Employee Relations*, 20(6): 610–27.

Casebourne, J., Regan, J., Neathey, F. and Tuohy, S. (2006) *Employment Rights at Work – Survey of Employees 2005,* DTI Employment Relations Research Series No. 51, London: Department of Trade and Industry.

Citizens Advice (1997) *Flexibility abused. A CAB evidence report on employment conditions and the labour market,* London: Citizens Advice.

Citizens Advice (2000) *Wish you were here. A CAB evidence report on the paid holiday provisions of the Working Time Regulations 1998,* London: Citizens Advice.

Citizens Advice (2001a) *Improving Employment Dispute Resolution: The CAB Service's Response.* London: National Association of Citizens Advice Bureaux.

Citizens Advice (2001b) *Fairness and Enterprise: The CAB Service's Case for a Fair Employment Commission.* London: National Association of Citizens Advice Bureaux.

Citizens Advice (2001c) *Birth Rights. A CAB evidence report on maternity and paternity rights at work,* London: Citizens Advice.

Citizens Advice (2004a) *The Geography of Advice: An Overview of the Challenges Facing the Community Legal Service,* London: Citizens Advice.

Citizens Advice (2004b) 'Employment Tribunals: The intimidatory use of costs threats by employers' legal representatives', March CAB Evidence, London: Citizens Advice Bureaux.

Citizens Advice (2006) *Citizens Advice Annual Report, 2005/2006,* London: Citizens Advice.

Citizens Advice (2007) 2006/2007 *Citizens Advice Bureau Information Survey,* mimeo, London: Citizens Advice.

Citron, J. (1989) *The Citizens Advice Bureaux, for the Community, by the Community,* London: Pluto Press.

Cully, M., Woodland, S., O'Reilly, A. and Dix, G. (1999) *Britain at Work as depicted by the 1998 Workplace Employee Relations Survey,* London: Routledge.

DTI (2001) *Routes to Resolution: Improving Dispute Resolution in Britain,* Consultation Document, July, London: Department of Trade and Industry.

DTI (2006) *Success at Work: Protecting Vulnerable Workers, Supporting Good Employers. A policy statement for this Parliament,* March, London: Department of Trade and Industry.

DTI (2007a) *Trade Union Membership 2006,* Employment Market Analysis and Research, London: Department of Trade and Industry and National Statistics.

DTI (2007b) *Better Dispute Resolution: A Review of Employment Dispute Resolution in Great Britain,* Michael Gibbons, London: Department of Trade and Industry.

ETS (2006) Employment Tribunal Service Annual Report and Accounts, 2005–06, London: Employment Tribunals Service, a Department of Trade and Industry Service.

▶

▶

Genn, H. (1999) *Paths to Justice: What People Do and Think About Going to the Law*, Oxford and Portland, Oregon: Hart Publishing.

House of Lords (2007) *Employment Bill HL 2007*, Parliamentary Copyright, House of Lords, London: the Stationery Office.

Kersley, B., Alpin, C., Forth, J., Bryson, A., Bewley, H., Dix, G. and Oxenbridge, S. (2006) *Inside the Workplace: Findings from the 2004 Workplace Employment Relations Survey*, DTI, ESRC, Acas, PSI, London: Routledge.

Labour Market Trends 2006 Labour Market Trends (2006), Public and private sector employment, Table S29, December 2006, Labour Market Trends, Office for National Statistics.

Lord Chancellor's Department (1998) *White Paper, Modernising Justice: The Government's Plans for Reforming Legal Services and the Courts,* Cm 4155 www.open.gov.uk/lcd.

Ministry of Justice (2008) *No win, no fee under scrutiny* 25 June 2008 http://www.justice.gov.uk/news/newsrelease250608a.htm

Pollert, A. (2005) 'The Unorganised Worker, the Decline in Collectivism and the New Hurdles to Individual Employment Rights', *Industrial Law Journal*, September 2005, 34:3, 217–38.

Pollert, A. (2007a) *The Unorganised Vulnerable Worker: The Case for Union Organising*, Liverpool: Institute for Employment Rights.

Pollert, A. (2007b) 'Britain and Individual Employment Rights: "Paper Tigers, Fierce in Appearance but Missing in Tooth and Claw"', *Economic and Industrial Democracy*, 28:1, 115–44.

Pollert, A., Danford, A., Tailby, S., Wilton, N. and Warren, S. (2008) 'Survey of Employment Rights Advisers from Citizens Advice Bureaux and Law Centres' TUC, Commission on Vulnerable Employment.

Richard, J. (1989) *50 Years of the CAB*, London: Citizens Advice Bureaux.

Russell, C. and Eyers, D. (2002). *Clutching at Straws, Rights at Work,* Briefing Paper No. 53, West Midlands Employment and Low Pay Unit.

Appendix

Table 4.2 Summary of experiences of 28 low paid, unorganised workers who sought help with CAB, 2004–2005

	Pseudonym	Age	Region and/or town and date	Workplace or occupation	Type of problem	Resolution to problem	CAB access	Opinion of CAB
1	Tina	18	November 2004, Norfolk	Hairdresser	Wrongful dismissal	Settlement: unpaid wages and holiday pay	Good (already sacked)	Very good
2	Christine	20s	November 2004, Norfolk	Holiday camp	Pregnancy dismissal	Settlement: £200 (hoped for £500–£1,000)	Good	Good but stressed
3	Marge	53	December 2004, Greater London	Labour club	Automatic unfair dismissal (procedural grounds).	Unknown	Good (already sacked)	Good
4	Becky	20s	May 2004, Stoke on Trent, 3 Midlands	Shop	Pregnancy dismissal	Settlement unpaid wages and holiday pay	Difficult	Good
5	Tony	24	December 2004, the North East	Animal shelter charity	Unfair dismissal and bullying	Constructive dismissal case not pursued.	Poor and Discontinuous	Poor
6	Iqbal	31	November 2004, Wolverhampton, West Midlands	Garment factory	Dismissal after asking for paid holidays	Settlement: £350	Difficult	Poor
7	Bill	30	November 2004, Scarborough the North East	Small firm (lorry driver)	Unfair dismissal for asking for rights	ET ruled in favour, £1,000 with friend in legal firm	Difficult	Respected CAB but found service poor

Table 4.2 Summary of experiences of 28 low paid, unorganised workers who sought help with CAB, 2004–2005 – *continued*

	Pseudonym	Age	Region and/or town and date	Workplace or occupation	Type of problem	Resolution to problem	CAB access	Opinion of CAB
8	Jacque	20s	November 2003, in Dudley, the Midlands	Security company	Unpaid wages	Successful ET claim, but not enforced	Good	Good
9	Graham	20s	May 2005 London	Security company	Unpaid wages	None	Poor	Poor (but so was solicitor)
10	Tom	28	October 2004, Staffordshire, the Midlands	Building company	Unfair dismissal or redundancy (no warning)	£700 from National Insurance funds	Good	Good, but failed to get £1,000
11	Sheila	40s	December 2004, the Midlands	Pub, general worker	Dismissal, no reason	None	Good	Good
12	Jane	40s	December, 2004, the Midlands	Pub barmaid	Dismissal, no reason	Settlement amount gagged	Fair	Poor
13	Pat	25	December 2004, Leeds, the North	Pub Training manager	Harassment, potential constructive dismissal	ET application withdrawn, no settlement	Good	Poor
14	Penny	33	December 2004, Worcestershire, the Midlands	Motorway service station, Fast-Food Team Leader	Harassment, potential constructive dismissal	Nothing	Fair	Poor
15	Alpay	40w	December, 2004, Newcastle, the North	Large hotel chain	Racial discrimination	ET application; £100 in settlement	Good	Good

Table 4.2 Summary of experiences of 28 low paid, unorganised workers who sought help with CAB, 2004–2005 – *continued*

	Pseudonym	Age	Region and/or town and date	Workplace or occupation	Type of problem	Resolution to problem	CAB access	Opinion of CAB
16	Lawrence	40s	December 2003, London	Hotel restaurant	Racial discrimination	'Satisfactory' but would not disclose	Went to Law Centre for ET form	Had paid solicitor
17	Jasmine	34	May 2005, London	Large hairdressing chain	Bullying while ill, potential constructive dismissal	No compensation	Difficult	Fair, but found Acas advice most helpful
18	Chitra	56	December, 2004, London	Multinational recruitment company	Bullying, unfair dismissal, multiple discrimination?	No outcome after more than a year	Good	Poor, changed to solicitor (not confident)
19	Moira (not in narrative, unionised)	40s	December, 2004, London	Major Airline	Harassment and victimisation	Union compromise	n.a	n.a.
20	Jane	59	December, 2004, London	University	Potential constructive dismissal	Redundancy package	Fair	Very poor
21	John	38	November, 2004, Doncaster, the North	Further and Higher Education	Potential constructive dismissal	Left, no compensation, debt	Fair	Poor

Table 4.2 Summary of experiences of 28 low paid, unorganised workers who sought help with CAB, 2004–2005 – *continued*

Pseudonym	Age	Region and/or town and date	Workplace or occupation	Type of problem	Resolution to problem	CAB access	Opinion of CAB
22 Joanna (not in narrative)	40s	May, 2004, the Midlands	Voluntary sector	Potential constructive dismissal	Left, settlement gagging clause	Fair	Fair, but union more involved in conciliation
23 Mary	55	December 2004, Blyth, North East England	Manufacturer, takeover	Unfair dismissal	£10,000 settlement	Fair	Poor. So was solicitor. Read up about employment law herself
24 Jean	45	December 2004, North Yorkshire	Care home takeover	Forced to leave	£200 settlement	Poor	Poor
25 Laura (not in narrative)	34	December 2004, Norfolk	Small manufacturer	Unfair dismissal	£1,000	Good	Good
26 Terry	40	November, 2003, Nottinghamshire, the Midlands	Sub-contract security company	Unfair dismissal, transfer of undertakings	Sacked, outcome unclear	Good	Good, but adviser left
27 Jenny	40	November 2003, Nottinghamshire, Midlands	Sub-contract security company	Unfair dismissal, transfer of undertakings	Sacked, £500 settlement	Good	Good, but adviser left
28 Mark	50s	December 2004 Leeds, the North	Sub-contract security company	Unfair dismissal while sick	Sacked, £500 settlement	Good	Good

Working in the Gold Rush: Polish Migrants' Careers and the Irish Hospitality Sector

5

James Wickham, Elaine Moriarty, Alicja Bobek and Justyna Salamońska

Introduction

In 2008 when tourists checked into a hotel in Ireland expecting a traditional Irish welcome they were often welcomed by a receptionist with a Polish accent. By then nearly 20 years of economic growth – the so-called 'Celtic Tiger' – had turned Ireland into one of the richest countries of Europe. The dramatic expansion of the number of migrants working in Irish hotels and restaurants was one of the most visible aspects of the employment explosion in the final years of the boom. Any casual observer would have noticed these migrants are mainly young women and men from Eastern Europe. How did they end up taking on work which has an international reputation for low pay and casual employment? What does such work involve and above all what relevance has it for their future plans?

The chapter begins by describing the extraordinary growth in employment in Ireland in the early years of this century. In what has been described as a 'gold rush' labour market large numbers of new arrivals took up an apparently inexhaustible supply of jobs. We show how this involved a massive rise in the number of well educated migrants working in the hospitality sector. In Ireland, as elsewhere, the hospitality sector is renowned for low wages and poor conditions, but using interviews with Polish migrants we reveal why migrants were prepared to accept such jobs and explore migrants' reasons for coming to Ireland, the way in which they have been recruited into the hospitality sector, their working conditions and their access to training. Somewhat surprisingly, the data undermines current theories of reluctant temporary workers and displays how the casualised employment contract is often as attractive for migrant workers as it is for the employers. This 'bargain' however depends on the job being seen as temporary by both parties to the employment arrangement, and some migrants in the sector now have developed a rather different orientation to employment. At the same time, the bargain can only work because there has been both a continual stream of new arrivals and a plentiful supply of jobs. These conditions are now ending as the gold rush is deemed to be finally over.

A gold rush labour market

Since the 1980s, Ireland's sustained and rapid economic growth became one of Europe's most impressive success stories. In not much more than ten years, Ireland moved from being one of the poorest West European countries to one of the richest. In 1986 Ireland GDP per capita was only 63.7 against an average of 100 for the pre-enlargement EU 15 member states; by 1999 it stood at 111.0 (Bradley, 2000: 12).

Economic growth meant that Ireland's unemployment rate fell from one of the highest in the EU in the 1980s to become one of the lowest in the 2000s: in 1987 unemployment had peaked at 16.9 percent, but by 2001 it had fallen to a mere 4.0 percent (O'Connell, 2000: 61; European Commission, 2007: 293). No other country in Europe has seen such an increase in the number of people at work and at the start of 2008 total employment was about two million, an increase of two-thirds in 15 years. At the same time, Ireland moved from being a country of emigration to a country of immigration, so that by 2008 nearly one in eight of those at work were born outside the country – again a figure that is one of the highest in Europe and on a par with a country such as Canada.

This much is widely known. However, it is usually ignored that immigration has occurred even though Ireland's employment rate (the extent to which people aged between 15 and 64 are actually at work) has never exceeded 70 percent, the 'Lisbon target' that the EU has set for all its member states. Some quite significant groups of the population, ranging from older women to young people in disadvantaged areas, have remained either outside the workforce or officially unemployed. This is important because it suggests that for Ireland importing labour has *de facto* been preferable to mobilising all the potential 'indigenous' workforce.

Mass immigration was especially important during the final years of the boom. In these years the overall economy continued to grow, but largely because more jobs were being added rather than because of increases in productivity per worker, or in income per inhabitant. Ireland, along with the UK and Sweden, was one of the few EU countries to completely open its labour market to workers from the new member states and the inflow of migrants from the Accession States was a multiple of that anticipated by all forecasters. The standard explanation is that such forecasts had assumed a

Europe-wide open labour market. Since, in fact, countries such as France or Germany kept their labour markets closed, the three countries which had opened their labour markets ended up with vastly more migrants than expected. This argument is convenient, but problematic. The forecasts assumed migrants would make migration decisions based essentially on comparing wage levels between (for example) Poland and Ireland, yet as we shall see, far more was involved than this. Movement to the West offers access to a different life style – and access to a wider labour market than just that of the initial destination. The sheer extent of movement into Ireland, the apparently limitless supply of jobs, the promise of novelty for the newcomers, all gave the Irish (and especially Dublin) labour market what we term its 'gold rush' quality.

A low paid and overqualified workforce

The growing number of migrants working in Irish hotels and restaurants can be traced at national level using the Quarterly National Household Survey (QNHS) carried out by the Irish Central Statistics Office (CSO). We use both the results published by the CSO[1] and our own analysis of the micro-data. Statistics are available at the level of economic sector, with the 'hospitality' sector including hotels, restaurants and catering. Between 2004 and 2007 total employment in Ireland rose from 1,894,000 to 2,141,000, an increase of 13 percent. In the same period total employment in hospitality in Ireland as a whole rose from 112,600 in final quarter of 2004 to 130,000 in the third quarter of 2007, an increase in the period of 15 percent. The sector was therefore growing somewhat faster than employment as a whole. Within the sector the total number of Irish employees actually declined slightly, so the entire employment gain came from migrants. Of these migrants, the majority came from the new Eastern European EU member states.[2] In 2004 there were just over 3,000 such employees, but by 2007 their number had increased more than sixfold to 22,500 (CSO, 2008a).

Hotel and restaurant work is commonly understood as low paid and precarious. Throughout Europe the hotel sector is a low pay sector with occupations such as hotel cleaners particularly likely to be working at minimum wages (Evans et al., 2005). Management controls costs by paying employees only for the precise hours they are needed, meaning employees effectively work 'on call' and contribute extra hours without overtime pay (Head and Lucas, 2005); a practice that has been identified as common in the sector in many European countries (Klein Hesselink, 2003: 30).

In Ireland, too, wages in hotels and restaurants are well below the national average. Indeed, average (full-time) wages in 'Accommodation and catering' are the lowest of the entire service sector (CSO, 2007). As we show

Table 5.1   Hospitality sector: occupational structure 2001 and 2006

	2001		2006	
	Hotels and restaurants (%)	All sectors (%)	Hotels and restaurants (%)	All sectors (%)
Managers and administrators	21.3	12.0	18.9	15.5
Professional	0.6	6.5	0.4	11.7
Associate professional and technical	0.2	5.6	0.2	8.5
Clerical and secretarial	4.9	8.5	5.5	12.3
Craft and related	0.6	9.0	0.4	14.2
Personal and protective service	50.0	7.3	53.4	10.8
Sales	2.5	6.0	4.2	8.8
Plant and machine operatives	0.3	7.9	0.4	8.3
Other (includes not stated)	19.6	37.3	16.5	9.8
Total	100	100	100	100

Source: QNHS 2001 Q2 (2nd quarter) and 2006 Q2 (2nd quarter) micro-data.

later, for migrants these wages are nonetheless an improvement on home earnings. Yet while wages have remained low, the educational standard of the Irish hospitality workforce has been rising. While it could be imagined this represents an upskilling of the workforce with jobs disproportionately created in managerial and professional positions, in fact change has been in the other direction, and analysis of the QNHS data shows that 'managers and administrators' comprised 21 percent of all those working in the sector in 2001 and only 19 percent in 2006 (Table 5.1).

As Table 5.1 shows, 'personal and protective service occupations' comprise the largest single occupational group in the sector. In Table 5.2 it can be seen that the educational level of both Irish and non-Irish workers in these occupations has been rising, but this is especially the case for migrants. In 2001 less than 3 percent of Irish workers in these occupations had a degree, but in 2006 this had risen to over 5 percent. Amongst migrants in these occupations the growth was larger: in 2001 4 percent had a degree, but by 2006 this had risen to just under 15 percent.

The hospitality sector is thus a particularly clear case of the general phenomenon that migrants in Ireland are underemployed relative to their skill level. (Barrett *et al.*, 2006). While most migrants in the sector are not graduates, it is surely remarkable that over a quarter of all migrants in the sector do actually have a third level qualification. We now use interviews with migrants to explore how and why people are prepared to accept poor work and working conditions that are apparently considerably below their qualification level.

Table 5.2   Unskilled workers in hospitality sector: nationality and education, 2001–2006

(Workers in 'personal and protective service' occupations)

	2001		2006	
	Irish (%)	Non-Irish (%)	Irish (%)	Non-Irish (%)
No formal/primary education	15.5	17.7	10.4	5.9
Lower secondary	26.3	24.9	21.5	7.8
Upper secondary	32.6	31.0	40.9	27.0
Post Leaving	11.8	10.1	9.2	8.4
Third level non degree	7.8	7.7	11.1	14.9
Third level degree or above	2.6	4.1	5.3	14.6
Other/not stated	3.3	4.5	1.5	21.5
Total	100	100	100	100

Source: QNHS 2001Q2 and 2006 Q2 (2nd quarter) micro-data.

Reasons for emigration: just taking what you can get?

The participants in our study are all Polish nationals and range in age from 21 to 29 years of age; some of them have only second level education, most however have a third level qualification such as a BA in Teaching, an MA in Engineering, or an MA in Tourism and Hotels. They each arrived in Ireland post accession and are employed in a range of hospitality sector occupations including receptionist, chef, waitress and manager. We interviewed them in Polish in Dublin in late 2007 and early 2008; the interviews were transcribed and translated. Respondents are identified here by their gender and age (e.g. 'male, 27').

For all our respondents, the initial rationale for moving to Ireland is primarily financial, including in particular accumulating capital in a way that would not be possible in Poland:

> It was a very simple reason: money. Better future...But in general it was a typical money purpose, to buy the apartment and possibly going back to Poland (female, 29).

Wages may be low by Irish standards, but they enable new possibilities compared to 'back home' in Poland:

> Life's easier. For example now with a minimum wage I can support myself, I can rent a room, I can buy the clothes, I can save up, I can go for

my *holiday* to Poland, I don't have problems with that. If I worked in Poland, as I say, for minimum wage, I could forget about being able to support myself and to save (female, 23).

However, there are also less straightforwardly instrumental reasons. Some made the decision to migrate in the spirit of adventure, travel and learning the English language.

It was totally by chance. It was during my second year in high school that I decided that I was going to go abroad somewhere. I wanted to take a *gap year* ... and I simply wanted to learn English and get to know let's say some more interesting cultures (female, 21).

Others saw Dublin in particular as a cool place to be.

Damn it, it's so cool in Dublin, there are so many opportunities, you go to work, then pints after work, there are some friends, this is a small city where everybody knows each other and it is cool (female, 29).

Just as Tormey (2000) has shown for part-time employment in the retail sector, within the hospitality sector even apparently casual jobs form some type of hierarchy. Work in city centre restaurants pays better because of higher tips; hotels with a well known brand or a higher star ranking are usually better employers; some enterprises have more sociable hours, etc. Thus as they gained experience a number of participants moved rapidly between low-skilled jobs, for example, from deli worker in a café to a cleaning job in a hostel to hotel work (female, 24). Another participant started as an *au-pair* before moving to a hotel and now to an Italian restaurant (female, 21).

These jobs were all secured by migrants on arrival in Ireland – none of our participants had arranged such positions in advance of arrival. And jobs in the hospitality sector demanded relatively limited English:

I was sending CVs, I even had a few phone interviews. I really wanted to work as a secretary, because I had the experience... But it was hard with the language. In the beginning I couldn't break myself into talking at all. So there was one time, then the second time, one interview, second one, third one, third one over the phone and they could see that the language is not as it supposed to be and thanks to that recommendation I found this job in the hotel and I went there, and that's how my cooperation with X Hotel started (female, 29).

Recruitment: hiring any one who shows up?

As we shall now show, one of the striking features of employment in the hospitality sector during the boom was the extent to which employers appeared to take on virtually anyone, apparently making no use of formal qualifications. On the one hand employers continually needed to recruit new employees, and so had little time for careful selection procedures, while on the other hand they faced large numbers of potential applicants between whom they had little way of distinguishing. In this situation informal recommendations from existing employees are an effective – and low cost-selection mechanism.

Some of our respondents did find their first job in Ireland through formal recruitment organisations, but this was usually only for skilled jobs. During the boom recruitment companies in Ireland have been doing good business and they provided one starting point for newly arrived migrants:

> So I thought come and find a job through an agency...In the beginning I was wandering around the city, we didn't have any experience in looking for a job in Ireland. That's why I was running around the city meeting six or seven recruitment consultants, although that wasn't perceived as appropriate[3]... And I was in fact offered such a job by X Recruitment (male, 22).

Online recruitment agencies have also expanded rapidly and migrants had frequently checked out Irish jobs on the internet before travelling to Ireland. However, this was only reconnaissance: when people actually obtained a job through an internet agency they had already moved to Ireland. Finally, migrants also used the state recruitment agency FÁS.

Such methods were geared towards the more skilled jobs in the hospitality sector however. Most of our respondents got their jobs more informally through social networks. This form of recruitment seems to be particularly important for semi-skilled work in hotels and catering, as is also reported for Northern Ireland by Devine *et al.* (2007). When employers recruit on the basis of a personal recommendation by an existing employee then they are effectively using their own employees as recruitment agents. Furthermore, since the existing employee is effectively providing a guarantee of good behaviour, the employer is using employees to make the recruitment decisions for them:

> And the job I got in the hotel of course through somebody's recommendation...You know, for them you are being recommended and if somebody is saying: 'Listen, this is my friend, could you hire her?'... So I went for an

interview but it was known before hand that...I already had this job (female, 29).

Indeed, employers will sometimes pay a reward to employees who recommend acquaintances:

And this friend that I recommended recently. He got the job, he works. Because we have it that if you recommend somebody and this person gets the job... It was only introduced now. You get 250 Euros. Pure money, you know... (female, 29).

In such situations, the recruitment process can appear astonishingly casual:

I dropped my CV and they called me in two hours time...I went there for an interview and I was waiting there 40 minutes for X before she came down...I wanted to get out but I was sitting at the reception so the receptionists would see...And she came, she apologised to me, said that something happened. And she asked me if I had my CV. Well, no, I left it there the day before. And she said: 'I lost it', and I said 'Ok'. And, all in all, she asked me where I had worked, so I said here and there. And she said they needed staff and that I could start work from the week after (female, 21).

And hard-earned academic qualifications appear meaningless:

In Poland lets say your academic background is important. And here nobody cares if one graduated or finished high school or anything else (male, 22).

Convenient hours – for the employer

In general casual employment means that the employment relationship involves low administrative costs. However, in Dublin in the boom this informality has a particular 'gold rush' quality: migrant workers are new to the country without any sense of established precedent, while workplaces are often new and have a high turnover. The result is that the workplace is not governed by any strong set of accepted social rules and the customary practices that govern established jobs are substantially absent. The fact that the relationship is informal means that the employer has extensive discretion. Once hired, most of our respondents found that work contracts, hours of hour and pay rates appeared 'flexible'. Contracts were non-existent or notional:

Do you have a contract signed or is it an oral agreement?
It is an oral agreement... But as far as I know there is a contract somewhere out there...but it just works on the basis that... Well, I don't know, I had never signed it (laugh) (male, 27).

And do you have a normal contract?
I never got it, you know... I have never signed one. There was only this form from the interview and that's all. It is on the basis of an oral contract (female, 29).

For some of the participants not having a written contract was itself an issue. Clearly this informality gives the employer the ability to change conditions at whim: one respondent without a contract was working in a shop with no holiday pay and no breaks during the working day. For our respondents, their primary concern was in relation to actual hours for which they were employed, since this of course impacted on their take-home pay. Confirming the findings of other studies of the sector (e.g. Head and Lucas, 2005), employers are recruiting 'full-time' workers who actually are offered less than full-time hours in any one week and are effectively working 'on call'. The employer thus only pays for work that is actually done and has a flexible labour force which will work additional hours if these are suddenly needed. This in turn makes employees look for other work, thus increasing turnover and so, in a vicious circle, increasing the need for more temporary staff:

So you work full time and you are hired directly by the hotel?
Yes, but this is not true, because I wasn't working full time many times.
And you wanted to?
Yes, I did, I mean, well, it happened to me a couple of times to work 45 hours, but usually it is around 33 or 32, which is a problem because lots of people quit a job because of it.
So though you have a full time contract you work less?
Yes and they absolutely don't care about it (female, 21).

In another case the employee did have a formal contract for 38 hours per week, but in practice people hired for this 'full-time' post would usually only work 33 or 36 hours. Employees discovered that even though they wanted to work the full number of hours, this actually did not usually happen. In this case, the existence of the formal contract was irrelevant and employers simply treated such staff as casual employees.

Minimal training – anyone can do the work?

Migrants soon discovered that employers usually assume that the jobs require no formal induction or training. Recruits are expected to 'know' how to perform a range of new tasks and to 'pick it up' from colleagues:

So I had to ask people I was working with. For example once, which was totally stupid, I was left alone on the floor, absolutely alone in the restaurant, and I simply had no idea how to charge people with credit cards. And two people wanted to pay with credit cards at the same time and everybody from the staff went to smoke, yeah. Well I was absolutely stressed, confused, I didn't know what to do... and then when everybody came back they were shouting at me without reason so I thought they were idiots and I went home (female, 21).

The level of training made available in most workplaces was limited. In general most participants were obliged to take part in health and safety courses and to a certain extent, manual handling courses. However, these are obviously more closely linked to employers' legal obligations rather than to employees' needs for promotion or career development. Other 'training' might include a brief introduction to customer service:

> *You mentioned before about the training, so exactly what training did you receive in your job?*
> I'm not sure if I can call it training, but we had that six hours long... it lasted the whole day, they obviously paid for that... It was called: *'Yes, I will.'*...and the manager from the reception department ran the training and, well, it concerned generally how to deal with customers. *Yes, I will,* so always, everywhere, wherever you were, whatever department you're from – you are ready and willing to help, you want to help the customers (female, 21).

Even this minimal level training is more prevalent in the larger hotel chains than in smaller family owned hotels and restaurants. At the same time, it is noticeable that our respondents might have been casually recruited, but in fact they did have the social skills and the motivation to quickly learn their new jobs. Employers, in other words, had chosen well: their assumptions about the commitment of migrants turned out to be correct.

As one of our respondents discovered, to the extent that employers do need to differentiate between applicants, they appear to be focusing on precisely those aspects identified as appropriate to 'aesthetic labour' (Warhurst *et al.*, 2000):

> My interview in here went in a funny way. My current manager came with some questionnaire and after she gave it to me, probably by mistake (laughing), with some documents I had to sign. And there was a list... it started with the impression I made on the manager...I mean, I shouldn't have got it, ... yes, it was with the assessment, attached, I don't know, for example: how I was dressed and there was an assessment from 1 to 5 (female, 24).

What employees want from work: flexibility, a job or a career

For most of our respondents their current jobs are merely temporary. It appears that this makes apparently exploitative conditions tolerable or not even noticed. Indeed, there is a convergence between some employers and some employees in defining the employment relationship as short term – for both sides, it is 'casual'. However, a job can be seen as temporary in several different ways. We also differentiate such *'temporary'* workers from those migrants who are – or have become – *'residents'*; those who have no immediate desire to move jobs and in different ways have become committed to their current employment. In addition, a third group of migrants are *'careerists'*, in that they see their current job as a stepping stone to something better.

A number of participants reported how convenient it was for them not to be tied to a rigid contract or working hours:

> I work there because of...there are really flexible hours. It is me who chooses the shifts, I ring them and say when I want to work... I don't know, if I had a whim of going to Poland for a month or two it is no problem, they simply get different staff somewhere from an agency...So...I do it for my convenience (female, 29).

And as another put it:

> Sometimes I work less than those 40 hours a week, it mostly depends on me, because practically I have the possibility of choosing my days off... it is mostly me who decides how many hours a week I work... (male, 27).

For such migrants, the flexibility which benefits their employers also benefits them.

A job can also be temporary simply because migrants intend to move on: simply a convenient way to earn money from which to live at the moment:

> God, my plans are changing from one day to another... France has always been there in my plans. And that's the target place. At least for now... I surely have also Argentina in my plans...as I dance the Argentinean tango and this is my big dream... And I would also like to go for a small trip around the world... And it's all related to the money. I would like to stay for a while in Brazil, in Argentina for a while... Somehow also get to New Zealand... So in my plans I would like to travel a lot. And then I will look

for a job in journalism, definitely something in journalism. Because that's what I want to do...I would like to study one more thing: photography. And that's one of my biggest dreams (female, 29).

Indeed, as other researchers have noted cities like Dublin and London are especially likely to attract such 'tumbleweeds' (Boyle, 2006) or those whose orientation to the future is one of 'intentional unpredictability' (Eade, 2008). They may have aspirations ('journalism', 'photography') but at least at the moment these are unconnected to any concrete plan of action.

These 'temporary' workers can be distinguished from a second group of migrants who have settled in their employment and indeed in Ireland: 'residents'. Such migrants have no immediate desire to move on and in different ways find their current employment satisfactory. One reason may be simply that they have no greater aspirations:

Is it an ideal job? Maybe it's not ideal, but simply I don't complain. I feel good in this job...The cooperation with people that I work with is excellent. The atmosphere at work is simply great. I feel like I'm at home there. Is it ideal...Well, I think that no job is ideal (male, 27).

In this situation a 'good job' means the same as for less transient workers: reasonable pay, good working conditions, and, a frequent theme in the interviews, being treated with respect. 'Residents' can also be prepared to take the job seriously:

Well...It's divided into two groups, and I would count myself into the group that thinks, I don't know how to phrase this, that is 'thinking *business*'...For example, if there is a situation when we basically have a full restaurant... the group that I'm a part of, we are simply happy that we are doing *business,* and the other part... in general don't care if we are making money or not... They simply want to do the job and go home.[4] So they are the ones that mostly complain, you know... (male, 27).

Paradoxically those who have settled in may well be offered training, although settling in may mean that this is of less interest to them:

I was offered by my bosses to go to France to do a range of training courses, so maybe I will go for that at some stage, don't know when...I was [also] offered a college; it was restaurant management and stuff like that. It was about a year ago...I was thinking about it for a long time, and...I'm 26 years old and I reckon that it's too late for me (male, 27).

For a third group their current employment is a stepping stone to another higher job. In this sense they are 'careerists'. Although their ambitions may be lower than some of the 'tumbleweeds', they do have strategies which link their current job to the destination they wish to reach. In the mid-20th century 'career' was usually understood as some form of upward movement through a clearly defined hierarchy of posts. We retain the notion that career involves a general improvement over time, and that one post is used to lead to another. However, while 'career' still involves purpose (even strategy) and improvement over time, today it can be 'boundaryless', involving moves between different organisations and even between different employment statuses (Arthur and Rousseau, 1996). Migrants appear especially likely to move jobs in this way.

> I would like to study here in Ireland just to make the time here as fruitful as possible. And I was thinking maybe in this area: hotels or something related to it. And I would like to change job...I mean also at the reception, I don't know. To a hotel with higher standard. And it would be nice to get a supervisor position or maybe a manager of the reception. I'm aiming at that and I want to aim my studies in that direction as well (female, 24).

Given the small size of most hotels, a better job means changing employers. Indeed, for some hotel work, further study is seen as a preparation for management in general. And these wider horizons involve no particular commitment to Ireland:

> I would definitely like to be a reception manager ...I mean I haven't decided yet for sure on the area of studies. I'm also considering sales management, or management. So definitely in this area, definitely a higher ranked position, basically not at the rank and file positions, and not necessarily in Ireland. Or not necessarily in the hotel area, maybe the business area in general (female, 24).

As we have seen, none of our migrants accessed their jobs in Ireland from Poland, but now employment in Ireland has opened up the possibility of intra-company migration.

> Through our intranet I can look for a job in the hotels from X chain everywhere in the world. I have access to that and priority in applying. I

also have assistance of my general manager and HR Manager, that support me in a sense.
And would you consider X Hotels here in Ireland?
Well, that's the problem, because there's only six X hotels in Ireland, and let's say three of them are very uninteresting hotels... (male, 22).

And finally, a career may involve more entrepreneurial plans based on the experience of working in the sector:

We want to open a café in Poland. And well that's our, it's our dream somehow... I have café experience, so well I know how it looks like from the technical side to run a café. I know what the costs are. And anyway, because we did a lot of different things, we know what we would like in that café (male, 26).

Conclusion: all good gold rushes come to an end?

Our respondents came to Dublin during an economic boom. Comparing the recent population growth of Dublin in the early 21st century to (for example) Melbourne in the 1850s or Johannesburg in the 1890s is an obvious exaggeration, but talking about 'gold rush Dublin' does highlight how the structure of the workforce has changed: there are not just more people at work, there are different people at work, so much so that in some workplaces the native-born are outnumbered. Gold rushes are times of mobility and transience; people arrive, but people also move on. Just as in a gold rush, everybody (or almost everybody) can win, or at least, hope to win. The demand for labour is such that, as we have seen, people can move jobs easily, simply abandoning employers with whom they fall out. Just as a gold rush town outgrows existing territorial boundaries which become irrelevant, so the existing labour market regulation is swept aside; in the Dublin case for example, trade unions simply do not appear in our respondents' accounts of their workplaces.

And of course, gold rushes are by definition short-lived. In early 2008 Irish employment finally ceased to grow, by July 2008 the number of those 'signing on' to the Live Register was about 30 percent more than the year before and unemployment had risen to very nearly 6 percent (CSO, 2008b). Yet after the gold rush, things do not revert to the *status quo ante*. One change could well be a shift towards a greater level of mobility within the Irish and indeed the European labour markets. After years in which Europeans in 'old Europe' were notorious for the extent to which they were immobile (Recchi, 2008), the enlargement of the EU has shaken up European labour markets and normalised movement from East to West and back again.

At the same time, while none of our respondents originally saw themselves as 'emigrating' to Ireland in the traditional sense, we have noticed how some of them already envisage staying in Ireland for longer. However, at the centre of the account has been the bargain of convenience between migrants and employers, with migrants tolerating conditions because they saw them as temporary. To the extent that this is no longer possible, then the basis for the bargain disappears.

Notes

1 We acknowledge permission for the use of the Central Statistics Office – QNHS Microdata Files © Government of Ireland.
2 In 2004 the Eastern European Accession states were the Czech Republic, Estonia, Hungary, Latvia, Lithuania, Poland, Slovakia and Slovenia; Bulgaria and Romania joined the EU in 2007 but their citizens do not have full access to the Irish labour market.
3 Recruitment agencies dislike job seekers using more than one agency.
4 For the phrase 'do their job' he used a pejorative phrase in Polish, that would mean 'do the minimum and leave as soon as possible'.

REFERENCES

Arthur, M. B. and Rousseau, D. M. (1996) *The Boundaryless Career: A New Employment Principle for a New Organizational Era*, New York: Oxford University Press.

Barrett, A., Bergin, A. and Duffy, D. (2006) 'The Labour Market Characteristics and Labour Market Impacts of Immigrants in Ireland', *The Economic and Social Review*, 37(1): 1–26, Spring.

Bradley, J. (2000) 'The Irish economy in comparative perspective', in B. Nolan, P. J. O'Connell and C. T. Whelan (eds) *Bust to Boom?*, Dublin: Institute of Public Administration, 4–26.

Boyle, M. (2006) 'Culture in the Rise of Tiger Economies: Scottish Expatriates in Dublin and the "Creative Class" Thesis', *International Journal of Urban and Regional Research*, 30:2 (June), 403–26.

CSO (Central Statistics Office) (2007) *Statistical Yearbook of Ireland 2007*.

CSO (Central Statistics Office) (2008a) QNHS, Revised Series Post 2002 Census of Population Table A2 http://www.cso.ie/qnhs/main_result_Post 2002.htm Accessed 1 July, 2008.

CSO (Central Statistics Office) (2008b) *Live Register July 2008*.

Devine, F., Baum, T., Hearns, N. and Devine, A. (2007) 'Cultural diversity in hospitality work: the Northern Ireland experience', *International Journal of Human Resource Management*, 18(2): 333–49.

▶

▶

Eade, J. (2008) 'The limits of the rational actor paradigm in understanding contemporary A8 migration to the UK: Should I go or should I stay?' Trinity College Dublin Migrant Careers and Aspirations Symposium, 5 June 2008. http://www.tcd.ie/immigration/careers/events.php.

European Commission – DG Employment, Social Affairs and Equal Opportunities (2007). *Employment in Europe.* Luxembourg: Office for Official Publications of the European Communities.

Evans, Y., Herbert, J., Data, K., May, J., McIllwaine, C. and Wills, J. (2005) *Making the City Work: Low Paid Employment in London,* Queen Mary University of London, Department of Geography, November.

Head, J. and Lucas, R. (2005) 'Employee relations in the non-union hotel industry: A case of "determined opportunism"?', *Personnel Review,* 33(5): 693–710.

Klein Hesselink, J. (2003) *EU Hotel and Restaurant Sector: Work and Employment Conditions,* Dublin: European Foundation.

O'Connell, P. (2000) 'The dynamics of the Irish labour market in comparative perspective', in B. Nolan, P. J. O'Connell and C. T. Whelan (eds) (2000). *Bust to Boom? The Irish Experience of Growth and Inequality,* Dublin: Institute of Public Administration.

Recchi, E. (2008) 'Cross-state mobility in the EU: Trends, puzzles and consequences'. *European Societies,* 10(2): 197–224.

Tormey, R. (2000) 'Cutting at the wrong edge: Gender, part-time work and the Irish retail sector', *Irish Journal of Sociology* 9: 77–96.

Warhurst, C., Nickson, D., Witz, A. and Cullen, A. M. (2000) 'Aesthetic labour in interactive service work: Some case study evidence from the "new" Glasgow'. *Services Industries Journal,* 20:3 (July), 1–18.

Housekeepers and the Siren Call of Hotel Chains

6

Christine Guégnard and Sylvie-Anne Mériot

As labour market segmentation and dual market theories state, on one hand a *primary* sector is related to qualified workers having attractive and stable positions and, on the other hand, a *secondary* sector includes low-paid labour with insecure positions, often in back-breaking working conditions. This gap can be observed in the case of housekeepers in the French hotel industry, where typically female and low-wage workers have very few career prospects. Indeed, the hotel industry remains France's emblematic low-wage sector, due to weak trade union organisation and few labour market regulations. Nevertheless, the rapid development of hotel chains leads to some changes in wage and labour organisation, building a form of high road practices.

Introduction

In France, as in most European countries, housekeepers differ from other hotel employees. They are almost invariably women, relatively mature, with the overwhelming majority being of foreign extraction, holding no qualifications, and paid wages that would hardly enable them to support a family. These are jobs that technological developments, training courses and the unions, pass by. Any real career prospects are remote, though in a few hotel chains management practices have brought some positive initiatives. The role of housekeeper is a female, invisible, activity that remains behind the scenes. Most employees are vulnerable and depend on their employer because of a lack of employability in the market. Thus, they represent a relatively docile form of labour power, confined to the status of low-wage workers, and yet they play an important role for the quality of the hotel business.

In this chapter, the life story of housekeepers in France is addressed from three different interlinked angles. First, the specificity of the hotel and catering industry, with regard to its labour market and industrial regulations, is presented with an emphasis on the strength of the employers' lobby. Second, the differences in managerial strategies assigned to hotel characteristics such as chain or independent status, which creates a form of dualism, is analysed. Housekeepers are often untrained and uninformed about their rights, and they have few means for fighting against intensification of work schedules or imaginative application of labour laws. Unequal access to full-time and permanent work underlines an increasing inequality in the labour market of which housekeepers are victims. Third, the difficulties housekeepers face in seeking to escape from the vicious circle that links precarious employment to low earnings.

The analysis presented in this chapter is built on the basis of three research surveys carried out in France. The first survey, '*Equilibre*', was financed by the European Commission (the European Social Fund) on the Equal programme. It was based on a set of experimental actions carried out from 2002–2004 in order to reconcile the balance between work and personal life (Guégnard, 2004). The second one, 'Managers Pluri*Elles*' was a project sustained by the European Social Fund in order to promote women's careers in hospitality (Bosse and Guégnard, 2005). The third one, involving Céreq and Iredu since 2004 at a European scale, was financed by Russell Sage Foundation (New York) and coordinated in France by Cepremap (Centre pour la recherche économique et ses applications) and related to the managerial practices of low-wage workers (Appelbaum *et al.*, 2003). All these studies have mixed quantitative and qualitative approaches, including a statistical and documentation review, monographs on hotels and 200 interviews with employees, employer organisations and trade union representatives (Guégnard and Mériot, 2005, 2008).

In the land of hotels

France, with its long history of tourism, was also a world pioneer ever since the introduction of its first luxury hotels in 1920. With regard to social progress for its workers, however, the hotel sector has never been much of a pioneer. The hotel industry differs from other French activities on more than one count. It remains mostly family-run, often marked by traditional norms of references, long working hours, a diluted application of collective agreements or labour rules, and undeclared work. In a sector dominated by very small independent establishments, the fragmentation of four employer organisations and five trade unions, and a very low level of trade union membership (2 percent), there are many obstacles to more positive labour regulations and working conditions. Small employers are '*protected by the natural weakness of worker organizations in their small, dispersed work force*' and by the variety of exemptions to the legislation, and minimum labour standards, as described by Piore (1978, p. 34).

A two-tier market

France has Europe's fourth highest hotel room capacity with over 612,000 rooms on January 1, 2007. For several years, the French hotel sector has stabilised at around 18,000 establishments, with an average of 33 rooms per hotel. This trend has benefited large hotel chains at the expense of smaller independent hotels. Nevertheless, the French hotel industry continues to be dominated by small units: 80 percent of hotels employ less than ten employees. They are often family-managed businesses whose assets are usually held by the hotelkeeper (and/or close relatives). Hotel chains are relentlessly gaining ground, however, and are concentrated in the upper and lower market segments.

Independent hotels have the lion's share of the market, in terms of number of establishments and of revenues. However, hotel chains are increasingly putting pressure on the market and this has led to a permanent price war. While large hotels and chains tend to rationalise the work, small and independent hotels maintain a cottage-industry approach to their employees, thus highlighting the French image of the hotel as a family-run micro-business. The chains tend to be dynamic in negotiations with unions and accept collective bargaining, while the small hotels are usually reluctant to discuss working conditions and seek to maintain lower wages, even for their loyal employees. Despite this contrast between independents and chains, a collective agreement for the entire industry was negotiated and adopted in 1997.

An emblematic sector

The hotel industry continues to be the archetype of low-wage sectors and could also set a bold example of labour market segmentation. It employs 27 percent of its workforce on low-wage[1] jobs and offers many part-time or short-term contracts, primarily to cope with yearly fluctuations. It stands out from other sectors because of its particular industrial and institutional regulations and the power of its employers' lobby when negotiating with the government and the trade unions. As a result, the hotel and catering trade is famous for the weakness of its negotiations in favour of employees and for its large number of employer dispensations from the French Labour Code (working hours, employment contracts...) – this last point underlines the strength of the employers' lobby and their electoral weight for French politicians.

For instance, until July 2004, the specific hotel industry minimum wage was lower than the real value of the inter-professional national legal minimum wage because hotel employers were allowed to deduct a number of benefits in kind such as meals or accommodation. The agreement in force makes no provision for automatic seniority allowance, and gives no occupational seniority rights to redundancy payment and no compensation for working on Sundays or many public holidays.

A specific workforce

The hotel industry employs 188,000 people (178,000 employees + 10,000 non-employees) in France. The main individual characteristics of the labour force in the *'secondary labour market'* (Doeringer and Piore, 1971) can be found here: youth, women, migrants, minority groups. Indeed, hotel industry employees differ from employees in other sectors: half of them are women, mostly under 30, and 10 percent are foreign workers, often with no qualifications. The hospitality industry attracts many young people and *non-citizen workers and illegal migrants*, because many of the jobs in this sector do not require qualifications.

In addition, there is a *black market* for labour, an expanding industry which totally escapes taxation and other legal restrictions. The black market sometimes corresponds to partly-declared situations, or to an unfair and excessive use of some precarious contracts, or to poor records of real working times. Illegal immigrants are especially likely to accept any kind of contract or schedule, sometimes working in conditions close to exploitation. The French government considers that undeclared work accounts for up to one-third of the hotel and restaurants' workforce.

Against this special backdrop, housekeepers, who account for almost 20 percent of the labour force, are different from other employees on more than one count. In a mixed sector, cleaning rooms is women's work. Another peculiarity claimed by hotel managers is that recruitment is easy and turnover is low, which contrasts with many other categories of hotel staff. Prospects of having a real career are remote, except in a few hotels where management has been making some positive initiatives, as discussed in the next section.

Facing managers' strategies

The tendency towards consolidation in the hotel industry, linked to the progression of chains, is nevertheless leading to some high road managerial practices. Accor, for example, led the way, when it adopted the 39-hour week several years ago. However, the same managers combine elements of the high and low roads in a profitable and flexible way. As the hotel industry is, by its very nature, subject to variability and uncertainty in demand, man-

agers offer jobs with career prospects to few employees and unstable contracts to others. Part-time work and subcontracting serve strategies of flexibility, rationalisation of work, and compression of production costs. As a
result, these human resource management practices lead to a dichotomy of
the market between stable and unstable jobs, which tend to disadvantage
those with lowest qualifications such as housekeepers, in particular.

The siren call of chains

The primary difference in management strategies relates to whether the hotel
is an independent establishment or part of a chain. However, we can also
see the emergence of other characteristics, such as category or size of hotel,
specific strategies within a single chain, the chain's employment history, or
the individual manager. In fact, the key element is often the hotel's management and the personality of the director can play a fundamental role
(Guégnard *et al.*, 2004). Because of the *domestic and behind the scenes* nature
of the work, employees are especially dependent on the director or a specific
manager, even in major hotels (Triby, 2004).

Working for a chain is often seen as opting for more institutional relations and compliance with current regulations (adherence to the Labour
Code or collective agreement, working hours, schedules provided) with
many benefits. One employee in a chain hotel relates:

> *Here we are paid on a 13th month basis,[2] we have sickness and pension schemes,
> surety bond, profit-sharing and guarantees, as well as the Accor card to get
> discounts on our travel expenses. In most hotels, they do not exist.*

The Accor Group employees, or 'collaborators', indicate that they have working
conditions which conform to legislation (a 39-hour working week, public holidays, bonuses, continuous training, and occasionally career prospects) that are
often lacking in independent hotels. Another housekeeper, in an Ibis hotel, adds:

> *Here, I enjoy the atmosphere and working alone, choosing my rhythm, as I
> want. My employer relies on me. We sometimes have meetings about things that
> went wrong, but we show solidarity, and we can express ourselves. We get on
> very well together.*

Furthermore, their work schedules are given in advance, making it easier for
employees to balance work and family commitments, as witnessed by the
'*Equilibre*' project implemented in Ibis:

> *Where I worked before, we had no schedule. It was weird. For example, we could
> not know how many days we were supposed to work, and how many days off we*

had collected. We used to make our own arrangements. But since I work here, the schedule is defined, for the whole month, so I know exactly my days off.

The Sofitel hotel chain, for another example, seeks to innovate on behalf of housekeepers by developing social monitoring (including social workers), limiting tediousness, isolation and stress through the possibility of working in pairs, encouraging good postural habits or using innovative equipment (such as the *'ergolit'* system that raises beds at the press of a pedal). These practices were proposed and initiated through a think tank with headquarters, when the MyBed concept[3] was introduced and resulted from some difficulties for housekeepers, related by one of them:

Since we've had MyBed, everyone complains of pains. I personally get pains in the arms.

In some up-market hotel chains, there have been recent moves to improve housekeepers' working conditions, while in mid- to low-range hotel chains, some managers are testing new forms of multiskilling (for instance, combining cleaning and reception activities). Other initiatives for housekeepers aim to make the working atmosphere friendlier or to include them more in company life. Thus, some chain hotels have launched group breakfasts, getting employees involved in festivities, and letting staff self-manage their holiday dates. In other independent establishments, guidance is given on interpersonal relations with colleagues and with patrons through periodic one-to-one interviews, organised meetings or breakfasts. And when Sofitel France introduced MyBed, some housekeepers were invited to take part in product testing, involving a free night and meal at the hotel. However, despite introducing these good practices, the same hotel managers do not hesitate to offer precarious contracts or subcontractors, especially for room cleaning.

Flexibility of employment contracts

As there is a large pool of available housekeepers, hoteliers can use a whole range of job contracts from numerical flexibility at the bottom of the hierarchy to fixed-term and permanent contracts at the top. Moreover, employees can also be divided between full-timers (39 or 37 weekly hours) and part-timers. Whereas numerically flexible workers often work for only a few hours a day, stable part-time workers are generally guaranteed around 30 hours a week in the hotels under study. This creates a reinforced dualism between permanent/non-permanent staff (*'tenured and untenured workers'*) and between part-timers/full-timers. There is competition for landing a full-time stable job, which comes hand in hand with better working hours and more regular work. Advancement through merit is thus a *right to work*, as the number of rooms allocated per day per person starts off very low, and only permanent hotel staff can be sure of getting a decent wage through their daily work.

In order to improve flexibility and mitigate absenteeism, employers often prefer to offer part-time work, and more than a third of hotel employees have part-time contracts. Part-time work is rarely requested by employees and can force them to take several jobs, with no real legal framework: one housekeeper gets up at 4 a.m. to spend three hours cleaning a pharmacy before going to her job in a hotel:

I would like to work full-time. I have been a part time worker for three years. They say to me that it is not possible to get employed full time. I make from 9 to 2 p.m., sometimes 3 p.m. when there is too much work to do. But working 25 hours per week, it is not enough!

Middle range hotels visited, whether independent or belonging to chains, mainly employ their floor staff as part-timers, with the exception of supervisors. This contrasts with deluxe hotels which offer very little part-time work, almost all their staff are on permanent full-time contracts.

The alternative is to hire 'extras' – temporary, numerically flexible workers, which allows managers to adapt schedules to fluctuations in room occupancy rates. Such temporary workers are specific to the French hotel and catering industry and cover a period of at least one hour, but for no longer than 60 days in any one quarter. In addition, employers are allowed to give staff these contracts within 48 hours of commencement, a condition which limits the Labour Inspectorate services' ability to monitor them and may encourage undeclared work, especially in small units. Indeed, when an inspector notices the absence of a written labour contract for an employee, employers always answer the same: their employee has just begun working for them when he arrived, and they were about to sign a contract together. Some managers also use such contracts to take their time over selecting the best staff. A temporary worker of this nature has to wait for a vacancy before she can expect to obtain a stable job contract and therefore has to prove she is highly committed to her work. This may take several years. One housekeeper relates: '*When we are extra, we have to fight every day*'. Indeed, these employees are particularly vulnerable and dependent on their employer's good practice. Accordingly, one extra works at the most 18 shifts per month and earns '*between €100–120 less than full-time workers at the same hotel*'. Some months, she only earns €400 and claims: '*Then I think it is poverty, and I cry*'.

One hotel director, along with many of his peers, admits that he is tempted to restrict the number of stable contracts, because '*sometimes, the people we hire lose their appetite for work.'* In an area blighted by unemployment, he can keep a large pool of labour available on unstable contracts. These are so vulnerable that they accept any type of requests, working hours or objectives (numbers of rooms to clean within a preset time, even if this is unrealistic). Many housekeepers are desperate about insecurity: one described herself as a *'permanent extra'*, prompting her comment that there is *'nothing extraordinary about the extra contract.'* She tells the following story: she arrived in France 20 years ago and took a two month short course to learn to speak French, then became a cleaner for several employers simultaneously (in a cleaning company). She worked up to 13 hours a day, then took a vocational course for housekeeping, and had now reverted to being an extra hired by a hotel, despite her qualifications and professional experience.

Flexibility in subcontracting

Some hotel managers look for greater flexibility by resorting to subcontractors for room cleaning. This allows them to overcome the constraints on personnel management and the associated social and administrative restrictions, along with the organisation of fluctuations in room occupancy. External subcontracting companies accept contracts with hotels for specific tasks, usually part-time cleaning of rooms (between 20 and 30 weekly hours for each room attendant). This gives the hotel adaptability in the management of personnel as well as the option of giving employees fewer overtime hours. The amount of work carried out by subcontractor employees is generally higher than those expected of hotel personnel. An ex-employee of one cleaning company confirms:

> We had to clean four and a half rooms per hour. It's impossible. In fact, to clean four rooms, we had to work one or two hours more each day, for no extra pay.

Subcontracting of room cleaning is used by one in two budget hotels, such as the Louvre Hotel Group, the second largest budget chain. However, market leader Accor has recently made a U-turn when its commercial image was dented by major industrial unrest at one of its subcontractors, Arcade. In 2002, Arcade's employees went on strike for better working conditions and work rates. While Accor's staff housekeepers were expected to clean 16 rooms in eight hours, the cleaning company's employees had to clean 20 to 23 rooms in six hours and were paid €7.16 per hour (only €0.49 more than the minimum wage). This inequity was a key factor in a huge and renowned strike (Puech, 2004) at Accor. It has now internalised part of the cleaning of its hotels and hired former cleaning company employees directly. When interviewed, these housekeepers considered that the decision had had a positive impact on their work schedules, wages and social relations. One of them adds:

> So it is heaven here, what I like is the atmosphere… When I come in the morning, there is some coffee and we can chat…

For some employers, subcontracting is part and parcel of their policy to seek flexibility and rein in costs as tightly as possible, paying a 'per room' charge at the lowest price. For others, the decision to keep internalised cleaning services is a way to get more loyal staff, and thus, to expect better quality in the service provided. Indeed, direct management tends to promote better staff retention, better quality services, and greater adaptability when multitasking is needed or when some patrons have specific expectations. The human factor is important, especially when guests insist on a room on a particular floor or the services of a specific housekeeper. The personal touch thus prevails in their choice as one manager confirms: '*In a hotel sector where we are competing on value-for-money, charm may come up trumps.*'

Employers and training

Continuing training is less widely practiced in the hotel industry than in other sectors, mainly because most of the companies are very small. In 2004, only one quarter of employees had participated in at least one course financed by their employers, against 38 percent of all employees in other industries (Continuing Training survey, Céreq). The mean duration of the training courses was 20 hours, versus 31 hours in all the other sectors combined. However, these statistics mask some disparities, since only large firms, such as chain hotels, actually gave percentages well above the legal minimum. At the Accor group, for example, continuing vocational training is central in Human Resource Management policies, and the company spends up to 2 percent of its wage bill for this purpose (whereas under French legislation, companies employing ten or more employees are only required to spend a sum equal to at least 1.6 percent for training purposes, otherwise they have to pay the same amount in taxes). The Accor Academy, the first corporate university to be created in Europe, aims to give all '*collaborators*' access to the career ladder, to give each employee '*one vocational training course per year!*'. One housekeeper confirm:

> Here, I enjoy everything I get. From the day I was engaged by Accor Group, I could benefit from several training sessions about cleaning products, I could learn how to make a room, what to do at first and last. I have learnt what positions to

adopt, how to make the beds and everything. I could also meet other workers from other Accor hotels, whom I could speak with... It is super.

Training for housekeepers is almost non-existent in small independent hotels. Only a handful of the visited hotels offer any kind of initiatives to the room attendants[4]: training days on ergonomic postures, room-cleaning techniques, reception in deluxe hotels, or customer satisfaction awareness building. Most training sessions have operational objectives and do not lead to industry-wide recognised skills certificates. They are aimed at retention and ensuring staff integration i.e. teaching the house style, improving in-house dialogue, rather than ensuring the housekeepers make career progress or rise in rank.

A shadow work force

The bedroom is at the heart of the hotel business and the quality of room cleaning is strategically important for the success of hotels, even if the housekeepers' activity remains a feminine and invisible form of work. The various profiles and career paths highlight the diverse, complex and *'cosmopolitan'* universe of housekeepers. In fact, employers often choose candidates with personal and ethnic characteristics for these secondary jobs (Reich *et al.*, 1973), especially people who belong to the same ethnic group, for example those coming from North Africa, Senegal, Madagascar, and from The Philippines. Working beside other professionals, these jobs can be considered as dead ends, in which it is difficult to find a positive way out.

A women's labour

Each morning a housekeeper is issued with her work schedule indicating which rooms need cleaning, sometimes with an order of priority or indications of guests' expectations. Her daily workload is 13–18 rooms (occasionally up to 24 rooms), at the rate of 2–4 rooms per hour depending on the hotel category. Sometimes housekeepers work to targets, and some managers take advantage of this to set unachievable goals. A housekeeper states:

Personally I find that the 30 minutes we are allowed per room, for a four-star hotel, isn't fair, as it takes at least 40 minutes to get a room spick-and-span.' Another one notes: 'We have to rush, and they tell us to work faster. The hotel should hire more staff. In eight hours, I am supposed to achieve my work, but whereas one hour is supposed to be enough to clean two rooms.

The work schedule is heavy and demanding, and all managers agree that housekeeping is very physical and tiring. One staff manager adds:

They are stressed out by the worry of being unable to keep up the pace to meet target times and a fixed number of rooms, since the guests leave their rooms in all sorts of states.

The European Foundation 2004 analysis of hotel workers' living and working conditions concluded that room cleaning involves uncomfortable physical positions (bending forwards, stretching and kneeling), carrying heavy weights (making beds and transporting equipment) and constant contact with water, cleaning products and disinfectants entailing a risk of allergy and biological infection.

Housekeepers have to keep up a brisk, testing working pace, as they testify:

– 'It is tiring, it is true that it is tiring, sometimes it gets you down';
– 'At the end of the day, when I have 24 rooms to clean on my own, to wash, rinse, wipe… my back is also broken';
– 'I think that it becomes increasingly hard. For me, the work is more difficult than before. Of course I am getting older, so I get tired earlier. I am 46 years old and when I began to work there, I was 27. But it is true that it is not an easy job';
– 'Physically I cannot do more especially in summer: I make about 100 breakfasts and then I go up to clean rooms. It is exhausting. I would enjoy cleaning two or three more rooms, to be paid one more hour, but physically I can not';
– 'As you know the housekeeper occupation is tiring. When I go back home, I can only watch TV. I am so tired!';
– 'I would really like to stop this work that tires me a lot. After a single working day, I am already broken. I even got problems with my muscles that I have never had before. And that tires me even more. I would like to take another job. If only I could stop!'

The work location defines which ethnic groups are represented and the local workforce characteristics may vary; some hotels mostly employ people from Eastern countries, others get more employees from North Africa or Sub-Saharan Africa. This is also encouraged by recruiting practices based on co-optation. One executive manager sums up this stereotype: '*We have to deal with many different ethnic groups:*

I have Muslims, Algerians, Moroccans, Poles, Chinese, Madagascans, Mauritians, and many Comorians. Their private lives are often a shambles, lots of children, their husbands are not always there or kind to them... They are often illiterate and their only experience is in cleaning, maybe domestic cleaning.

Some have fled from poverty, others from conflicts in their home country. Few of them have been to secondary school before migrating. Hard family or social events are often responsible for the lack of qualification, as house-keepers mention:

– 'Concerning my education, my father fell ill when I was very young. My mother had to take care of the children, so I left school when I was about thirteen. I had to get a job and I only worked in hotels';
– 'You know, school in Congo isn't like it is here. There was a war all the time, and so school was not a priority.'

A woman vividly presents the housekeepers' situation:

To be honest, a housekeeper's work does not suit anyone. I personally have to work and we have to work with the abilities we have. I have not any qualifications, so... as it is obvious that I have to work, I have chosen this occupation. If one day I can find something better to do, then without doubt I will take it. It is not always easy. It's a very hard, physically demanding job. But it is life, so when we have no choice, we do it as long as possible, do you understand?

One feature common to all housekeepers is the need to earn a living, however tedious the job may be. In fact, taking a job as housekeeper is often a question of Hobson's choice because no other occupation is open to these women. To be sure, men are also assigned to clean in some hotels but are usually allocated different tasks such as cleaning public areas, performing harder physical tasks (carpet cleaning) or handling jobs (linen, guests' luggage). Thus, there is a division of labour by gender within the cleaning sector. Women's work in hotels is an extension of their domestic activity.

A hidden job

Housekeepers occupy a special place in the hotel industry; a subordinate position within the ranks, invisible to guests, engaged in a tedious and servile activity. They, and the technical staff, are excluded from face-to-face contact with guests in a service activity centred on customer relations (Monchatre and Testenoire, 2004). All the managers agree that it's also, to use their words, *'the hotel's image'*, *'the hotel's calling cards.'* Rooms must be cleaned when the guests are out, to avoid disturbing them with their presence, so they are instructed to remain inconspicuous, or even apologise, when they come across a guest. In most hotels, housekeepers are isolated, out on the edge of the collective life of the establishment and reduced to spending many hours alone or only occasionally meeting their colleagues or supervisors.

Over and above the issue of gender, the profile is defined without resort to pre-recruitment criteria, as one manager states:

> *The person must be serious, inconspicuous and cleanliness is an essential criterion. A housekeeper does not need to have any special skills; she just needs to know how to use the color codes, namely, read figures.*[5]

Thus, even in deluxe hotels, there is no real need for any qualifications. There are very few housekeepers with a hotel or catering diploma, such as a CAP/BEP (a two-year French vocational training course for 14–16 year olds). Regarded as an *unskilled* job, training is basic, generally carried out on the job, by observing, imitating and shadowing an experienced colleague, usually over no more than one or two days depending on the hotel category. By the third day, the person is broadly expected to work independently and as fast as experienced staff, as one newly appointed housekeeper comments: '*I personally have had no training (…) I worked for one day at Hotel B. and the following day, they wanted me to clean twelve rooms!*'

While housekeepers appear to abound in the employment market, employers pay more attention to their supervisors. Some of them, especially in the luxury segment, go by the epithet of '*rare gems*'. Occasionally they are promoted internally, but more often than not, they have received several years' hotel training. This managerial practice creates another dichotomy, in both hotels and the cleaning departments, between selected qualified supervisors, and rarely promoted low qualified housekeepers.

A lower wage for the heart of the hotel

A housekeeper complains about her daily life:

> *The first thing I can tell you, it is that I do not earn enough. My wage is not sufficient, therefore as I live alone the ends of months are difficult, and when I have to pay for everything, I have nothing more. I find that I am not paid for the work I do.*

The room is at the heart of the hotel business and quality of room cleaning is decisive for customer loyalty. However, wages are pegged to the national legal minimum wage rate and only individual negotiations or bonuses, such as the payment of a 13th month by chains, make a slight difference. The net monthly wages declared by the housekeepers interviewed are in the range

€800–1,200 for permanent staff (part-time and full-time for 30–39 hours per week). A housekeeper working 39 hours per week in a chain hotel declares:

> *I think it is true, when people say it is a hard job. They could pay us more. But we get the minimum wage… We get just under 1,200 euros per month.*

The most recent survey, conducted in 2005, emphasises that the gross average monthly wage for housekeepers (€1,350) is considerably lower than all the other hotel occupations (€1,608).[6] Other data shows that about 27 percent of hotel employees can be considered as low-wage workers, compared to 10 percent of the total working population. Women represent about two-thirds of the workforce considered as low-paid workers. Moreover, this share is increasing (23 percent in 1995) whereas the general trend in France is a decline in low-paid workers. These results are underestimated because these data do not include undeclared or illegal work and family help. Wages in the hotel and catering industry are lower than in most other sectors, partly due to the low job skills and the weakness of labour market regulation.

Finally, many attributes of women's occupations in France are to be found combined in the housekeeper job: continuity between their domestic and workplace activity, short-term or part-time contracts, and low-wages. However, if they want to achieve high quality service, it may be in the interests of chain or deluxe hotels to gain the loyalty of their floor staff. An example is Sofitel, with incentives for housekeepers, explained by a supervisor: '*We operate a points system. Every task is worth a one or two-point credit, and these one or two points are worth euros.*' The measure is very popular with low-paid staff: '*We were really pleased because we sweated blood over our work. We really want to prove that we work well, that we make a good job.*'

A symbolic promotion

In-house career possibilities are few and far between, and symbolic. They are limited to positions of assistant supervisor and executive housekeeper, which only large establishments can offer. As many hotels are small and run by their owners, such as in the case of family hotels, there are few possibilities of being promoted to supervisor since this function is usually held by the hotelier's wife. Most housekeepers either have no certificates, or only a certificate obtained abroad and not recognised in France. Among the chains, geographical mobility may clinch access to a supervisor's job and this may conflict with their family situation.

Some hotels are exceptions to the rule, with promotions awarded through convenience during periods when manpower is scarce, rather than by deliberate strategy. A deluxe hotel, for instance, promoted one individual to *first housekeeper* and gave her half a day's training. Another small hotel chain promoted a woman to *first housekeeper* with a new administrative role, but insisted that she retains her hourly cleaning rate of three rooms as before. Here we see the *'internal market'* at work, allowing employers to avoid the cost of recruitment and reduce the cost of training. This situation contrasts with the Cinderella story told by a former housekeeper in a recent study for Accor (Bosse and Guégnard, 2005). Of African origin, she arrived in France at the age of 20 and started working in a three-star hotel: room cleaner to executive housekeeper, then trainer, she travelled widely from Russia to Cuba, Egypt to Latin America before settling down in France as the head of a hotel, because in the course of her travels, as she puts it, *'she found her Prince Charming'*.

Housekeepers hope to become supervisors and to be recognised as *'real supervisors'* one day. They cannot see any other opportunities for making good use of their professional experience. They try to remain hopeful about their prospects, even if they know they have very little opportunity to reach their dream. Such hope helps them make their daily lives easier. Some of them explain:

– *'My hope is to become an executive housekeeper. At the reception desk, you wait and stand up in front of customers, or to answer the phone: it is not interesting. I prefer to be a worker and in the back office';*
– *'To be a supervisor means to be financially independent. Even when the husband works, that means that you can have your own life';*
– *'I would like to work full-time but for now, it is not possible… I have neither personal nor professional projects. For now, I think about nothing. I have no prospects.'*
– *'I like what I do. I have always worked in this occupation. I am a well-known housekeeper, I am usually congratulated for my job… My husband tells me that I have to take another job. But as I have no diploma, I have no choice… Even to become a supervisor, English is to be learnt. For now, I do not think I am ready for that';*
– *'It is really hard work. I have been working here for nearly eight years. But for a long time, with the previous managers, housekeepers had no tenure because this work is really hard. But I do not want to leave because I like my work […] So I keep it and I like my position. It is my home';*
– *'I live from day to day. I do not have any personal goals. I would like to have one, but anyway, being housekeepers, we are not supposed to have any personal goals'.*

Segmentation, vulnerability and exclusion

In France, housekeepers have secondary market jobs reinforced by industry conditions and legislative provisions: low-paid, back-breaking working conditions and few chances of promotion. In fact, the working life of a housekeeper often falls into three phases. During the first phase, she works as an extra or for a subcontractor (external management). Next, she is hired by the hotel on a more stable contract (internal management). But this phase is quickly compromised by the constraints of intensive productivity and increasingly hard work which it is impossible to sustain for more than ten years. Then when her physical health begins to suffer (for instance, back pains and/or allergies to cleaning products), or quite simply she is incapable of maintaining the same work schedule, she is forced either to reduce her hours or to leave the workforce, slipping into a new period of vulnerability, or worse, into social exclusion. It is, therefore, difficult for her to escape from the vicious circle of precarious contracts and low earnings.

Housekeepers build up their job year after year, sometimes hour after hour. They have to deal with job insecurity and all the disadvantages of flexibility and segmentation in the industrial labour market. Housekeepers have to overcome the same obstacles as many low-wage earners, given the difficulty of obtaining a stable job, and sometimes the impossibility of keeping it. Even though in France the Labour Code and procedures provide high protection to permanent workers and a legal framework for industrial relations, these women are caught in a spiral of vulnerability and low salaries, and at the whim of managerial strategies, which is reinforced by certain government policies. In this special context, hotel chains that take the high road in employment practice, doing their utmost to get more satisfied and loyal staff, sometimes appear like a mirage in a barely innovative industry.

Housekeepers provide a perfect illustration of Piore's argument (1978, p. 48) that *'In France, the dual labor market is not a matter of small and large enterprises. Much greater reliance is placed in institutions which creates islands of flexibility (and insecurity) within the enterprise itself'*. Housekeepers have very few opportunities to develop individual strategies and to escape from their professional destiny, a fate common to low-wage workers in labour market segmentation.

Notes

1 Definition of low-wage: a wage less than or equal to two-thirds of the median wage (rate calculated by Cepremap). The net hourly cut-off corresponded to an average of €5.09 in 1995 and €6.23 in 2003, all sectors taken into account (DADS surveys, Insee).

2 In France, some employers, especially larger companies, offer employees a '13th Month' double wage as an incentive – usually in December

3 The *My-Bed* concept comes from the US. *'A new way of sleeping and dreaming'* according to the advertising, but to make this bed with a featherbed,

thick comforter and four down pillows may take 12–20 minutes according to the housekeepers.

4 In one small chain hotel, all the housekeepers have been on 2–8 short vocational continuing training courses.

5 In the many hotels visited, the housekeepers have colour-coded boards for identification purposes *'marked in blue, they are the rooms due to check out and in yellow, the rooms that will be slept in again... and the crew is high-lighted in orange...'* explains one supervisor.

6 Survey carried out by *CHD Conso* in 2005, based on a sample of hoteliers and restaurant owners (342 establishments) (L'Hôtellerie, 2005).

REFERENCES

Appelbaum, E., Bernhardt, A. and Murnamer, R. (2003) *Low-Wage America: How Employers are Reshaping Opportunity in the Workplace*, New York: Russell Sage Foundation.

Bosse, N. and Guégnard, C. (2005) *Mixité, carrières et performances*. Céreq-Iredu/Cnrs Report.

Doeringer, P. B. and Piore, M. J. (1971) *Internal Labour Market and Manpower Analysis*, Lexington, Mass.: Heath Lexiton Books.

Guégnard, C. and Mériot, S.-A. (2008) 'Housekeepers in French Hotels: Cinderella in the Shadow', in Caroli, E. and Gautié, J., *Low-Wage Work in France*, Russell Sage Foundation, 168–208.

Guégnard, C. and Mériot S.-A. (2005) *French Hotel Industry: Traditions and Social Developments*. Report for Russell Sage Foundation. Céreq-Iredu/Cnrs.

Guégnard, C. *et al.* (2004) 'À la recherche d'une conciliation des temps professionnels et personnels dans l'hôtellerie-restauration', *Relief*, n°7. Céreq.

L'Hôtellerie Restauration (2005) Paris: supplement n°2930.

Monchatre, S. and Testenoire, A. (2004) 'Les carrières entre mirage et réalité', *Relief*, n°7. Céreq: 39–67.

Piore, M. J. (1978) 'Dualism in the labour market. A response to uncertainty and flux. The case of France', *Revue Economique*, vol. 19 n°1: 26–48.

Puech, I. (2004) 'Le temps du remue-ménage. Conditions d'emploi et de travail des femmes de chambre'. *Sociologie du Travail*, 46 n°2: 150–67.

Reich, M., Gordon, D. M. and Edwards, C. (1973) 'A theory of labour market segmentation', *American Economic Review*, Vol. 63 n°2: 359–65.

Triby, E. (2004) 'Le travail entre le professionnel et le domestique', *Relief*, n°7 Céreq: 27–38.

Balancing Trays and Smiles: What Restaurant Servers Teach Us About Hard Work in the Service Economy

Mary Gatta

It is 8:30 on a Saturday night. The restaurant is on a 20 minute wait and you are 'in the weeds'; all your tables need something and you have to determine how to get everything done. Table number 601 needs a beer; 602 asked for their check five minutes ago; you still have to put 603's order into the micro-computers (and there is a line of servers at the only two computers that work!). Finally, table 605 has been waiting 33 minutes for their meal. You have been working since noon without a formal break, and only ate a cold chicken sandwich at 2:00 p.m. Then you see that the service station is out of ice and filling the ice is your sidework responsibility.

You go over to 605 to apologise for their meal delay and tell them the manager will buy them a round of drinks for their inconvenience. However the free drinks do not make things better and instead the customer starts yelling at you. He is trying to catch a movie, which he will now miss, because his dinner is taking so long. He goes on to say that his whole night is ruined and you should not even think about a tip! This makes you angry, but you have to maintain your composure. You still have to bring their food out; put other tables' orders in; and, of course, you can't forget to fill the ice, as you hear a fellow server scream, 'We need ice. Whose sidework is ice tonight?'

This scenario, and many others similar to it, plays out almost daily for the 2.3 million restaurant servers in the United States (US DOL, 2006). An integral thread in the fabric of restaurants, servers are both ubiquitous and invisible. Americans spend almost a billion dollars a day on dining outside the home (Ginsberg, 2000), interacting with many waiters/waitresses in their daily lives. Yet while restaurant servers are the main point of contact between the customer and all other restaurant employees (chefs, bartenders, and even managers), patrons typically do not remember their server's name or even physical attributes. In fact, customers are most aware of their server when he/she is not there. The moments when a customer needs extra napkins or another soda, are the times when servers are most visible in their consciousness. It is then when one is likely to hear, 'Where is my waitress?'

Delving into an analysis of restaurant service is important for many reasons. Similar to other interactive service work, restaurant service jobs are growing. Employment opportunities for waiters/waitresses are expected to increase by 14 percent through 2016 in the United States, translating into about 993,000 new jobs (US DOL, 2008). Moreover, this work cannot easily be outsourced or replaced by technology because it requires face-to-face service work and emotional labour that the worker must personally perform (Blinder, 2006; Gatta, 2002; Callaghan and Thompson, 2002). Yet while plentiful, these jobs represent some of the lowest-wage work, with millions of workers far from achieving economic self-sufficiency. Given the large current and projected growth in restaurant service, we need to understand exactly what is going on in service work – namely the conditions of work, along with the job and skill demands.

Waiters/waitresses raise serious questions to the conventional notions of standardisation and routinisation of service work. George Ritzer (1996) famously refers to this as the 'McDonaldisation' of service jobs where speed and scripts are the central components of work and employers enact routinised jobs. Ritzer envisions a future of service work characterised by continued integration of technology and streamlined services, thus relegating workers to low-skill, standardised, and boring work.[1] Characterisations of service work as 'McJobs' insinuate that service work is easy and natural, along with unsatisfying and dehumanising. Interpreted as a new form of alienation in the service economy (Hochschild, 1983), interactive service workers 'sell' themselves as part of the product with their actions and emotions subjected to routines and scripts which eliminate much scope for creativity or authenticity.

While there are extensive in-roads to routinisation in restaurant work, including the use of computers to both relay orders to the kitchen, and control and monitor stock and order patterns (along with restricting customer's choices), this depiction does not capture the actual work experiences of servers. In this chapter, building on ethnographic research conducted in American restaurants, I share the experiences of wait staff to illustrate not only the complex practices and interactions involved in waiting tables, but also what this teaches us about work in the new economy.

Studying restaurant work

This study emerges out of larger work I conducted on the emotional labour and emotional balancing practices of restaurant servers, which occurred in two phases over three years. In the first phase I conducted interviews with

30 servers (nine men and 21 women) in restaurants ranging from local diners to fine dining establishments. Then two years later, I expanded the study to engage in eight months of participant observation at a franchised casual dining restaurant located in a suburban shopping mall. During my participant observation at Café Red,[2] I experienced all the duties of a server. Upon completion of a training programme, I was 'on my own on the floor.' Throughout my shifts I attended meetings, took surprise quizzes, worked in different table sections, and on different shifts. Like any other server I was completely responsible for my section and my daily work. I took field notes after each shift to record my experiences. Although I disclosed myself as a researcher from the start, as I continually worked at the restaurant I was treated just as another co-worker. In addition to my participant observation I also conducted 20 more server interviews (ten men and ten women), and eight interviews with managers. These interviews, in conjunction with my participant observation, allowed me to delve into the everyday lives of the men and women who are charged with the responsibility of serving us our dinners.

A day in the life of a server[3]

The daily work practices of restaurant servers involve physical prowess, communication and technology skills, emotional labour, and the ability to multitask quickly and efficiently.

Income

Restaurant servers derive their income through a combination of hourly wages and customer tips. However, since hourly wages are typically below the US minimum wage, tips comprise the most significant portion of their income. The median hourly (including tips) wage of waiters/waitresses is $7.14. The middle 50 percent earn between $6.42 and $9.14, with the lowest 10 percent earning less than $5.78, and the highest 10 percent earning more than $12.46 an hour (US DOL, 2008). For most waiters/waitresses, higher earnings are primarily the result of receiving more in tips rather than higher hourly wages. Although American custom dictates that the tip should be between 15 and 20 percent of the total meal bill, there is no true mechanism to ensure that the server receives this amount, and instead he/she is dependent on the customers' whims. Sometimes regardless of the service received; the customer will not tip. As one waiter told me:

> Sometimes I think that people come in just to harass the waiter. They either had a bad day, problems at home, or something. I'm the only person that they can take it out on, they can pretend I'm their

servant...lots of times they won't leave me anything or just like 5 or 10 percent which is basically a stiff.... I think they come in prepared to stiff the waiter.

The tipping system structures the server's work as workers attempt to maximise their earnings via tips. Yet, this does not mean that the tipping system is fully deterministic. Instead workers may adapt, resist and challenge the tipping practice. In addition, workers also do not see the tip as the *only* measure of their success or worth. As a waitress notes:

This guy comes in everyday for the past few years and never tips. He is a truck driver and runs up an eight to ten dollar bill, but he will never tip me. I still give him the same nice service even though I know that he won't tip. I know that I am still doing my job at my best.

While certainly important, the tip is not necessarily the defining moment for a server.

Physical work and work intensity

Much analysis of service economy jobs focuses on its interactive elements, often ignoring or overlooking the physical dimensions of such work. Yet many service jobs also require physically demanding work and restaurant service is no exception. Wait staff typically work on their feet for at least an eight hour shift, carrying heavy trays of food and drinks. At Café Red shifts are scheduled 10 a.m. (opening shift), 10 BD, 11 a.m., 12 BD, 4 p.m., 5 p.m. (closing shift). On a BD shift, common in many US restaurants, a server works both the lunch and dinner shift until the 'business declines'. (Indeed this is a preferred shift at Café Red as servers have 'double' the opportunity to earn money.) Most opening shifts are cut by 4:00 p.m., and 11 o'clockers are usually completed by 5:00 p.m. BD's work through lunch and dinner, typically finishing by 10:30 p.m. 4 o'clockers serve customers until about an hour before the restaurant closes. Those working a closing shift have additional duties, such as vacuuming and cleaning light fixtures, completed after the customers leave the restaurant. Yet these quitting times are just estimates, as there are no guarantees when a shift will be complete. If there are no or few customers, servers are cut early; if the restaurant remains busy, no one is cut. As I overheard one waiter tell his daughter: 'I only know when I am to come into work, not when I am going to leave.'

The uncertainty concerning how many hours servers would work also corresponds to uncertainty in their pay. Since they work for tips, no customers translates into no tips. It is then in their best economic interest to work when it is busy. Yet it is quite possible for a server to work a shift and wait on very few or even no customers, leaving with very little income for the day. Such uncertainty also makes it difficult for servers to manage responsibilities outside of the restaurant, such as childcare or educational commitments. This requires servers to find flexible arrangements – sometimes quite difficult to do – to integrate their work and life commitments.

The long hours contribute to the heavy toll waiting tables puts on servers' bodies. Servers carry heavy, hot plates quickly through the dining room, sometimes balancing up to six or seven plates at a time. As floors in kitchens are very slippery and backstage service spaces tend to be quite crowded, servers need considerable agility to manoeuvre. As Karla Erickson (2004) notes in her study of restaurants, the 'skilful use of the body is necessary for this work: a staff that communicates well will get so accustomed to passing each other, switching places, transferring trays, sharing space and helping each other that words no longer are necessary during the busiest part of the evening.' (p. 80). The physical rhythms of the restaurant are therefore essential for servers to learn and become part of. Of course, sometimes the rhythms break down and accidents occur, forcing servers to respond quickly and maintain composure. As this waiter shares:

> A server bumped into me when I was weeded and carrying lots of plates. All the plates fell and all the food, which I was going to wrap for the customers to take home, was all on the floor. I was pissed.... I then slammed my way into the kitchen, told the cook to get me all new food to wrap on the fly.... I was mad at her, but I handled what I had to do, I was in the weeds and she put me more in the weeds, because now I had to wait for new food to be cooked, before I could turn over that table.... She then avoided me for awhile, then she tried to apologize, but I ignored her. Because if I did not ignore her I would have gone off and yelled at her. She was so stupid, she stopped right in the doorway, you're not supposed to do that.... I had to repress my anger because I was busy... if I had the time to rip into her I would have, but I had to get my shit done with the six tables I had.

Erickson (2004) refers to this as the 'dance' of restaurant work – just one misstep in that dance and everything hangs in the balance.

The degree of physical work is further compounded as servers do not often get formal breaks in their workday and can work ten to 12 hours without once sitting down. Café Red managers told me that they provide servers with a 'choice' regarding breaks, but many times servers would rather continue taking tables than take a break (as taking a break means forfeiting at least one round of tips). Yet my field observation showed that during busy times managers would inform servers that they would *try* to give breaks, but if the restaurant remained busy the servers would have to work through their break. Breaks therefore became a privilege. In lieu of formal breaks, servers must squeeze in time between serving customers to go to the bathroom and eat meals Often they will get food, and then place it somewhere in the kitchen. This food may sit for hours, with the server nibbling at bites whenever a free second is found. Quite astutely, Erickson (2004, p. 80) comments, 'You need to be in good shape to wait tables, but you don't get in shape doing it.' Clearly, such a lifestyle when performed long enough puts strains on muscles, bones, and digestive systems.

Sidework and sections

The server's shifts begin somewhat routinely everyday with what is termed a 'pre-meal' or 'line-up' at most American restaurants. Part inspirational, part informative, during the line-up at Café Red a manager shares the expectations for the shift, what foods are out of stock, quizzes servers on menu knowledge, and assigns them their sections and running sidework. Per shift, each server has a section consisting of three to six tables. Some sections are considered better money-makers than others. At Café Red sections containing tables closest to the bar, larger tables, or booths are believed to be the 'best sections.' Although managers there claim that sections are randomly assigned, discovering one's section can be either a moment of joy or contention for the server, as this becomes his or her territory for the shift. As Greta Foff Paules (1991, 145–7) noted, servers refer to their tables with possessive pronouns (such as those are *my* customers; those are *Sue's* people; I have to fill *my* mustards on 102). The server is responsible for everything that occurs in his/her section, often with little help from other workers. This responsibility is further solidified by the rule on walkouts. When a table 'walks out on the check,' (meaning that they do not pay the check), it is the server who is financially responsible for the unpaid meal.

In addition to bearing complete responsibility for his/her tables, servers also have sidework responsibilities including: filling items (creamers, ice); prepping foods (lemons, tomatoes); cleaning (sweeping floors, wiping counters, emptying bus buckets); and/or stocking hardware (glasses, plates, silverware). As Paules (1991: 143) notes, although 'the term sidework fosters the view that these tasks are peripheral to the waitress's work... the thorough completion of sidework duties is critical to the smooth functioning of each shift and to peaceful relations between shifts.' Running sidework allows servers to work more efficiently. However, when the restaurant is busy, servers have to partition their time effectively to be able to complete sidework and wait on customers. Servers have to wipe down their tables, fill and clean the condiments on their tables, 'pop' booth seats to wipe down the crevasses, and sweep underneath and around their tables. Finally, they are assigned a closing sidework job which involves cleaning, breaking down coffee and iced tea machines, stocking products for the following shift or sanitising the soda machine. All in all, a server can spend between 30 and 45 minutes doing sidework after a shift is officially over.[4]

Emotion work

The heart of restaurant service work is literally serving tables. Servers are responsible for greeting customers, taking orders, answering questions, getting drinks, processing orders in the computers, bringing food, balancing as many plates as possible to save on trips to the kitchen, and making change for customers, all the while being as nice and friendly as possible. Similar to Arlie Russell Hochschild's (1983) flight attendants, servers have to both *deliver* friendly service and find it within themselves to *feel* happy as they are serving each customer – and engaging in such emotion work is central to a successful server.

Restaurant managers do not assume that servers know the emotional labour required of them and instead mandate each server (regardless of previous experience) attend a training programme. In addition to learning about the menu items and computer systems, servers also learn the 'official scripts' of the restaurant. In the case of Café Red, staff are provided with detailed sample interactions, and instructed that it is their responsibility to 'take care of the customers'. Such scripts specify both the act of serving tables (including greeting customers, taking an order, delivering food and presenting a check), and the emotion work expected, with an emphasis on the demonstration of authenticity. As the training manual at Café Red states:

> being a server means more than just taking the order. Each customer that walks in the door should be treated with the basic courtesy and respect that you would treat a customer in your own home. A smile and professional greeting help create a good first impression and make the customer feel at home....Two basic ingredients to a good welcoming greeting are briefness and sincerity. The purpose is to establish a friendly courteous relationship with the customer. We want the customer to feel good about having made the choice to come... A sincere greeting doesn't sound like you are just going through the motions.

The implication here is that servers consider customers through a personal lens and yet are not to take the emotional responses of the customer personally. The training manual offers 'professional hints' to equip the server in the interaction.

> Don't respond to a customer or situation emotionally. In other words, do not take a customer's mood or difficult situation personally. Avoid getting angry and showing it to the customer.... When you are 'in the weeds' during a busy time... try to remain calm, cool and collected... Don't show the customer hurried behaviour.... Realize the importance of the customer's self-image. Make the customer feel important by your courteous and professional service.

It is clear that the servers understand that this is the 'official' script and would help each other to ensure that their emotional balance (Gatta, 2002) was in check. For example, while I was working at Café Red one server encouraged me to 'squash' my own emotions in the interaction and continue with my work (excerpt from my fieldnotes):

> After dealing with a demanding and rude table, I felt pretty frazzled. I then had to bring the table another round of drinks. Since I could not carry them all, I had to ask Mark [a waiter] to help me. As we were carrying the drinks I was telling him that this table was bothering me, specifically that they had me running all over the place and spoke to me in a condescending manner. As I was telling him this I was getting upset. He told me to stop and 'squash it right here.' If I continued to think about the table and let it get to me, my emotions would, as he stated, 'spread like a disease' to all my other tables. They would notice my frazzledness and I would make unnecessary mistakes that would emotionally get to me. However, if I just put that table out of my mind, I would be able to carry on without affecting my work.

Emotion work is central to servers' work lives. Servers also deal with many emotional hazards from customers – those who are not happy with their meals, those who may have a particularly long time waiting for a table, or those just having a bad day – while serving them their meals (Gatta, 2002). This articulation skill-work (Bolton, 2004, 2005; Hampson and Junor, 2005), while less visible, is critical to successfully completing one's job. Going beyond simply enacting routines and scripts, articulation work involves a blend of emotional, cognitive, technical, and time management skills, performed often at speed and at varying levels of complexity and autonomy (p. 176). While customers come to the restaurant for a meal, they also expect a service experience. Typically they anticipate sincere pleasant service, with all their dining needs met. In some cases customers make this quite clear to servers. As one server told me:

> Once this woman was so superior as she talked to me. She ordered a Chicken Caesar without the chicken or croutons. I put the order in right

but there was some mix up; I did not know because I did not bring the food out, but there was chicken and croutons on the salad. When I went to see how everything was she handed me a napkin with the chicken and croutons on it and said 'here, I did not order this.' I said 'I am sorry.' She then said 'I don't care, this is why I don't eat out, you people always make mistakes.' She never looked at me when she talked or handed me the napkin.

Although there are fairly exacting scripts to guide the service inter-action, and in particular the emotional labour process, waiters/waitresses need additional skills to successfully complete the interactions. Though each server knows the official prescriptions for emotional labour, they do not always follow them, often for good and necessary reasons – in other words, there is a definite difference at times, between officially espoused emotions, and those necessary to get the job done on one hand, and to deal with the emotions that they are experiencing within workplace interactions, on the other. Servers therefore choose, disregard, alter, and create different scripts based on the unique characteristics of the micro-social context and flexibility, creativity, and adaptability become important work attributes.

A waitress of 15 years at a diner describes situations where she would adapt the official script: 'when customers are rude and make me feel like I am their servant, especially when they don't make an effort to reciprocate the friendliness that I gave them.' When these instances occur the waitress would 'still smile, but not go out of my way. Customers never know that they made me mad.' She would continue the service but withhold what she referred to as that 'extra something... being there to refill their drinks, try to entertain their kids, just making sure that their stay was pleasant.' This server, by way of sanction, thus removed the expressive behaviours that con-stituted the good service she was expected to provide.

It is clear that wait staff must be able to read and interpret customers' needs, judge what the customer expects, select service actions and scripts, and then deliver that service to the customer. Bolton and Boyd (2003) describe this, in their analysis of flight attendants as 'multi-skilled emotional managers' who 'juggle and synthesize' each service interaction. Such skills are also central to successful restaurant work. In a study of a luxury hotel, Rachel Sherman (2007) found restaurant servers readily defined their ability to read guest demeanour as a skill. She shares examples of servers who 'gauge from the beginning how a table wants [them] to be', so as to treat each customer distinctly and anticipate their needs. Restaurant servers must be able to effectively assess and react to situations quickly; and read customers' cues as to whether they need to be handled distinctly. For example, a waitress told me that she would try to keep a magazine in her locker at work. She went on to explain:

> The magazine is not really for me. Sometimes when a customer dines alone they are really uncomfortable when they are waiting for their food. They will look around at other tables and the workers, and just be really fidgety. When I see this, I will bring them a magazine to look through. It just gives them something to do, and makes them feel a bit more comfortable. It is so simple, but it makes a big difference.

This waitress notes that servers do not just use formal guidelines to assess the service interaction, they go beyond scripts to find creative ways to make the restaurant experience enjoyable. This not only makes the customer feel good, but the server also takes joy in that experience. Articulation work of this nature can also bring practical benefits: For instance, a waitress shares an instance when she asserted that work to a customer.

> A man wanted me to serve him immediately, as soon as he sat down. But I had other tables and I had to get them in the order that they came in. So I told him, 'Sir you have to wait a minute.' Then he told me, 'If you don't wait on me now you aren't getting tipped.' So I told him, 'Sir you can keep your tip and I will still wait on you. I will wait on you and you don't have to tip me.' So then I got the other tables' orders and then his, just like I was supposed to, in the order that they came in. He ended up tipping me three dollars, which was surprising 'cause I thought he would not leave me anything, but I had to make him understand that I have a pattern to my job and that is important to me. I was upset that he felt that I didn't have a set way to do my job.

Hochschild (1983) has argued that emotional labour is not only challenging, it can 'transmute' employees own connection with their feelings and create a 'managed heart'. Yet, while emotional labour is hard work, it is also clear from so many of the servers studied that the labour does not always result in the 'transmutation of feelings by the organization', and indeed can at times provide opportunities for heightened sense of dignity in that work. For example, one waitress told me:

> I get a feeling of pride knowing that I did a good job while waiting on the table. That I helped them to have fun and relax while I was waiting on

them. Even if it was something small like bringing out candles for a birthday, they had a good time and I was a part of that.

Her sense of personal pride is coming from the work interaction. She is not distanced or alienated from the work, but instead defines the emotions that she feels as part of her personal lived experience.

Hard work in the service economy

From the foregoing it is clear that restaurant servers bear the brunt of the responsibility for their tables. Servers, among other things, must manage multiple tables at once, perform extensive side work, engage in creative rapports with customers, use technology skills to input and manage customer food orders so that they can be processed, and in some restaurants, steer customers to higher priced foods and drinks without appearing manipulative. They have to learn and often juggle the prescriptions of service. They need the knowledge to answer customers' questions regarding food and drink ingredients, cooking specifications, and appropriate pairings of food and drink. They also need to be aware of how to communicate customers' special requests to kitchen and bar staff. Service presentation also matters and servers need to know the appropriate silverware and place settings for different points of the meal. All of this requires a complex web of social, technical, emotional and physical skills as servers simultaneously manage the customer, the computer, the food product, other workers, and time; and all as seamlessly as possible.

In addition to the physical, mental and emotional work all of this involves, servers must of course finally finely balance their relationships with other staff and management, being at once interdependent, and in some ways, in competition. While servers can attempt to control their physical and emotion work, many aspects of the service experience – tasty and timely food, clean tables, perfectly made cocktails – are beyond their immediate control. Instead servers have to actively negotiate with other restaurant workers to ensure a successful customer experience – to find ways to manage and elicit work from other workers over whom they do not have power. For example, a waitress noted how sometimes the flow of work can be disrupted.

The bartender did not have too many tickets up, but I had an order come up and he did not make my drink.... I was waiting for my drink, it was four minutes then he finally started making my drink, then at six minutes, he stops making it to take a phone call, then I think he forgot about the drink... it took like ten minutes to get the drink out to the table, by that time the appetizer was out.. I was livid. I was trying to be calm at first, because I don't like to get upset at work. But the bartender then got mad at me, he's yelling at me, I'm yelling at him... go get the manager and tell him... the manager made a table visit to take care of everything... what amazed me was that the bartender did not admit that he was wrong.

This tension stems, as Gordon Marshall (1986) has noted, from the culture of the workplace as a restaurant injects customer initiations into staff status order. High status customers initiate their demands for efficient service and goods to lower status workers (servers), who in turn must demand prompt action of their somewhat higher status superiors (cooks, chefs, bartenders) (Marshall, 1986, p. 34). This relationship puts the server in the precarious status position of demanding work of his/her status superiors. Not only must the server demand that work is performed efficiently and at the highest level, he/she is also dependent on that work. If the food is not prepared efficiently and well, or the bartender is taking too long to make drinks, it is the server who must be the buffer to the customer and more often than not, it is the server's tip that is negatively affected.

The interdependence of workers, along with a highly charged fast paced work environment, leads to feelings of teamwork among servers and servers often turn to each other to deal with trials of service work. Many times this is accomplished by finding 'new' backstage areas where they can escape for a few moments during the shift. At Café Red, one of the most common places for workers to meet is in the handicapped stalls of the men and women's bathrooms. These stalls are quite large and can house three to four servers. Servers sneak in there to smoke a cigarette and to vent to each other. This backstage area is out of most customers' sights and also out of the managers' watchful eyes. Even though they are officially 'on the clock,' the workers could communally come together and vent, share stories, or just help each other get their minds off their emotions.

Perhaps the clearest examples of worker camaraderie are when workers sacrifice portions of their own income for another worker. One waiter recounted such a moment.

A server lost her money... she was definitely upset, in fact she started crying.... I felt bad for her, it kinda made me ill, like in my stomach.... I told her that that really sucked to lose your money, it was like $100, which means she had to pay for the bills out of her tips and walked with nothing. Then everyone else felt bad too... so we all chipped in a couple dollars for her, so at least she made something for the day.

However while teamwork is important to a successful restaurant staff, servers are also in competition to ensure that they wait on the highest number of tables possible per shift, in order to increase their tip income. Keen servers learn early how to 'scoop the door'. That is, as soon as a server spots customers enter the restaurant, he/she will greet them and then seat them in their table sections. 'Scooping the door' is strongly discouraged by managers as it disrupts the table rotation (which is in place to ensure that all servers get tables in turn), but many servers see scooping the door as a survival strategy, especially during slow times. Moreover, servers may also make strategic alliances with hostesses in attempts to get additional tables or direct tables that could result in higher tips (such as larger parties or regular customers at the restaurant) to their sections. Such behaviours cause tensions and in-fighting among servers.

Throughout this account it is clear that restaurant service work is hard work. It is a fast paced work environment that requires quick thinking, physical agility, and the ability to multitask effectively. Servers have to engage in emotional labour to ensure the customer feels special, but they also need to manage their emotions so they can quickly move from table to table without letting negative emotions carry over to other customers. Waiting tables is also exhausting work. Barbara Ehrenreich (2001) in her participant observation noted how her feet, legs, and back all throbbed in pain after a day of waiting tables. Yet it is not just throbbing muscles that remain after the shift. It is quite common for the smell of the food to linger on one's uniform, and one's skin can bear the marks of table service for hours. As a waiter told me:

Some days my fingernails are red when I leave work. This is because we have to garnish our drinks, and when there is no spoon available I put my hand in the maraschino cherry jar. You know the way auto mechanics have black oil under their nails, I have red cherries!

Conclusion

While the knowledge workers of the new economy continue to gain much attention, the real job growth is among low-wage service work. As service work continues to grow we must revisit these occupations to understand work practices, job skill contents, training procedures and expectations. We will always need a waiter to bring us our food, or a waitress to negotiate with the chef when our steak is not cooked to our liking. Yet restaurant servers continue to be among the lowest wage earners. Restaurant work, especially non-unionised, tends to have short term and high turnover. Yearly earnings are low because of both bad pay and insufficient hours (Lane, 1999), along with the fact that these jobs are much less likely to offer healthcare and pension benefits (Glomb, Kammemery-Mueller and Rotundo, 2004; Bernstein and Gittleman, 2003). Servers also have little control over their hours – if there are no customers, they have no work and no income.

Technology, while complementing the work of servers, cannot replace them. Waitresses may use computers to tally up their orders, but, at least for now, only a human can carry trays, take orders, fill water glasses, complete sidework, and smile – all at the same time. This work is hard in terms of its physical, emotional, communication, technical, and articulation skills. Yet often in the new economy, restaurant service is simply regulated to broad categorisations of low-wage, low skill 'McJobs.' We then must engage in a dialogue to better understand restaurant service work and other interactive service occupations which will help us not only better prepare workers for these jobs, but also ensure that we are able to value the work they are performing.

Notes

1 Such conceptualisations are further fuelled by the decline of manufacturing work which has often been seen as being replaced by less demanding and prestigious service work. Tim Strangleman (2007) relays a quite telling 1998 *Guardian* headline summing this up: 'We once made ships, now we take calls' (p. 90).
2 Café Red is a pseudonym for the restaurant where I conducted my participant observation.
3 This section is adapted and updated from my detailed ethnographic account of this study, see Gatta, 2002.
4 At Café Red, during end of shift work, servers are not earning tips, but instead are being paid just $2.13 an hour.

REFERENCES

Bernstein, J. and Gittleman, M. (2003) 'Exploring Low-Wage Labour with the National Compensation Survey', *Monthly Labour Review*.

Blinder, A. (2006) 'Offshoring: The Next Industrial Revolution', *Foreign Affairs*.

Bolton, S. and Boyd, C. (2003) 'Trolly dolly or skilled emotion manager? Moving on from Hochschild's Managed Heart', *Work, Employment and Society*, 17: 289–308.

Bolton, S. (2004) 'Conceptual Confusions: Emotion Work as Skilled Work', in Warhurst, C., Keep, E. and Grugulis, I. (eds) *The Skills that Matter*, pp. 19–37, London: Palgrave.

Bolton, S. C. (2005) 'Women's Work, Dirty Work: The Gynaecology Nurse as "Other"', *Gender, Work and Organisation*, 16(2): 169–86.

▶

▶

Callaghan, G. and Thompson, P. (2002) 'We Recruit Attitude: The Selection and Shaping of Routine Call Centre Labour', *Journal of Management Studies*, 39: 233–54.

Erickson, K. (2004) 'Bodies at Work: Performing Service in American Restaurants', *Space and Culture* 7: 76–89.

Ehrenreich, B. (2001) *Nickel and Dimed: On Not Getting By in America*, New York: Metropolitan Books.

Gatta, M. (2002) *Juggling Food and Feelings: Emotional Balance in the Workplace*, Lanham, MD: Lexington Books.

Ginsberg, D. (2000) *Waiting: The True Confessions of a Waitress*, New York: HarpersCollins.

Glomb, T., Kammeyer-Mueller, J. and Rotundo, M. (2004) 'Emotional Labour Demands and Compensating Wage Differentials', *Journal of Applied Psychology*, 89: 700–14.

Hampson, I. and Junor, A. (2005) 'Invisible Work, Invisible Skills: Interactive Customer Service as Articulation Work', *New Technology, Work and Employment*, 20: 166–181.

Hochschild, A. (1983) *The Second Shift*, New York: Penguin Books.

Lane, J. (1999) 'The Role of Job Turnover in the Low-Wage Labour Markets', *The Low-Wage Labour Market: Challenges and Opportunities for Economic Self-Sufficiency*, Washington DC: The Urban Institute

Marshall, G. (1986) 'The Workplace Culture of a Licensed Restaurant', *Theory, Culture and Society*, 3: 33–47.

Paules, G. (1991) *Dishing It Out: Power and Resistance Among Waitresses in a New Jersey Restaurant*, Philadelphia, PA: Temple University Press.

Ritzer, G. (1996) *The McDonaldization of Society*, Thousand Oaks, CA: Pine Forge Press.

Sherman, R. (2007) *Class Acts: Service and Inequality in Luxury Hotels*, Berkeley, CA: University of California Press.

Strangleman, T. (2007) 'The nostalgia for permanence at work?: The end of work and its commentators', *Sociological Review*, 55(1): 81–103.

US DOL (2006) Occupational Employment and Wages, 2006, US Department of Labor, http://www.bls.gov/oes/viewed July 2008.

US DOL (US Department of Labour) (2008) Bureau of Labour Statistics. http://www.bls.gov/emp/, data accessed July 2, 2008.

Inequality Street? Working Life in a British Chocolate Factory

Benjamin Hopkins

This chapter offers a glimpse of the contemporary experience within what once may have been regarded as a quaintly traditional workplace – the English chocolate factory. However as this case study will reveal, today's English chocolate factory is characterised by short term and agency employment, multiethnicity, and highly deskilled work. Far from quaint, stories from the factory floor reveal a picture of a divided and frustrated workforce who are seeking opportunities where few are forthcoming.

In 1979, when the Conservative government took power in the United Kingdom, 6.9 million people worked in manufacturing out of a total workforce of 24.7 million. By the time the Conservatives were voted out in 1997 the workforce had remained relatively static at 24.5 million, but the number employed in manufacturing had fallen to 4.2 million. Ten years later, when this case study was conducted, the total workforce had grown to 27.1 million, but the numbers employed in manufacturing had fallen to 2.9 million (Office for National Statistics, 2008a). With a diminishing number of people employed in manufacturing, contemporary studies into these workplaces are rare, particularly long-term investigations such as the classic studies of Roy (1952), Lupton (1963) and Burawoy (1979), with jobs at the bottom end of the labour market being particularly neglected in recent years (Bach, 2005). However, despite the smaller numbers of people employed in this sector, the make up of workers in this area has changed significantly. On 1 May 2004 the UK opened its borders to the European Union A8 accession countries. By the time this case study was conducted over 600,000 people had registered on the Worker Registration Scheme (Cooley and Sriskandarajah, 2008), a figure far higher than the government's predicted figures of between 8,000 and 13,000 (Dustmann *et al.*, 2003). This figure has been supplemented by successful asylum seekers from countries such as Iraq and Afghanistan (Holgate, 2005). There have been changes, too, amongst workers from the UK. Temporary work has grown rapidly from 1.2 million in 1990 through the recession of the 1990s to a peak of 1.8 million in 1998, after which it has levelled out to the current figure of around 1.5 million (Office for National Statistics, 2008b). This reduction in security has altered the perception of the low skill manufacturing job, from a comfortable working class permanent job with a guaranteed income or as a stepping stone into higher skill roles or management, into a hoped-for stepping stone into some kind of permanent role, of which few may be forthcoming.

When writing about the low skilled manufacturing job in 1974, Braverman (1974, p. 57) noted that deskilling of jobs leads workers to 'surrender their interest in the labour process, which has now been "alienated"'. The aim of this chapter is to examine how companies use deskilling and short-term employment as a strategic response to cope with variable demand, and the consequences for workers. By reducing jobs to small repetitive tasks the training times of new starters are reduced, allowing companies to employ new starters with little extra cost in training. This has made it easier and more cost-effective for companies to react to changes in demand for their products or services by employing short-term workers, rather than use other methods of meeting variable demand, such as stock accumulation, or by attempting to influence demand, such as through price promotions. Although workers conduct the same tasks, organisations have divided their workforces by employing them on differing contractual statuses. Deskilled work also means that the ability to understand English is no longer a prerequisite, as workers can be physically shown their job rather than having it verbally explained to them, a fact which has facilitated workers from the newly-enlarged EU or from the Middle East who cannot speak English to take employment in the UK. These new and differing routes into low skill manufacturing affect workers' experiences of these jobs and the meanings that these jobs have to them. By exploring the case of ChocCo, this chapter takes a detailed look at the lived experience of contemporary factory work, how these different workers perceive each other, and how this fragmentation causes tension between different groups.

The case company: ChocCo

ChocCo is a confectioner based in the Midlands of England. ChocCo has been trading for nearly 100 years, spending most of its early years in a town-centre site in the Midlands, and more recently at a purpose-built factory on an industrial estate around ten miles from the town-centre site. This new location was chosen because of its proximity to the motorway network, and is equidistant between two large cities, each being around 15 miles away. The workforce traditionally came from the local town when the factory was in the town centre, whereas now the workforce comes from both the local area and the two cities, although public transport to the factory is scarce. No trade union is recognised, although there is a Joint Consultative Committee.

Methodology

Fieldwork with ChocCo was undertaken over a period of three weeks in July 2007.[1] In addition to 20 semi-structured interviews with managers, permanent workers, directly-employed temporary workers and agency workers, the research was conducted through a semi-ethnographic approach that included informal interviews, observation of work and recreational areas, observation of recruitment interviews for temporary workers, and a morning spent on the induction programme for new factory workers. In keeping with Kochan's (1998, p. 35) view that a key aspect of industrial relations research is its 'reverence for and appreciation of history' a key consideration of this research analysis was the evolutionary development of the company and how this affects its current operations.

Work organisation

The factory has a core workforce of around 1,000 manufacturing employees, and these are supplemented by around 400 directly-employed temporary workers and up to 100 agency staff for the periods when the company experiences heightened demand. These are mainly holiday periods such as Easter, Valentine's Day, Mother's Day and Father's Day, with the key period for the company being Christmas. Production for the Christmas period starts in June as the products have a shelf life of nine months and thus can be stored either in warehouses or, to increase the shelf life, in cold store. The company does not experience any peaks or troughs in the supply of its raw materials, as chocolate is delivered pre-made to the factory and other ingredients such as sugar and milk do not have high degrees of seasonality. New starters employed directly by the company were paid £5.50 in July 2007, which was 15 pence above the national minimum wage at that time. The rationale behind this was explained by the HR manager as attracting a 'better class of worker', who added that if the job was minimum wage then it would become interchangeable with other low-skill jobs such as supermarket work. By contrast, agency workers, who made up around 5 percent of the work force at the time of this research, received the minimum wage of £5.35.

The factory is split into five main areas based upon the products that they make. These are Assortments Manufacturing and Assortments Packing, which produce and pack chocolate assortment boxes; Boilings, which produces boiled sweets, fudge and rock; Eggs, which produces Easter eggs; and

Moulded, which produces bars. There are also storage areas for work-in-progress between Assortments Manufacturing and Assortments Packing, and storage areas for raw materials and finished goods. This study was concentrated in the Assortments Packing department, which is formed of several smaller lines that comprise between seven and 30 people, and is responsible for packing the chocolates that have been made by Assortments Manufacturing and placed in the work-in-progress store. The number of people working on each line is determined by how many chocolates will go into the box. At the start of the line cardboard is brought from the raw materials store to make boxes and, once this is constructed, the pre-formed plastic tray that the chocolates will sit in is placed into the box. The boxes are then placed onto an automated belt which passes them down the line. On most lines the workers stand or sit down one side of the belt, and have chocolates brought to them from the work-in-progress store by a worker known as the 'filler-upper', which they then place into the cavities in the tray. Each worker is responsible for placing one chocolate in the tray. Once the tray is full it passes to the end of the line where another worker known as the 'lidder' places the lid on top, and the box is then put into a larger outer box by another worker and is taken away to the finished goods store. Owing to the layout of the work, and the relatively low noise of the machinery, it is easy for workers to speak to their colleagues on either side of them. The radio is played for two hours a day in the department, but cannot be played for longer as the company would have to pay for a licence, currently priced at 7.55 pence plus VAT per half hour for every 25 employees (MCPS-PRS, 2008). The shifts run from 7:30 a.m. until 4:45 p.m. on Monday to Thursday, and then 7:30 a.m. till 11:30 a.m. on Friday. Overtime is used over the weekend, but only as a buffer in case the week's production targets have not been met. Directly employed workers are paid time and a half for working on Saturdays, and double time on Sundays, whereas agency workers receive a premium of 30 pence an hour for overtime, less than 6 percent extra, whichever day they work.

It is reasonable to describe jobs at ChocCo as deskilled, with most workers repetitively placing one chocolate into a box that passes in front of them on a belt, when compared to, for example, the chocolate factory examined by Scott (1994) which had attempted to introduce job enlargement and make operatives responsible for maintaining the machinery. Such deskilling allows ChocCo to hire workers on a short-term basis, often on week-to-week contracts through agencies, to cope with variable demand, as the work requires just one morning's induction. A new dimension shaping the experience of work for people in this factory is the increase in migrant workers, both from the Middle East, and also from Eastern Europe following the expansion of the European Union. This has greatly varied the reasons for people taking jobs in the factory and the meaning of work to each of them.

Career paths into ChocCo

The workers in Assortments Packing had taken a variety of routes into their current roles. Many of the younger directly employed workers had worked in other low or semi skilled roles, both in other factories in the area, and also in jobs like gardening or working in a petrol station. There were also a number of older workers who had previously held higher skilled jobs, but that had lost these jobs through redundancy, and had been forced to re-evaluate their position in the job market, such as this comment from a worker taking his first factory job:

> Now I realise that the forklift driver's job prospects are better than mine, so now he is earning more money than I am. Issues like that have really brought me down and made me look at things, someone stacking shelves is just as good as me.
>
> *Permanent worker*

As an indication of intense job competition in the area, some of these workers had also found themselves forced to take a short-term job for the first time and resented the loss of permanent income, as seen in the case of a former printer who had been made redundant and who had taken a temporary job at ChocCo as competition for printing jobs was so fierce:

> I think a lot of people here come at my age and they are temporary – temporary because they have moved into a different field from what they were doing. Like print training, you might get one [job] every four months that comes up, when I went for interview there were 45 printers that went, so you can imagine the probability of you getting that job.
>
> *Directly-employed Temporary Worker*

This frustration was exacerbated for some of the British workers by many of the competitors for these jobs coming from abroad. Some of these tensions were based on cultural differences, others on language difficulties, but for many the key anxiety was increased competition for low skill jobs such as those in the chocolate factory. Some of the British workers felt this to be particularly true since the EU expansion in 2004, giving rise at times to some negative, arguably racist, sentiment, such as:

> We should be more entitled to the jobs before the Polish and this lot... The British people feel let down because of people coming in and taking their jobs who can't talk English. People have generally thought 'I can't get a job and they [foreign nationals] come and go to an agency and go

straight into a job'. I think if you put a questionnaire out to the Brits here about what you think the worst issue is they will say all these immigrants taking our jobs... I used to read in the papers they are all coming in taking our jobs, but until I came here I didn't know. Where I used to work there was no immigrants at all. I mean Poles, not coloured people. If you didn't talk English you wouldn't get through the door.

Permanent worker

It is difficult to measure the exact number of migrant workers in the UK, a fact reported upon by much of the UK media (Pillai *et al.*, 2007). The largest group of workers on the Worker Registration Scheme are Poles, who make up 58 per cent of all registrations (Gilpin *et al.*, 2006). The main reason cited for leaving Eastern Europe is high levels of unemployment, which for example was almost 20 per cent in Poland at the time of accession (Drinkwater *et al.*, 2006). The majority of Eastern European workers have ended up in low skill jobs (Gilpin *et al.*, 2006; Green *et al.*, 2005) paying an average wage of £5.94 an hour (Anderson *et al.*, 2006), although this is still higher than the £5.35 received by agency workers in the chocolate factory. This is despite their relatively high levels of education (Drinkwater *et al.*, 2006), providing another difference with the British workers who tended not to have a university education. Most of the Eastern European workers who came through the agency into the chocolate factory were not attempting to secure a permanent job as many were still in higher education, working at bachelor's level or higher in their native country, and were working during the university holidays. These students had little or no previous experience of manufacturing work and their main challenge was to find work quickly. This could be a problem owing to English language skills, and so they used the agency to get low skilled jobs that did not require fluency in English. Those workers that did have previous experience or skills often could not communicate these to managers at the factory because of language difficulties, and in one instance this had led to a Polish master confectioner working on a lidding job, an example of underemployment common to many migrant workers' experiences. Many Middle Eastern workers had also come through the agency route to avoid a formal interview because of language difficulties, even though several had been in the UK for several years, and some had worked at the chocolate factory for a number of seasons.

The meaning and value of work

The low skill jobs for the workers in Assortments Packing are broadly similar, and the largest numbers of tasks are based around packing individual chocolates into pre-moulded plastic trays as they pass down the belt. Conversations with these workers suggests that the meaning and value of work in the Assortments Packing Department depends on the route the workers have taken to their job, and the contractual status they work on.

Permanent workers

All the permanent staff who were interviewed had initially started as directly employed temporary workers. They described the key benefit of getting a permanent job as the removal of financial uncertainty, because as a temporary worker they had only been guaranteed work for the next week. The permanent belt job was seen by most as the natural summit of a progression from temporary to permanent worker, which for some had been a long process involving three or more temporary contracts and a three month probation period. Although many of the line managers had worked their way up from shop-floor jobs, often temporary ones, there was little confidence that a career path into the higher skilled area of process management could still be achieved.

> All you can do is wait for that break, and it is very rare that break will come to someone on our line. I think basically this is going to be a dead-end job.
>
> *Permanent worker*

At best, these workers hoped that they would now be able to attend the training courses that were only open to permanent workers in order to increase their skill set and to therefore receive higher pay. Although they had alleviated the financial worries of being on a temporary contract, many now felt that they faced higher levels of workplace stress which they attributed to having to work harder to cover the lower work rate of newer short-term workers. Permanent workers were involved in the training of temporary workers, and found that they were getting placed onto trickier jobs when new temporary people joined, even though they would not be paid any more money until they had been on training courses.

> This lad who has started with me, he is so laid back. I will be doing one in four and he will be doing one in eight. He will miss one so I have to do his one...When I used to be a temp I wasn't bothered, but now I am permanent I have gone back to a regular income so I have to do as I am told.
>
> *Permanent worker*

This highlights a view amongst the permanent staff that work ethics and standards amongst the temporary workers were lower than their own:

> You are trying to do everything properly like you have been shown, and not let shoddy work go out, like we were told to straighten the chocolates

out before we put the lid on them. I know that there is not always time to straighten them but they [short term workers] don't even try to straighten them, and if you tell them they will look at you and they will do it for a bit but then they just go back to their own sweet way, so it is a bit disheartening in that respect.

Permanent worker

These findings are similar to those of Smith (1998), who observed divisions between workers who believed they were good enough to be offered a permanent contract, and those who they saw as 'bad' temporary workers who they felt embodied the negative stereotypes of temporary workers as uncommitted and therefore undeserving of a permanent contract. Use of short-term workers created informal hierarchies amongst the staff at ChocCo, with the permanent workers acting as mentors to newer staff, and although permanent workers saw no need for an official hierarchy they felt that their role as mentors warranted a higher level of pay than new starters – a premium that was not forthcoming. Smith (1994) describes this as the construction of 'hidden hierarchies' – informal hierarchies where permanent employees have to take on the role of managers of shorter-term workers. Permanent workers at ChocCo felt that their contractual status had given them a higher place in this informal hierarchy.

Directly employed temporary workers

Many of the directly employed temporaries had followed similar routes into the factory to permanent workers, and were following similar career paths, hoping that short-term work would provide a stepping stone into permanent employment (Booth *et al.*, 2002; Holmlund and Storrie, 2002; Korpi and Levin, 2001). However, a number of directly employed temporary workers had come through the Job Centre, and process managers reported that many coming via this route made no effort on the first day, hoping that they would be removed without losing their Job Seekers' Allowance. Managers suggested that, as a rule of thumb, out of 25 new starters around twenty would arrive on the first day, seventeen would return on the second day, and around a dozen would return the next week. Some new starters find that the factory environment is too difficult to work in, or they are put off by the smell of the confectionery or get motion sickness from the belt. This high drop out rate meant that ChocCo attempted to use short-term work as a trial period rather than setting workers straight onto a permanent job (see also Maguire, 1988). For those workers who stayed, the main aim was to be offered a permanent job in the factory, although again few saw it as a place to build a long-term career. They wanted the financial security of having a permanent job, and found themselves trying to plan their lives around rumours:

> I want a permanent job, but they were advertising for six months worth of work so at least you have got the run-up to Christmas...Most of the workers say they will extend contracts anyway up until Easter or after, and then there are some that say they very rarely set on, so you don't know what to believe... I have been looking at other jobs, because you don't want to be out of a job right after Christmas.
>
> *Directly-employed Temporary Worker*

However, temporary workers thought that the deskilled nature of the job meant that it would provide little in the way of experience to take to another company, and that it would not help them to get a new job if their contracts were not renewed.

> I do like the job, but I don't think it provides you with any relevant experience. You couldn't take working with chocolates to another factory. When you work on the belt that is good because a lot of other factories use belts as well, that shows that you can use it, but other than that I don't think it provides anything that's of any use to you.
>
> *Directly-employed Temporary Worker*

Despite perceived lack of skills development and the low wages, directly-employed temporary workers generally found the job to be better than comparable jobs in other factories because of the relatively pleasant working environment, as explained by one worker with previous factory experience elsewhere:

> The job is what it is, you can't expect it to be anything more, it is monotonous, sometimes it can be a right bastard when the line is moving fast and you can't get your fingers to work fast enough. The money is shit, the money is appalling, I hate being on low wage, I've never been on it before, but I would say that on the whole there are a hell of a lot worse jobs out there.
>
> *Directly-employed Temporary Worker*

Overall, views amongst directly-employed temporary workers echoed that of permanent workers, which is perhaps unsurprising as they were at an earlier stage of a similar career path. However, although workers did broadly the same tasks, their differing contractual statuses had fragmented them into groups, and short-term workers in various ways described themselves as alienated from ChocCo as it had not committed to employing them on a permanent basis. Although short-term work may sometimes provide a 'stepping stone' into permanent employment, at ChocCo it was just the first of a number of steps, including contract renewals and probationary periods, that the short-term workers would have to take before getting a permanent belt job.

Agency workers

The agency workers interviewed were all foreign nationals, representing the two largest non-British groups in the factory from Poland and Iraq. Very few of the agency workers were British. Agency workers tended to live in the neighbouring large cities, and travelled in on agency buses at a cost of £5.50 per day (for comparison, the off-peak public transport cost from the cities to the nearest town was £4.20). However, these buses were unreliable, and some of the agency workers had missed days of work through the failure of buses to arrive. Amongst agency workers there tended to be a split between those of Middle Eastern origin who had been with the company and agency for a long time, and Eastern European workers who as discussed earlier were often highly educated working in Britain temporarily during university holidays. Working in Eastern Europe in a similar job would earn around £200 a month, and this caused many workers to express themselves as satisfied with the work based on earnings. However, the desire to earn as much money as possible in a short space of time led to the peculiar problem of some workers taking another eight hour shift in another factory on the industrial estate, and then falling asleep on the belt in the chocolate factory. These workers were not aiming to build a career path with the company, and therefore not using the job as a 'stepping stone' into permanent employment, but rather were trying to earn as much as possible before returning home, mirroring the findings of Grzymala-Kazlowska (2005). They displayed little commitment to either the agency that employed them or the company at which they worked. Although generally displeased with the agency, the longer-term agency workers, who tended to be from the Middle East, had stuck with the agency often because they felt that their English was not good enough to pass the interview to get a permanent job. While these workers hoped that short term work would provide a stepping stone into permanent work, they generally found themselves trapped in the agency jobs because of their lack of language skills and personal transport.

Group relations

In Assortments Packing workers tended to be on the same jobs along the belt irrespective of contract status, and during formal working time separate group formation was not overtly evident. This was in contrast to earlier years when temporary workers were visually differentiated and there had been more hostility between the groups based solely on contractual status:

> When I first started we used to have different coloured collars and hats, so we as temporary staff, we stuck out like a sore thumb and, going back all those years, you were treated differently. A lot of the permanent staff said 'If you are temp I'm not speaking to you'. Now because you don't really know who is who, everyone seems to mix a lot better.
>
> *Process Manager*

Although new directly-employed temporaries and agency workers wore blue overshoes and overalls without their names, this was of less concern to them than the safety of the overshoes which could be very slippery. In fact, some directly-employed temporary workers described how they welcomed the opportunity to bed in to the job anonymously with no name tags so that any mistakes were less likely to be attributed to them. One such man was particularly pleased that he did not have his name on his overalls:

> They all call me Bob on the line anyway – 'Bob the Knob'. I wouldn't want that printed across my chest.
>
> *Directly-employed Temporary Worker*

Although the low noise level allowed conversation on the line, as workers were assigned to a different line each morning there was little real opportunity for friendship groups to form. One notable exception was 'Mister and Missus', an elderly Polish couple whom the managers allowed to sit together. However, at break times noticeable sub-groups could be seen (see also Lupton, 1963). These developed what Tajfel (1970) and Tajfel and Turner (1979) refer to as 'outgroups' from the directly-employed workers, based on those workers who were not British. At break times a whole line would be stopped and all the workers from one line would go to the canteen and sit together. However within this main group would be smaller groups of workers based upon their country of origin, most noticeably Polish workers and Iraqi workers, who were invariably from the agency. The influx of foreign workers had led to differing reactions amongst the British workers, with some stating that the mix in the work areas was one of the greatest benefits of the job:

> This is one of the things I love about the place, it is totally multiculture, multigeneration, multigender. You have got Asians from Pakistan, you have got the Asians from India, you have got people from the Arab nations and you have got Poles and people from Eastern Europe. You have got

Scots, and there are probably some Irish and Welsh in here, you've got English, and you have got English like me from other parts of England. It's brilliant, absolutely brilliant. And it does make things interesting when the guy next to you is singing in Gujarati.

Directly-employed Temporary Worker

However, some of the British workers felt that having foreign workers proved detrimental to the quality of the work, particularly as the deskilled nature of the jobs did not require new starters to be able to speak English.

There is one guy who came here, and he doesn't even speak English, and he is on the same money as me...The thing is, what is happening with our line, everybody seems to be like, how can I say, there are different races coming on all the time. There is not a constant. I think if you want to keep a line busy and working more efficient you want the same people.

Permanent worker

This again shows the divisive effects on the workforce of deskilled jobs. As the tasks are simple enough to pick up by being shown, workers who cannot speak English are able to get jobs in the factory. However, their inability to speak to their workmates had caused them to form separate groups from the English-speaking workers. Although agency workers could not group together in the workplace they would cluster at breaktimes, and this had caused some resentment amongst the directly-employed workers, and tended to heighten stereotypes:

When I first started here I thought I was at [local airport], there were so many different people here. I didn't know the country was in such a bad state...If I had an Indian who talks Indian and he tells me I come from [local city] and I'm British, I joke and I say you all look the same to me... I think they tend to keep all to themselves. They have their own little groups. I wouldn't go and sit on a table of Polish, I would be lucky if I got out.

Permanent worker

The managers at ChocCo were aware of the feelings of some of the British workers, but were unwilling to formally reprimand such views when expressed during breaks.

You've got to be careful what you say now, how things you say are interpreted. And I have reminded my department of that policy that is in place at [ChocCo]. They [the British workers] can be very vocal on what they think, and its offensive. And I have on one occasion this month reminded them of it. But in their breaks and in their own time you can't stop them saying what they want to say.

Process Manager

The main barrier between British and non-British workers was language, but cultural differences also caused some ill-feeling, with a particular area of tension being the Middle Eastern workers allegedly standing on the toilets to use them and breaking them. There were also a higher number of locker break-ins when there were short term workers on site, although there was suspicion amongst process managers that this was perhaps permanent workers taking advantage of the situation. As well as tensions between directly employed and agency workers, there were often disputes between agency workers themselves. Arguments between agency workers tended to be about religion, and had occasionally turned violent, with one agency worker recently being hospitalised after being struck by his colleague with a steel cooling tray. This violence was also experienced by some of the managers, who reported that they had been threatened with knives and that the police had been called to the factory. This had led to a distinct uneasiness from the managers about the use of foreign labour, and it is significant that many of the more uncomfortable sentiments expressed by the permanent British workers were also voiced by the managers, such as:

When they're stood there yacking in their own language I find that most ignorant. And its upsetting to others to listen to it, because they're very loud when there's a good bunch of them.

Process Manager

I am not prejudiced or anything, but I can walk in the morning and I am probably the only one what's speaking English. With different bus loads coming in, you feel 'God, am I in the right country'?

Process Manager

I'm not racist in any way or anything, but you know when it is busy and I walk down from the car park, I walk in and not one person's speaking English, I feel uncomfortable when I come into work. And so that's how it makes you feel. And I've spoken to a couple of our guys who've been here a long time, and they say when they go into the changing area, again, you know, only jokingly, and they don't mean nothing by it but they'll say 'God, its like we're on holiday. Its like we're in Mecca. There's people praying and all sorts on the floor'. They're not doing it in a nasty way, its just I feel uncomfortable. I don't feel as if I'm in England.

Process Manager

This suggests that one of the key reasons for permanent workers escaping reprimand for their views is that these views were, in fact, shared by the process managers at ChocCo.

Concluding remarks

This chapter has attempted to illuminate the experience of work for people in low skill jobs in UK manufacturing, providing a contemporary rejoinder to earlier studies into these workplaces such as the chocolate factory examined by Andrew Scott in *Willing Slaves* (1994). Much remains the same in manufacturing workplaces since Braverman wrote of alienation from the labour process in 1974 – factory work of this nature is monotonous and unpleasant, and workers tend to fragment into different groups who often distrust each other. However, in some ways the work has got worse, with a proliferation of short term work and agency employment, increasing financial uncertainty away from the workplace, and distance and alienation from the company. Whereas once low skill manufacturing jobs could be seen as stepping stones into higher skilled work or management, workers now have to take several steps through short term jobs, contract renewals and probationary periods just to get a permanent job on the belt.

A clear theme of the contemporary picture is the issue of migrant work and the associated multiculturalism or racial division of the workplace. The influx of migrant workers is clearly an important issue for many British people in the factory, both workers and managers, and although some welcome the opportunity to mix with people from other cultures, others resent the idea that people from foreign countries are 'taking their jobs', and also resent the impact on their working environment of different languages and cultures. This also relates to the issue of contractual status of workers, with some feeling that foreign workers are pushing them into more precarious forms of employment, such as short-term work, and alienating them from the company that they work at. The issue of hostility towards groups of foreign workers in a factory is certainly not a new one, the caveat of 'I'm not racist, but...' being a depressingly frequent continuation of earlier industrial studies of similar jobs. However, this case study has illuminated how deskilled work has allowed for changes in the makeup of groups of workers in factory jobs, such as the increases in numbers of Middle Eastern and Eastern European workers, showing that, although fragmentation amongst UK manufacturing workforces is not new, the groups towards which these hostilities are directed have changed.

Note

1 This case study forms part of the author's PhD, which has been funded by the Economics and Social Research Council.

REFERENCES

Anderson, B., Ruhs, M., Rogaly, B. and Spencer, S. (2006) *Fair Enough? Central and Eastern European Migrants in the Low-Wage Employment in the UK*, COMPAS Research Report, University of Oxford.

Bach, S. (2005) 'Personnel Management in Transition', in Bach, S. (ed.) *Managing Human Resources*, Oxford: Blackwell.

Booth, A. L., Francesconi, M. and Frank, J. (2002) 'Temporary Jobs: Stepping Stones or Dead Ends?', *The Economic Journal*, 112, F189–F213.

Braverman, H. (1974) *Labour and Monopoly Capital: The Degradation of Work in the Twentieth Century*, New York: Monthly Review Press.

Burawoy, M. (1979) *Manufacturing Consent: Changes in the Labour Process Under Monopoly Capitalism*, Chicago: Chicago University Press.

Cooley, L. and Sriskandarajah, D. (2008) 'Facts and Figures: A Context for Understanding the Issues', in Flynn, D. and Williams, Z. (eds) *Towards a Progressive Immigration Policy*, London: Compass.

Drinkwater, S., Eade, J. and Garapich, M. (2006) 'Poles Apart? EU Enlargement and the Labour Market Outcomes of Immigrants in the UK', *Institute for the Study of Labor*, Discussion Paper No. 2410.

Dustmann, C., Casanove, M., Fertig, M., Preston, I. and Schmidt, C. (2003) *The Impact of EU Enlargement on Migration Flows*, Home Office Online Report No. 25/03.

Gilpin, N., Henty, M., Lemos, S., Portes, J. and Bullen, C. (2006) 'The Impact of Free Movement of Workers from Central and Eastern Europe on the UK Labour Market', *Department for Work and Pensions*, Working Paper No. 29.

Green, A., Owen, D. and Wilson, R. (2005) *Changing Patterns of Employment by Ethnic Group and for Migrant Workers*, Warwick Institute for Employment Research, National Report.

Green, A. E., Owen, D. W., Jones, P. with Owen, C. and Francis, J. (2007) *The Economic Impact of Migrant Workers in the West Midlands*, West Midlands Regional Observatory, Birmingham.

Grzymala-Kazlowska, A. (2005) 'From Ethnic Cooperation to In-Group Competition: Undocumented Polish Workers in Brussels', *Journal of Ethnic and Migration Studies*, 31: 4, 675–97.

Holgate, J. (2005) 'Organizing migrant workers: a case study of working conditions and unionization in a London sandwich factory', *Work, Employment and Society*, 19: 3, 463–80.

Holmlund, B. and Storrie, D. (2002) 'Temporary Work in Turbulent Times: The Swedish Experience', *The Economic Journal*, 112, F245–F269.

▶

▶

Kochan, T. A. (1998) 'What is Distinctive about Industrial Relations Research?', in Whitfield, K. and Strauss, G. (eds) *Researching the World of Work: Strategies and Methods in Studying Industrial Relations*, Cornell: Cornell University Press.

Korpi, T. and Levin, H. (2001) 'Precarious Footing: Temporary Employment as a Stepping Stone out of Unemployment in Sweden', *Work, Employment and Society*, 15: 1, 127–48.

Lupton, T. (1963) *On The Shop Floor: Two Studies of Workshop Organization and Output*, Oxford: Pergamon Press.

Maguire, M. (1988) 'Work, Locality and Social Control', *Work, Employment and Society*, 2: 1, 71–87.

MCPS-PRS (2008) Mechanical Copyright Protection Society and Performing Right Society http://www.mcps-prs-alliance.co.uk/playingbroadcasting-online/music_for_businesses/officesandfactories/Pages/officesfactories.aspx, date accessed 07 July 2008.

Office for National Statistics (2008a) UK Statistics Authority http://www.statistics.gov.uk/STATBASE/tsdataset.asp?vlnk=341, date accessed 07 July 2008.

Office for National Statistics (2008b) UK Statistics Authority http://www.statistics.gov.uk/STATBASE/ssdataset.asp?vlnk=7924, date accessed 07 July 2008.

Pillai, R., Kyambi, S., Nowacka, K. and Sriskandarajah, D. (2007) 'The Reception and Integration of New Migrant Communities', *Institute of Public Policy Research*, London.

Roy, D. (1952) 'Efficiency and "The Fix": Informal Intergroup Relations in a Piecework Machine Shop', *American Journal of Sociology*, 57: 255–66.

Scott, A. (1994) *Willing Slaves?: British Workers Under Human Resource Management*, Cambridge: Cambridge University Press.

Smith, V. (1994) 'Institutionalizing Flexibility in a Service Firm: Multiple Contingencies and Hidden Hierarchies', *Work and Occupations*, 21: 3, 284–307.

Smith, V. (1998) 'The Fractured World of the Temporary Worker: Power, Participation and Fragmentation in the Contemporary Workplace', *Social Problems*, 45: 4, 411–30.

Tajfel, H. (1970) 'Experiments in Intergroup Discrimination', *Scientific American*, 223: 5, 96–102.

Tajfel, H. and Turner, J. (1979) 'An Integrative Theory of Intergroup Conflict', in Austin, W. G. (ed.) *The Social Psychology of Intergroup Relations*, Belmont: Wadsworth.

The Forgotten Factories: Supermarket Suppliers and Dignity at Work in the Contemporary Economy

Kirsty Newsome, Paul Thompson and Johanna Commander

...few people now toil under arduous or hazardous conditions. Most people work in safe, clean environments...Increasingly work environments look, feel, sound and even smell great. (Reeves quoted in Bolton, 2007: 5)

It is a commonplace now to observe that most – by some estimates 80 percent-work takes place in service settings. Whilst the time when service jobs were wrongly associated with high skills, autonomy and status is long past, the emphasis on the nature and growth of mass service work has led to some degree of neglect of the significance of factory work in the contemporary economy. Even now, when social scientists examine factory work it tends to be associated with the dynamics and defects of high performance practices in sectors such as motors and aerospace. Though there is useful recent literature on employment relations in small, often manufacturing, firms (e.g. Moule, 1998; Ram and Edwards, 2003), much low-end factory work remains hidden and often neglected. While diminishing in scale and scope, factory work remains heterogeneous. Moreover it is often more connected to the service sector than commonly assumed. For instance, behind the glossy façade of the new economy and consumer-facing internet firms are drab warehouses and distribution centres whose semi-skilled work is driven by computerised stock control systems. Just as we are now encouraged to 'look behind the label' on high street fashions to the sweatshop labour thousands of miles away, so we need to look up and down the retail supply chain to see how the goods that we take from supermarket shelves actually got there.

In our case, this would take you to the food-processing factories at the end of supermarket chains. This chapter draws on a wider research project which is concerned with power dynamics between customers (the super-markets) and suppliers (the food processing firms) in a number of product lines, and the impact of such dynamics on work and employment. In this chapter, we turn to a more specific focus on the lived reality of the labour process, consistent with the traditional themes and concerns of the book. Whilst we will draw on some of the more general evidence to establish overall patterns of work and employment, we will examine three cases, from one product line, in more detail. This will allow us to explore employer pol-icies, employment conditions and, most especially, worker responses in greater depth. While the research continues, the picture that has emerged so far has been one of a highly controlled and constrained labour process. In addition to attempting to identify the causal influences in the market and other conditions that can explain such outcomes, the in-depth case studies allow for an exploration of worker perceptions and responses, including those of the migrant workers who form an increasing proportion of the workforce.

In other words, we examine how the labour force experience, adapt, survive and sometimes resist their work. Of course, there is a rich tradition in labour process theory that can potentially illuminate such issues. Yet there are limits. The control and resistance model that underpinned second wave labour process theory and research was largely built on the experiences of large workplaces and well-organised workers. At the end of the supermarket supply chain, we find labour that has limited power resources and low levels of unionisation. 'Resistance', whether expressed through powerful informal job controls or formal, collective action and organisation, does not seem to provide an adequate conceptual template for analysing the work and its experiences in forgotten factories.

There are a number of potential sources of correction to this parti-cular agency problem. As two of us have observed elsewhere (Thompson and Newsome, 2004), second wave LPT became a control, resistance *and consent* model. Burawoy's (1979) hugely-influential theorisation of consent expanded our vocabulary of worker behaviour and restored a certain kind of agency through a focus on active participation in workplace games and organisational choices. However, the consent concept was elaborated pri-marily to solve the puzzle, why don't workers resist, or at least resist more often than they do? The insights were large, but the scope of explanation was comparatively small. Something is still missing for our subject. In part, the gap can be filled by the vocabulary of organisational misbehaviour (Thompson and Ackroyd, 1995; Ackroyd and Thompson, 1999), given the emphasis on a variety of largely informal and less organised employee actions in the spheres of time, product, work and identity. But we also want to consider the utility of the idea of dignity at work in the hope that the emergent debate on the concept can help to illuminate the factors that shape the availability of 'good' and 'bad' work, and labour's responses to such trends.

Dignity?

There have been a number of contributions on dignity at work by scholars sympathetic to LPT, including the major work by Hodson (2001) and the more recent collection by Bolton (2007). The latter is strongly influenced by the work of the social theorist Andrew Sayer (2007a, 2007b). Sayer locates dignity in a broad philosophical, practical and theoretical frameworks, conditions and feelings, autonomy, trust, respect, dependence and seriousness are fundamental to our social being and psychological well being. Much of this discussion treats dignity as a relatively free floating concept, but it is applied to the economy and work relations. Systematic inequalities of power and inequalities of treatment and distribution of resources erode the possibility of mutual recognition. Persistent absence of respect and recognition result in a range of subjective responses from habituated low esteem to resistance. The latter is described as a compensation mechanism that substitutes for the absence of respectful treatment. In turn such responses can be regarded as expressions of voice mechanisms and the broader exercise of human powers to shape circumstances.

In the introduction to the *Dimensions of Dignity* volume, Bolton positions the concept primarily as a means of addressing questions about the constraints on the availability of 'good work' in a supposedly high skill, service economy that has largely eliminated dirty, hard jobs. Drawing on a variety of popular and academic evidence she rightly notes old and new forms of routinisation and intensification that limit the opportunities for achieving interest and autonomy. She goes on to distinguish between dignity *in* work and at work that broadly correspond to work and employment relations. This sensibly allows for the possibility that employees may have poor work, but good or at least better terms and conditions.

Hodson's (2001) categories offer an ambitious, comprehensive framework for analysing the objective and subjective conditions that shape dignity at work. Dignity at work is regarded first and foremost as deriving from the purposeful, strategic actions of workers to attain and maintain dignity within work, and management-influenced conditions that destroy or deny it. We will look briefly at each in turn.

Dignity is asserted to be the overarching goal of worker behaviour (Hodson, 2001, p. 60) and within this context, a range of 'alternative behavioural strategies' exist to pursue it. These strategies encompass actions that are normally seen as antithetical: on the one hand resistance and on the other, citizenship. Whereas the former involves the conventional array of behaviours (sabotage, absenteeism, work avoidance) familiar to industrial sociology and LPT, the latter focuses on the tendency to take pride in work accomplishments and 'transform jobs with insufficient meaning into jobs that are more worthy of their personal stature, time and effort' (p. 45). Both are strengthened by other 'meaningful actions' of workers, notably the creation of independent meaning systems and attention to the social climate of the workplace through co-worker relations and other aspects of friendship and group solidarity. Whilst such activities are played out in daily work life, they 'may be only tangentially related to management demands and organizational agendas' (p. 18).

Turning to Hodson's depiction of the challenges to dignity, the first two, chaotic, disorganised and abusive workplaces, coupled with overwork and exploitation, are more likely to occur in situations where management has unilateral control over production. The second two, constraints on autonomy and new demands of involvement, occur where employees have some greater degree of discretion over their work tasks. Indeed the often contradictory demands of enhanced employee involvement are highlighted as providing the opportunity for greater dignity, but simultaneously being open to abuse.

This framework is seen by Hodson as expanding the capacity of social science to 'describe and analyse workers' complex and sometimes contradictory behaviours' (p. 16). On that score it succeeds. Our understandings of agency are enhanced and a variety of actions are interrogated and explained through a systematic analysis of workplace ethnographies (many from a labour process tradition). However there are flaws that limit its explanatory power. We would highlight two interrelated issues. First, what are the dynamics of the workplace behaviour described? Conventional notions of agency are, in effect, inverted by Hodson. Worker actions to create meaning systems and dignity are presented as the driver, with management actions as the 'challenge' to them. There is an equivalence problem here. Whereas worker actions are 'strategic', it is never clear what drives management action, and whether such action is purposeful, reactive or a reflection of lack of purpose (as in chaotic practices). The four types of 'challenge' lack any coherence as categories – employee involvement could be seen as a variant of responsible autonomy, but abuse is hardly a strategy. In fact, the whole concept of abuse and mismanagement is problematic, at least as a means of understanding the conditions for 'good' and 'bad' work. Abusive and 'poorly managed' (p. 260) workplaces are associated in the book with arbitrary and autocratic power. The implication can only be that normal, rational management and work organisation is not or is unlikely to be an attack on dignity. The overwork category is much more circumspect and therefore more useful. Though underconceptualised (as stress and chronic pressure) and conflated with 'exploitation', as a driver of poor work experience, it is consistent with a growing body of research on work intensification (Green, 2001; Burchell *et al.*, 2002).

This relates to a second problem. For Hodson, the pursuit of dignity is seen as independent of the employment relationship – work is just another arena in which dignity is sought and contested. Whilst a case could be made that dignity is a goal of worker action, it is dangerous to subsume all other goals – particularly the range of collective interests pursued via the effort bargain – within that overarching notion. In contrast, the idea that denying dignity *in itself* could be a driver of managerial behaviour, is not persuasive. It seems unlikely that dignity is the moral or practical lens through which managerial choices on work, poor or otherwise, is made. By partially abstracting dignity from the dynamics of the employment relationship, Hodson's framework overestimates the capacity for common interests within work, for example on citizenship actions (see p. 46). Relatedly, by neglecting and inadequately explaining managerial agency, the analysis underestimates the structural, market constraints on 'normal' companies providing good work and dignified employment.

Despite these objections, we retain Hodson's broad framework of conditions that constrain or attack dignity and worker responses to those conditions as a way of structuring our case study evidence. Whilst not a detailed ethnography, the cases are consistent with the kind of qualitative studies influenced by a labour process tradition discussed extensively in Hodson's book. The categories, though we seek to modify them, also provide a useful way into discussing the salience of factors that shape the supply and nature of 'good work' in an underresearched sector. We divide our research evidence into three sections. The first section highlights that work organisation in these supermarket suppliers is predicated upon assembly line production which limits the opportunity for autonomy, discretion or interest within work. However within the next section we wish to highlight that the opportunity for dignity within work is also predicated upon relations outside the workplace; in this case the relationship with the customers of these supply organisations notably the major supermarket multiples. In essence we are concerned with exploring the market constraints which impact on these supply organisations' ability to offer good work. The final section explores the 'meaningful actions' of workers and their attempts to safeguard dignity within work. However we indicate that the opportunity to access the mechanisms to 'safeguard' dignity within work is increasingly fractured on gender and ethnic lines.

Research evidence

In order to delve into the qualitative experiences of factory work this chapter focuses on three UK case-study organisations within one product line in the supermarket supply chain; notably fruit and vegetable processing. Within the constraints of a number of potential supplier firms and access issues, cases studies have been selected where reasonable comparisons can be made across size, ownership, type of customer, nature/quality of product and workforce/unionisation (see Table 9.1 below). The selection of case study companies was organised to include those who supply the multiple supermarkets via third parties, those who supply to a number of multiples, as well as those engaged in sole-supplier agreements.

In each organisation semi-structured interviews (an average of six per company) with managerial respondents (including supervisors) were undertaken, combined with a number of focus groups with a typical number of five employees in each group. In one company, *Asar,* it was not possible to utilise focus groups and data was gathered from a total of nine semi-structured interviews with managerial and employee respondents.

In terms of organisational background, *Asar* processes fresh fruit and vegetables for processed food manufacturers. Whilst it does not directly supply supermarkets its products are components of the burgeoning ready meal sector, with the supermarket shelf being the ultimate destination. *Skin* is a large unionised organisation involved in the processing and packaging of fruit and vegetables for a number of major retailers. It is predominantly concerned with supplying the higher end of the market, offering a value-added element to their products. By contrast *Stir-Fry* is a larger firm with a single-supply agreement with one of the large multiples.

Table 9.1 Case studies overview

	Fruit/Vegetable Processors		
	Asar	Skin	Stir-Fry
Size	Employees: 100 Small	Employees: 850 Large	Employees: 200 Medium
Type of customer	UK multiples via 3rd parties	UK multiples	Single multiple
Nature/ Quality of product	Own-label/ Premium & Standard	Own-label/ Premium & Standard	Own-Label Standard
Unionised	No	Yes	No

Attacks and constraints on dignity: the tyranny of assembly work?

With regard to the internal systems of work organisation all of the organisations utilised assembly-line production based upon monotonous, low-skilled and low-paid repetitive work. The experience of this has some variations, which we now discuss in turn.

Stir-Fry had invested in technology to facilitate the large volume of product that is required. From goods inward the product is routed along a series of conveyor belts to the picking tables, predominantly operated by women workers, where defects are removed. The speed and flow of the picking area is determined by the quality and size of the product. Rejects are binned, however these bins are checked to ensure women do not reject any acceptable products – if they do they will lose their bonus. The product continues to the production area along differing lines where it is labelled and bagged, according to the specific yet often fluctuating requirements of their one customer. This area is highly labour intensive and, in contrast, male dominated, requiring someone to sit at the end of each line sticking promotion stickers onto the bags in exactly the right place. Overall it is a very noisy and dry atmosphere with a constant and seemingly ferocious speed of work.

As a result the work is physically demanding and tiring, and line operators commented upon not only the long hours but also the tedious nature of the work itself. One operator stated:

> It's a long day when you're on the machine because your legs get sore, your back gets... you're twisting so it is a long day when you're on the tables, see people just see a bag of veggies at the supermarket but they don't know the work that's got to go into that bag.

Moreover, the growing levels of automation had increased the speed of the line and the intensity of work. Product lines are expected to meet daily production targets, though supervisors acknowledged that often machine breakdown or poor quality products prevent the line meeting its target. Often this intensity is exacerbated by the high levels of absenteeism that the organisation experiences, resulting in operators covering for absent colleagues.

By contrast *Asar* did not have the resources to invest heavily in technology. However in order to ensure the necessary flexibility of response to their multiple and sometimes competing customers, managers deploy overstaffing. *Asar* is similarly organised around a number of product lines, which clean, peel, slice, chop and/or cut to the exact requirements of the customer. These limited automated lines are supplemented by hand-preparation areas. Again, there is a gendered division of labour with women working in the hand-prep areas.

Moreover it was highlighted that the growing numbers of migrant workers in the organisation are often allocated the most tedious jobs.

Overall, working in *Asar* is acknowledged by many employees as being deeply monotonous, with the apparent unpleasant conditions at work exacerbated by a noisy, cold and unpleasant smelling factory. One migrant worker line operator commented upon the difficulties of working in a factory for long hours whilst undertaking a tedious, repetitive job:

> I think biggest problem in ten hours work is …it's impossible to work, you cannot feel the feet and you can't feel your fingers […] you have to use your hands and you can't because it is very cold.

The management within the organisation recognised the tedious and repetitive nature of the work process and highlighted that they had attempted to introduce some limited aspects of job rotation in order to limit not only the effects of boredom but also the possibility of repetitive strain injuries. The speed of work was described as dictated by the requirements of *Asar's* multiple customers. Moreover, prioritising the competing demands of the customers was often regarded as a battle between concerns over ensuring the quality of the product and getting the goods out of the factory.

Within both *Asar* and *Stir-Fry* women workers are predominantly based in hand preparation areas or on picking tables. These areas of production are more physically constraining and, for example at *Stir-Fry* the constant demands of assembly line production curtail the opportunity to physically move about during working hours. This situation is particularly acute for women workers on the picking tables where physical movement is limited to moving from side to side. Alternatively the physical space in the packaging and dispatch areas ensures that male workers have greater opportunity to move around. As a female worker at *Stir-Fry* laments:

> If you stand on that line for eight hours a day, its bloody tiring…. you can move to this side or move to that side, that's it.

Work organisation within *Skin* is similarly based around a series of product lines, with additional 'value added' areas which package oven-ready packs. *Skin* had recently instigated a major restructuring of the work process that sought to move away from a reactive fire-fighting response and to create a more pro-active organisation. This restructuring had also resulted in a redundancy programme. The organisation invested heavily in technology and further automation to facilitate the restructuring. For example, plasma screens were introduced onto the line so that employees were aware of production levels and whether they were satisfying daily targets. The training manager highlighted that the restructuring programme was concerned with not only ensuring that employees increased their levels of technical skills (which would include food hygiene, routine maintenance of the machinery etc) but required behavioural change. This behavioural change coincided with a change in remuneration from piece rate (where employees traditionally were encouraged to 'job and finish' i.e. work intensively to get home as soon as possible) to formalised standard hours. Managers recognised that this shift took away the incentive to work hard, and hence the focus of behavioural changes was regarded not only as a way of counteracting this disincentive but simultaneously ensuring consistent performance. As one production manager commented:

> The behavioural side of things is that we're trying to, not force them, but try to see that there's a more consistent level of performance with them whatever job they happen to be doing at that time. So you see a lot of areas that have, where there's not piece work now, we have target levels for them within that.

Line operatives by contrast painted a less positive picture of working at *Skin*. It was widely acknowledged that despite the management rhetoric of involvement the job remained highly repetitive and tedious. The introduction of the new technology had facilitated massive increases in the speed of work. The speed of the lines is often so intense that it causes motion sickness. One line operator reported that she took travel sickness tablets to try to deal with the effects of motion sickness from working for long periods on the line. It was also highlighted that the constant flux of promotions coupled with the speed of the machines made it difficult to adhere to the strict labelling requirements of customers. It was reported that the company was fined if promotional stickers were not on every package when the product arrived at the supermarket depot. The Team Leader present commented that 'more and more is expected of you but it is never enough'.

What then lies at the heart of these constraints on dignity and good work? Hodson (2001, 76) is right to note that food processing is one of the industries in which assembly work survives in a modern economy, but this is about more than 'the tyranny of the assembly line'. We need to broaden the frame of reference in such instances to encompass the supply chain and the role of the customer. All organisations highlighted the power imbalance between themselves and their dominant customers, the major supermarkets. They described how the supermarkets instigated and expected high degrees of external auditing, traceability and monitoring. The constant and merciless pressure on price, coupled with the unpredictable demands for goods, also heavily impacted upon these supply organisations. Satisfying the demands of a seemingly insatiable customer clearly affected the conditions of work and employment within these supply organisations.

Asar juggled the competing requirements of demanding and also numerous customers – third parties who themselves are subjected to the pressures of their own dominant customers; the supermarkets. As one manager commented, 'They use us; we get them out of jail on a lot of occasions'. The pressures from their customers appear to manifest in a number of guises. Alongside the pressures over price, is the additional difficulty of the fluctuating and often sporadic call for goods. Despite the organisation's best efforts to 'double guess what the customer wants', often the call for goods comes with little notice and changes considerably from provisional schedules. They are also often 'caught out' by additional promotions and new product launches that the manufacturers simply have not communicated to them.

Although having only one customer, managers within *Stir-Fry* also alluded to pressure and recurring difficulties. It was apparent that the price pressures were acute, creating a very tough environment within which to conduct business. *Stir-Fry* was also expected to resource an ongoing series of product promotions. The cost implications of these promotions was apparent not only in terms of the amount of 'free' products it was expected to provide the consumer with (such as buy one get one free campaigns) but also the additional labour costs associated with attaching promotional labels to packaging. Managers within *Skin* highlighted the power imbalance between themselves and their customers; as one manager stated, 'you're never on an equal footing'. For *Skin* one outcome of supplying a number of retailers is the highly unpredictable requirements to supply from these competing organisations, often with the added pressure that failure to satisfy the order incurs a series of fines.

These levels of unpredictability, coupled with the perishable nature of the product, have a particular impact on working patterns and work allocation. Each of these fruit and vegetable processors has to be able to accommodate these fluctuating requirements and ensure customer demands are satisfied. Whilst this pressure on working time is reminiscent of the notion of 'overwork' it is apparent that the instigator for this pressure operates outside the confines of these particular points of production. Within *Skin*, for example, the constant pressure of matching staffing levels to output in a sector that is subjected to fierce competition was highlighted. The Operations Manager commented, 'Sometimes it means that we carry too many people, or you can be too light.' Other managers highlighted that they deliberately use the importance of satisfying the customer as a way of 'coercing' employees to undertake overtime. One Manager argued, 'there is an element of pressure put on the staff saying "look guys we need you to work", they'll just go elsewhere, which is true.' Employees in *Skin* complained that often Saturday orders are not confirmed until 4 p.m. despite an 8 o'clock start. All staff have to stay on site until the orders are completed. As a result it is never possible to predict when a Saturday shift will finish. It was commented that 'Supermarket X determines the hours'.

Asar, alternatively cope with the fluctuating demand for goods by operating the factory 24/7. As a result working patterns in this highly labour intensive organisation are directly predicated upon servicing the fluctuating demands of their multiple customers. The production manager acknowledged the difficulty of balancing working-time with customer orders. Most of its employees therefore work a six day week with long hours. In *Stir-Fry* the high levels of unpredictability similarly impact upon working patterns. As the factory manager stated:

> because you're dealing with such a fresh product you can only pack so far and then it comes to a point where you've got to stop....but if the order went ballistic you'd maybe be here an hour or so after that, I mean you've always got to deliver no matter.

As a result of this unpredictability workers in *Stir-Fry* often have very little notice if they are required to either stay late to finish a rush order or, indeed, go home early as the orders have been less than expected. Faced with the unpredictable demands of their seemingly insatiable customers it is not only working time that is scrutinised by all of these organisations but also workplace attendance. As such, absence management techniques are regarded as a key aspect of overall drive to satisfy customer requirements.

The discussion so far has raised issues about managerial and corporate agency. Much of the debate on dignity and good work focuses on worker agency and it is to this that we now turn. Our concern here is to highlight the distinctions within employee attempts to safeguard dignity.

Employee experience and action: safeguarding dignity?

Despite the constraints on workplace dignity within these supply organisations, often clearly exacerbated and/or legitimised by the requirements of dominant customer(s), examples of employee initiated safeguarding of dignity were witnessed and highlighted. Notwithstanding the rigid and often stultifying requirements of assembly work, employees deployed a variety of strategies of reshaping or recasting the requirements of the working day. Such efforts were based around limited attempts to control the speeds of work as well as escaping and disengaging from the pressure and the monotony. Within *Asar* for example employees highlighted that despite the often competing demands of their multiple customers they were still to some extent able to control the speed of their work. As one operator commented:

> Oh yeah we have a laugh and all that which I think breaks it up you know if you're sitting, standing there doing a job all the time and you're not talking it can makes it a long day you know but we can have a laugh and all that.

Some employees indicated that they were able to vary the pace of work in order to be able to 'take it easier'. Such attempts to garner some autonomy, one of Hodson's criteria for safeguarding dignity, are however predicated upon the prevailing division of labour within these organisations. For example, as we indicated earlier, the gendered nature of the location of women workers constrains their ability to move about the plant. And yet, no constraint entirely removes opportunity for misbehaviour, as the following quote indicates: 'But you can also have a very slow walk to the toilet and then you sit on the toilet for a couple of minutes [laughs]'.

The opportunity to further safeguard dignity through the role of and relations between co-workers provides a valuable mechanism for many line operators. Often some notion of worker cohesion is based upon a mutual recognition of the difficulties of meeting production requirements, juggling scheduling demands usually with little support and/or recognition from management. Support from co-workers within all the organisations meant that despite the attacks on their dignity at work, they still took some pride in their work and gained some level of satisfaction from meeting the competing demands of customers. A particularly hostile employee relations climate in *Stir-Fry* perversely facilitated further unity amongst workers. In response to the growing absence problem *Stir-Fry* had instigated a draconian attendance policy linked to the bonus scheme. The bonus scheme had initially been introduced as a way of managing absence by linking continued and punctual attendance to additional pay. One manager stated, 'it started to encourage people to come to their work.' The scheme was regarded as being both unreasonable and inconsistent, with managers arbitrarily adding further misdemeanours which would result in operators losing their bonus. Many line operators referred to the 'bonus' scheme with a degree of disdain and resentment, often simply disengaging from it, recognising that the loss of their bonus, often amounting to little more than 48p a day after deductions, was, by reason of one rule infraction or another, inevitable.

Within *Stir-Fry*, there was ample evidence of open forms of resistance – for example, employees changing the figures of the 'efficiency boards' which management required as a visual display of productivity levels, as emerged at one of the focus groups:

> We've got an efficiency board out there that ....all the machines that are running every hour, [it's been] blagged for the last four months and every manager goes out and they're looking, they don't know what they're looking at...

Indeed an additional effect of monotonous low skilled poorly paid work is that management in these organisations are finding it difficult to recruit local labour. The growing numbers of migrant workers was apparent across each of the case companies (see James and Lloyd (2008) for parallel evidence). Yet, this fact appeared to create tensions and divisions amongst relationships between co-workers. Despite the low-skilled nature of the work process, migrant workers appeared to adopt a different work ethic to their local co-workers. As a Polish worker at *Stir-Fry* commented:

> I've noticed that we just really want to work because that work is very important for us, especially because you've got five times more money than in Poland for that kind of job, so we really work hard and you want to work but it is different [laughs] lazy you know. I have got nothing against British people but we work even more hard than them...it's not fair.

On the other hand, at each case site, local labour highlighted the difficulties of working with co-workers who they weren't able to communicate effectively with. One particular incident was highlighted in *Stir-Fry* that indicated the potential dangers of such communication difficulties when working in highly pressured environments:

> ...health and safety it's bad that way, yeah it's a bit dodgy, coz Steve was shouting 'gonna turn the machine off' and they didn't understand him and he lost the top of this finger, you know what I mean. But then again that's foreign people when they don't understand.

In terms of more collective attempts to safeguard dignity only one of the organisations was unionised. *Skin* had secured a recognition agreement through the recent legislative changes. The suggestion was that an autocratic management style coupled with the recent redundancy exercise had increased interest in securing union membership within the organisation. Being a union member meant having a vote on the recent pay deal as well as on the new shift pattern adopted. The suggestion here was that growing levels of union organisation within Skin had indeed curbed some of the excesses of this autocratic style. One shop Steward argued:

> Well, it was abusing ... not physically abusing you but mentally abusing you, bringing you down in front of other people, shouting at you, swearing at you. And I've seen a lot of the managers in here [leave] women, especially women, just broken down and cry. And I say don't take that, and they say I've no option. And I say there are options, don't take that and I just couldn't stand it anymore so I just went and got the union in.

By contrast attempts to secure recognition in *Stir-Fry* were less successful. Despite the very apparent 'them and us' culture of the organisation, often exacerbated by the draconian bonus policy, the management had blocked attempts to secure recognition. Some respondents suggested that the massive growth of the use of migrant workers in the organisation was linked to limiting the possibility of further attempts to unionise by recruitment of an allegedly more compliant labour force. Workers reflected on the experience of trying to get a union in:

> We tried to get them in a couple of year ago and they went mental, they threatened to close the factory and they tell us out in the middle of the floor, 'if a union comes in here we'll just shut the factory, we don't care', that was two years ago, there's some of the guys that are still here but most of them are not here now and there's less interest. Focus group, *Stir-Fry*.

Reflections and conclusions

The case studies discussed in this paper paint a fairly bleak picture of a new form of factory life at the end of the supermarket supply chain. This pessimism is matched in a recent wide-ranging study of food processing in five European countries (Grunert, James and Moss, 2008) and more specifically on the indirect pressures on occupational ill health of supply chain pressures in the sector (James and Lloyd, 2008). If there is little sign of the kind of good work that might confer a degree of dignity, there are, conversely, few glimpses of the 'good worker': employees who commit Hodson-style acts of 'citizenship' or who are compliant with the factory regime. This is not to say that the workforces resist in any significant way – the imbalance of power resources induces disaffection, but little beyond.

To return to our opening theme, to what extent are the conditions for denial or destruction of dignity outlined by Hodson (2001) present in these workplaces? There are certainly commonalities. These are factories with high levels of work intensity and 'overwork', filtered through assembly lines subject to largely unilateral technical controls. Though assembly work is seldom pleasant, the nature of the product in many of these instances adds a further dimension of *hazardous* work environments through extremes of temperatures, smells and noise levels. It could be argued that these conditions are of long-standing in the food processing sector. Think of Upton Sinclair's description of Chicago meat packing plants in *The Jungle* (Sinclair, 1906).

However, in a crucial respect, the circumstances differ sharply from Hodson's argument. Whilst there have been limited instances (such as at *Skin*) of abusive behaviour, management, authority and work organisation in these plants is not, by and large, 'abusive', 'chaotic', or 'anomic'. Such terminology creates the unavoidable impression of prerational workplaces based on arbitrary, personal power. In our cases, the plants are not so much 'mismanaged' as managed rationally, albeit often with great difficulty, according to direct and indirect pressures exerted through supply chain power dynamics. Much of the distinctive and destructive attacks on dignity only make sense in that context. Work intensity becomes work *intensification* as lines are speeded up and work stretched out to meet cost cutting supermarket or other purchaser requirements. But it is in the sphere of *time* that the most significant effects take place. Dignity comes, in part, from a regulated effort bargain that generates a degree of consistency and stability. What we have much of the time in these cases is a form of *hyper-flexibility* in which the worker's tasks and times are at the whim of the employer, though, in fact, the employer is really dancing to the customer's tune. In this sense, the direct employer and its management, contra the implication of Hodson's framework, cannot guarantee dignity, whose primary source lies largely outside their control. Or put another way and returning to Bolton's (2007) distinctions – whilst the suppliers shape some of the conditions *in* work, the customer constrains the conditions *at* work. Such outcomes are exacerbated in product lines characterised by perishability as at *Stir-Fry*. The negative consequences for dignity are seen not just in the work itself, but in the impossibility of an adequate work-life balance, whether through compulsory overtime or compulsory availability.

The existence of the minimum wage provides an important floor from which further gains can conceivably be made. Otherwise adverse conditions affecting the effort bargain, such as the punitive requirements for bonus payments at *Stir-Fry*, can be offset by the assertion of worker voice mechanisms. Some of these may be expressed through participative measures in work or employment relations initiated by employers. The largest of our cases – *Skin* – did show some evidence of work restructuring and redesign measures, but these were very limited and perceived as such by employees. The best that could be probably said of management in these cases is that there is a degree of paternalistic concern for the (traditionally local) workforce, but benevolence is frequently accompanied by low trust that is manifested in various combinations of poor communication and increased surveillance. The depth of the problem is indicated by the fact that their own version of absence of voice with respect to their customers was an issue consistently raised by managerial respondents, as in the comment from the manager at *Skin* who said that it was difficult to respect somebody who was continually kicking you. Supply chain pressures were felt particularly by supervisors, who often acted as a form of limited voice and protection for employees. The existence of a union at *Skin* was a counterweight to the previous excesses of abusive behaviour, but has not been able to exert significant bargaining power. Concerns about union leverage are likely to lie behind the ambivalent attitudes revealed elsewhere. A previous campaign to achieve recognition at *Stir-Fry* had been outweighed by aggressive tactics from the employers and senior managers. Workers now appear to be divided about the prospects and potential of a union presence. In the absence of formal, collective organisation, the cases reveal the normal variety of informal actions from group-based output norms, to minor acts of misbehaviour such as absenteeism and reappropriation of time. But coping strategies and disengagement, such as those reported by respondents at *Asar*, are far more typical responses than any form of resistance.

There were claims from some employees (at *Stir-Fry*) that migrant workers had been brought in to weaken unionisation efforts, but this is almost certainly confusing intent with outcome. Even that judgment is too stark to grasp the complexity of the impact of migrant labour. On the one hand, the willingness to work hard or harder than their local counterparts is clearly a source of dignity and pride to many Polish and other migrant workers. And this, in turn, supports the perceptions of managers about this (extra) willingness to work. On the other hand, there appears to be evidence that disaffection and misbehaviour may be more a function of time and experience than ethnicity. Similarly there is no evidence that migrant workers are anti-union or less willing to join. What does appear to be the case, however, is that the dignity and social solidarity that workers traditionally seek through peer networks (co-workers in Hodson's terms) is weakened, at least in the short term, through greater workforce heterogeneity. Voices are raised, but multiply as experiences and mechanisms for expressing it vary. Such fragmentation also has potentially negative implications for positive citizenship behaviours that rely, in part, on shared norms concerning appropriate levels and types of effort.

Factory work need not be low waged or low skilled and, as Bolton argues there can be dignity in and at work. Neither is present here to any significant degree. The primary reason is that supermarkets have engineered a double transfer of risk: first from them to the owners and managers of the supply firms themselves, then from them to the labour force, which is in itself fractured on gender and ethnic lines. In the absence of better regulated labour markets, innovation or greater independence in the product market by suppliers, or successful unionisation drives, these circumstances are unlikely to alter.

REFERENCES

Ackroyd, S. and Thompson, P. (1999) *Organizational Misbehaviour*, London: Sage.

Bolton, S. (2007) *Dimensions of Dignity at Work*, London: Butterworth Heineman.

Burawoy, M. (1979) *Manufacturing Consent: Changes in the Labor Process under Monopoly Capitalism*, Chicago: Chicago University Press.

Burchell, B. J., Ladipo, D. and Wilkinson, F. (2002) (eds) *Job Insecurity and Work Intensification*, London: Routledge.

Green, F. (2001) 'It's Been A Hard Day's Night: The Concentration and Intensification of Work in Late Twentieth-Century Britain', *British Journal of Industrial Relations*, 39(1): 53–80.

Grunert, K., James, S. and Moss, P. (2008) Chocolate Chicken: Bittersweet Implications for Low Wage Work in the Food Processing Industry, Report to Russell Sage Foundation Conference on Low Waged Work, Paris, 1–3 February.

Hodson, R. (2001) *Dignity at Work*, Cambridge: Cambridge University Press.

James, S. and Lloyd, C. (2008) 'Supply Chain Pressures and Migrant Workers: Deteriorating Conditions in the United Kingdom Food-processing Industry', in C. Lloyd, G. Mason and K. Mayhew (eds) *Low-Wage Work in the United Kingdom*, New York: Russell Sage Foundation.

Moule, C. (1998) 'Regulation of Work in Small Firms: A View From the Inside', *Work, Employment and Society*, Vol. 12, No. 4: 635–53.

Ram, M. and Edwards, P. (2003) 'Praising Caesar Not Burying Him: What We Know About Employment Relations in Small Firms', *Work, Employment and Society*, Vol. 17, No. 4: 719–30.

Sayer, A. (2007a) 'Dignity at Work: Broadening the Agenda', *Organization*, 14(4): 565–81.

Sayer, A. (2007b) 'What Dignity at Work Means', in Bolton, S. C. (ed.) *Dimensions of. Dignity at Work*, London: Butterworth Heineman.

Thompson, P. and Ackroyd, S. (1995) 'All Quiet on the Workplace Front? A Critique of Recent Trends in British Industrial Sociology', *Sociology*, 29/4, 1–19.

Thompson, P. and Newsome, K. (2004) 'Labour Process Theory, Work and the Employment Relation', in Kaufman, B. E. (ed.) *Theoretical Perspectives on Work and the Employment Relationship*, Cornell: Cornell University Press.

Sinclair, U. (1906) *The Jungle*, reprinted 1986, New York: Penguin Classics.

Life on the Supermarket Floor: Replenishment Assistants and Just-in-Time Systems

Kate Mulholland

This chapter examines the contemporary work experiences of supermarket employees, based on a case study of hourly paid male and female part-time workers in a major supermarket, with a focus on the implementation of just-in-time systems and the implications for stock replenishment assistants in particular. Although, service sector employment has largely replaced manufacturing and predominantly better paid male employment, and Marchington and Harrison (1991) report that food retailing now employs 10 percent of all those employed in the sector, this critical shift has attracted surprisingly little attention. Some important studies of retailing (Ogbonna and Harris, 2002; Rosenthal, Hill and Peccie, 1997) discuss different aspect of the 'new' organisation culture in supermarkets, primarily articulating a managerial perspective that unsurprisingly sheds little light on the employee experience. For example, Rosenthal *et al.* claim that the politics of flexibilisation had little impact on the way workers experienced autonomy, control, surveillance, and work intensification, concluding that workers internalised major features of corporate culture. Contrarily, Ogbonna and Harris's (2002) examination of a culture change initiative found that at most, worker behaviour may have altered, but doubt there was any major change in worker values.

By contrast, Kenny (2001) focuses on the structural transformation of employment relations for South African supermarket workers demonstrating that post-apartheid globalisation resulted in casualisation and flexibilisation, practices that greatly eroded the hard won trade union gains made during the emergence of democracy. Similarly, Newsome, Thompson and Commander (see Chapter 9, this volume) find that poor industrial relations exist for workers in the small and medium-sized food manufacturing sector, insisting on the need for dignity as part of the work process. A deterioration in working conditions is the underpinning thread characterising these later studies, coupled with the inexorable link between emergent practices of food production and food consumption. In this context, Wright and Lund (1996) and Lund and Wright (2003) have extensively explored the Australian food distribution sector, the mediating link between food manufacture and food retail, suggesting that alongside organisation efficiencies, the labour process has been subject to a series of rationalised restructurings that has transformed employment relations and the character of work in this sector facilitated by the introduction of new information technologies and the philosophy of the lean production model. Drawing on the managerial concept of Supply Chain Management (SCM) they reveal the logic that underpins the notion of the 'product flow cycle time' which arguably is the equivalent of the traditional assembly line (Clarke, 1990) – is to connect discrete aspects of food production and groups of workers, from the producers, to the warehouse workers, through to drivers and replenishment assistants. Each cluster of workers are then subject to similar rationalisation principles, such as work measurement and surveillance technologies. Furthermore, Wright and Lund (2006) also argue that:

> Major retailers have begun to focus on cost reduction within retail outlets and supermarkets rather than solely focusing on distribution centres: as some observers have suggested that as much as half the cost of retailing may lie in getting stock the last fifty metres to the customer (p. 70).

This suggests that the search for efficiencies has shifted *down the line* to the supermarkets themselves. In this context this chapter will explore the experiences of a particular cluster of supermarket workers, the Replenishment Assistants (RAs). This group alongside Checkout Assistants are on the lowest rung of the job hierarchy, receive the same pay rate, and their jobs are interchangeable. Drawing on the concept of lean production, this chapter will also explore how teamworking amongst RAs was transformed with the introduction of the lean model. Lean production according to Womack *et al.* (1990) is a standardised model that has wide applicability across different industries. Rooted in Japanisation, and claiming to transcend Fordism, it also claims to offer maximum efficiency through the elimination of the stockroom, a just-in-time response, apparently accompanied by harmonious industrial relations exemplified in multiskilled workers, plentiful training opportunities, continuous improvement, flexible working, teamworking and good communications based on high trust industrial relations. In their critically comprehensive interrogation of the different aspect of this concept in the manufacturing sector, Danford *et al.* (2005), Garraghan and Stewart (1992), Moody (1997), Rinehart *et al.* (1997) and Williams *et al.* (1992) strongly challenge these claims for the enhancement of worker experience. Shifting the focus to a supermarket, this chapter will examine how an aspect of the lean model, the elimination of the stockroom and the application of just-in-time in fact resulted in the demise of teamworking and limited worker autonomy in the investigated case study.

The study

Using an ethnographic approach the research for this study was conducted in two phases at ShopCo, a typically large store, which is part of a major supermarket chain. In the first phase, the researcher took a part-time job (16 hours weekly) as a Replenishment Assistant and used covert participant observation (Burgess, 1982) from 2005 to 2006 to explore the dynamics of the workplace relationship. The advantage of working alongside other workers doing the same job was that the researcher was able to share the experience of doing the work with other workers and to directly observe how the politics of the employment relationship and the contradictions between managerial goals and practice, service and productivity was played out on a day-to-day basis. I and the other workers found the work to be generally monotonous, tedious and physically hard, features that were magnified by management's constant insistence on greater speed and productivity. The pace of the work and the fact that I was studying the work covertly often defined the boundaries in which I would have liked to further explore the logic of some aspects of work organisation with management in particular. However, the covert approach was the only option open as I was persistently refused access, when I used an open approach explaining that I wished to research employment relations. I was able to gain open access for the second phase by redefining the research agenda in terms of exploring the logistics of SCM with management members, and I interviewed six managers in another store in the same supermarket chain. I also conducted a pilot study in the food distribution depot that supplies the store. The data from the first part of the study was used iteratively and influenced the range of questions put to the managers in the second phase regarding work reorganisation, teamworking and productivity. For the managers productivity and efficiencies transcended all other considerations.

Employment relationship

In order to understand the context in which the just-in-time system was introduced it is important to comment on the character of employment relations at ShopCo. Typically workplace relations at ShopCo are reminiscent of Guest and Hoque's (1994) *'bleak house model'* of industrial relations. Pay is set according to the minimum wage for all hourly paid workers with small premiums awarded for week-end and overnight work. Although, wages are no longer debated in the context of dependency (Barrett and McIntosh, 1982), the research shows that all the part-time workers relied on other sources to supplement their earnings. This includes men and women with partners who were the main earners, women and men with childcare responsibilities, workers with second jobs and students. ShopCo had weak union organisation, and indicative of this is how little influence the union had in the reorganisation and the subsequent surge for productivity as a result of just-in-time. According to Gregory and O' Reilly (1996), in the UK, this weakness goes back to the Thatcher era, when USDAR was forced to adopt a flexible position towards employers' demands in order to sustain some influence in negotiations. Indeed the impact of the weak bargaining position of the union is again noted by Gregory and O'Reilly (1996) who argue that in British supermarkets the application of *'a more detailed Taylorist labour measurement is allowed'* (p. 223), and is used extensively in the organisation of part-time workers. Such work patterns are underpinned by numerical flexibility and a managerial rigidity that is distinctly formulaic and bureaucratic (Thompson and McHugh 1995, p. 39). One example of bureaucracy and the low trust model in action is the draconian security practices upheld by ShopCo ironically referred to as 'Stop and Search'. For example, staff are searched repeatedly during work time and as they leave the premises after work, and notably during lulls in trade. A manager will ask them to empty their pockets and will record the contents using a clipboard and pen. The research revealed that staff are very careful and generally only take house keys, car keys and a mobile phone to work. This practice is greatly resented and is one of several dimensions of an intensive control regime that translates in high rates of labour turnover, sickness and absence.

The labour process at ShopCo – old ways of working

The size of the retail floor at ShopCo is typically large and is divided into four product zones, fresh produce, frozen foods, dry grocery and health and beauty. A major task of any supermarket store is regular and ongoing stock replenishment to ensure constant availability and saleability of supplies. To accommodate the competing demands of customer service and the arrival of deliveries, the peak times for stock replenishment at ShopCo, typical of most supermarkets, are during unsocial hours, when the store is closed to customers. This pattern of replenishment requires flexible shift patterns that include a full-time night shift and part-time evening shifts. At ShopCo, the overnight shift from 11.00 p.m. to 7.00 a.m. employs full-time male workers. Although gender was not a formal specification the physically arduous character of the task in the replenishment of very heavy dry goods and frozen foods perhaps explains the absence of women. A second strand of four-hour, part-time evening shifts commencing at varying times starting from 6.00 p.m. are set aside for the replenishment of lighter dry grocery goods, illustrating the extent that work patterns are flexibilised. These shorter shifts are female dominated consisting of 75 percent women and 25 percent men, although many work overtime working up to 30 hours on a weekly basis. While workers are obliged to strictly adhere to set shift patterns, the politics of flexibility allow management to respond to the variation in labour requirements simply by offering or withdrawing overtime at will echoing Gregory and O'Reilly's (1996) arguments over flexibilisation. The research shows that overtime is a regular feature, and some workers who grow accustomed to the extra earnings face difficulties when overtime is withdrawn or reduced, evident after the introduction of just-in-time and in periods of slack trading. However, the typical number of hours worked are approximately 16.

Teamworking

At ShopCo, part-time evening shifts are organised in three teams of five to eight workers depending on the volume of work, and the overnight shift is a separate team. Each team works a particular aisle and product zone. Prior to the introduction of just-in-time, teams comprised a number of permanent members, who had acquired their positions through seniority, and a few 'floaters', newly appointed staff who had yet to negotiate their position in any team. The negotiation into the desired teams depends on fitting in with the specificity of team culture and establishing an identity with the preferred team, and not least the management concern with the allocation of labour during the particular shift. Although, there is no formal team leader position, informally each team is headed by a senior worker who has emerged organically having long work experience and product knowledge reflecting Benders and Van Hootegem's (1999) notion of a quality circle. The importance of such workers to management is that they depend on them to train new staff and to ensure the smooth running of the shift. These senior workers have no formal status as team leaders, they are on the same pay as other workers and are expected to meet similar productivity quotas.

These team leaders adopt very different management styles, broadly reflecting Proctor and Mueller's (2000) dichotomy of a 'coach' versus 'cop' style. The research shows that such difference in work organisation affords a degree of autonomy, particularly for teams adopting the 'coach' style approach. On the one hand, teams A and B headed by the 'coaches' are more interactive and democratic, and at the start of each shift the division of tasks is negotiated between the members. On the other hand, the team leader in team C pursuing a 'cop' style is autocratic and partial, and makes decisions which leaves the majority of team members little discretion, nor voice over task choice. This causes tensions, which are not acknowledged by management, although they are well aware of them. Frequently the 'floating staff' protest when allocated to team C and staff tolerance of an evening's work often rests on avoiding working with this team.

These styles and experiences also reflect patterns of working for the particular shift, since teams A and B use a more collective, democratic and shared method of working which takes account of individual preference and strength. By contrast, work organisation amongst team C members is individualised and fragmented. Members in the more democratic teams enjoy some limited autonomy in the choice of work, thus they are better able to cope with the continuous pressure for increased effort, while those workers in team C, who have no choice, are left to struggle as best they can. Moreover, the individualised style of working makes an individual worker's productivity more transparent to management surveillance when such workers are deemed to be underperforming and vulnerable to discipline. All four night shifts are managed by two first-line female managers, who rely very heavily on the cooperation and good will of the team leaders and the teams, despite their relentless driving to get the work completed.

Teamworking and productivity

Traditionally, when deliveries arrive the shelves are replenished and surplus products are kept in backroom stocks. However, as Wright and Lund (2006) report, in the Australian context the central concern for management is the cost of handling storage and the shelving function. Similarly at ShopCo, a product on arrival is handled four to five times on its journey to the shelf within the store alone. For instance, the first step in this process is to sort the deliveries into product types, placing them in seven foot high metal crates, which are then wheeled from the delivery bay onto the appropriate aisle. RAs then lift packs of produce, containing six to 12 items, from the holding crate, and place them on a shelving trolley, which has a large storage shelf, low to the floor, and a three foot high bench and steps. The next manoeuver is to release the items from the outer packaging using a knife, placing them on the bench, and using the steps, to lift the goods onto the shelf. The productivity target is a case of items shelved per minute, or the hourly completion of the seven foot crate per team member. However, prior to the change initiative, which will be discussed in the next section, individual output was not strictly measured. Nevertheless, the overarching team concern was to ensure that all necessary replenishment is completed by the end of the shift.

It is important to note that late deliveries cause backlogs disrupting the shelving routine, and in such circumstances items are stored. However, it is not at all clear prior to the change initiative that management operate an individual target system, since the research suggests that the two line managers are singularly interested in the completion of the evening shelving, rather that in how the teams organise the work tasks.

Moreover, it is also not at all clear that the variations in the team working methods result in big productivity differentials, but the advantage of the democratic team approach to the workers is that it acts as a coping mechanism in a stressful work situation. For instance, replenishment is very physically demanding and the experienced 'coach' style leaders try to match the particular jobs with individual capability, notably strength, agility, and dexterity. There is a tacit acceptance that some workers prefer to handle heavier goods, since they can be processed more rapidly, while others dislike handling small 'fiddly' goods, contradicting unconscious gender matching, when it is often assumed that women are suited to tedious work (Phillips, 1983), such as the preparation of merchandise, a task that is time consuming requiring fastidious attention to detail. Such limited autonomy provides a limited coping mechanism to manage the physical rigours of stooping, stretching and lifting speedily over the head on a repetitive basis, offering some protection against occupational injuries. The research shows that almost every member of staff including the line managers experienced some injury, such as repetitive strain, muscle, joint and back injuries at some point. Although occupational injury seems to be a common feature of such work, no figures are available from management.

Business strategy and change

Towards the end of my research with ShopCo, the introduction of the lean model was precipitated by a crisis in the supermarket's market strategy. Competing on quality ShopCo had nationally been losing market share to two major rivals, who were competing on price. The first step the business took was to make a major managerial change at national level with the appointment of a senior executive, who initiated a two – pronged recovery strategy. The first part of the strategy involved a shift from quality competition to price competition. Gregory and O'Reilly (1996) and Turnbull and Wass (1997) argue that the character of market competition influences the quality of employment relations, and indeed this thinking is reflected in the second aspect of StoreCo's recovery strategy, which was to cut costs through a focus on the labour process. The RAs were one of the most likely clusters of workers to be identified in the search for efficiencies because they handled the goods a process that is considered to be too costly.

Proposed change

The recovery strategy was to bring about changes in work organisation that would result in the reshaping of the replenishment task, underpinned by the logic of the lean model. First, the proposed work reorganisation began with a dramatic and immediate decrease in the stock inventory. Secondly, the two existing trolleys, simple but necessary technologies for the shelving task, were to be made obsolete and a single trolley introduced that would reduce the number of times goods were handled during the replenishment process. As will be discussed in the next section, this substitution proved a major point of contention and subsequently was modified. However the biggest problem for management was that no reduction could be made in the handling of goods. As a result management shifted focus to the productivity issue and each worker's output was evaluated using time and motion study and an engineering performance standard, a development that resulted in the break-up of team organisation. Finally, there was an increase in work speed up and further work fragmentation.

Team briefings

However, if increased productivity is what the management intended, few of the implications were explained, and those that were proved not to be relevant in the presentation of the company's 'recovery strategy', which involved a series of briefings between management and the evening shifts. The first two meetings were addressed by middle managers and there was a final meeting with the store manager. In the first meeting, the manager explained neither the character of the company's market difficulties, the character of the proposed change, nor more importantly, the implications of the proposed changes for the staff concerned. While the key issues of the RAs were working practices and productivity, the manager engaged in what was opaque discourse to the staff, but dotted this with references to *'the need for increased efficiency'*, *'the out of stock problem' and 'the need for greater team co-operation'*. This immediately created tensions amongst the staff. They were angry, confused and could not understand the particular manager's intention. In seeking clarification a few raised questions. Typically:

> Denise: I am at a profound loss to know how we can be responsible for the 'out of stock problem', this is not our job. Maybe, you can explain.

At this meeting this particular team leader challenged the manager over the suggestion that a local *'out of stock'* problem was related to the lack of cooperation within or between teams, and pointed to the problems with delivery timeliness. His reply was:

> We have a solution to the deliveries problem now.

This exchange demonstrates the misunderstanding between the staff and management. From a management perspective, there is a problem with the ordering system, while from a staff perspective, late deliveries are the problem, since they disrupt the pace and flow of work practices. Indeed, late deliveries are inevitable and it is only with the staff commitment and extra effort that goods are shelved on time. Emphasising these sentiments and practices, the team leader argued:

> You say we have to focus on cooperation and team work. Well, my own view is that there is no (management) commitment to teamworking here. I mean it's about talking to your colleagues, which we do. It's getting their confidence and trust in you, and helping each other out. I tell you, on the rare occasions that my team finishes three minutes early, we go and help our mates out. That's not something everyone does.

This statement challenged an implied inference about the lack of cooperation and productivity amongst the RAs, and reflects the custom and practice for the teams to deploy to other aisles once they complete their allotted shelving. It is not surprising that this team leader, who has been a ShopCo employee for 30 years, is angry, for she works very hard putting into practice her understanding of teamwork as cooperation. Her experience, consistent with my observations, is that the company gives little support to teams.

The authoritarian character of ShopCo's managerial style was again illustrated the following evening, when the shift supervisor separately questioned each of the members who had raised questions at the meeting. Most of the team saw this as intimidation, and a member commented:

> It's just A...'s way (the company) of stifling our opinion, and at the end of day, you have to ask yourself whether it is worth the hassle. Another ruefully added: It's a bit like the master servant relationship here.

Team members well understood that management at ShopCo expected obedience, whilst assuming that staff questioning of management was tantamount to dissonance. The difficulties faced by the first line supervision are that such managers have to manage divided loyalties, between their responsibilities as the agents of senior management and their working proximity to the staff, where goodwill and trust go a long way.

At the second meeting, the teams were informed of three proposed changes, including the elimination of stock inventory, the substitution of a new shelving trolley in place of the two existing trolleys, and the requirement for team involvement in the 'ordering' needs for the different aisles. Although this necessitated additional work, the staff were visibly reluctant to raise questions as they felt intimidated by the earlier meeting. The team insisted that the job needed the two existing trolleys, but agreed to try out the new trolley provided they could use the old trolleys simultaneously. In this instance, the shift managers supported the staff over the unsuitability of the new trolley, since they fully understood how critical the old trolleys were to the operationalisation of the job. It is notable that the team's broader concerns regarding how the restructuring would affect patterns of working and particularly the character of the team organisation was decentred in the struggle to retain the existing trolley and the old way of working.

The elimination of the inventory

The elimination of the store inventory, was the first critical step in job reorganisation at ShopCo, and is an efficiency measure that mirrors cost reduction in the American and Australian grocery and distribution trades (Lund and Wright, 2003). The stockroom at ShopCo was cleared of all merchandise and the floor-to-ceiling shelving racks were removed. The implications this had for the RAs is that the inventory had helped the replenishment teams to manage late deliveries. In sharp contrast, the logic of Supply Chain Management and just-in-time goods ordering systems, is that both manufacturers and depots are able to respond immediately to store orders. This means that orders can be initiated at store level and once a product is about to run out, it is supplied quickly, eliminating the need for the stockroom. However as the following section illustrates it was not until the new system was put into practice that the problems associated with just-in-time fully appeared.

Once the stockroom was cleared deliveries were to be loaded onto the new single trolley and shelved immediately. The clear advantage of this to management is that just-in-time in conjunction with the trolley considerably reduces goods handling, in addition to making a cost saving on storage. The logic of the system is that delivered goods are immediately made available for sale. One of the implementation difficulties is that deliveries are invariably late, for despite the Global Navigation Systems that are in place, management are unable to anticipate road delays. In such instances, a late delivery in the absence of the stockroom translates into acute productivity problems for the replenishment teams who are driven to speed up the pace of work so that shift's work allocation is complete. In these circumstances the RAs are less able to control the rate in which they work.

The second problem to emerge was with the new shelving trolley. The teams found it to be poorly designed, impractical, difficult to use and unsafe. Importantly it disrupted the momentum for movement slowing the work pace. It necessitated excessive stooping, because it was too low to the floor, which made the job very difficult to do. However, the major flaw was that unlike the sturdier old shelving trolley it did not have a shelf and steps, from which items could be lifted onto prior to the second lift, whereby the operatives using the steps could more safely reach overhead shelves. Reminiscent of the lean production model (Rinehart et al., 1997) and Frederick Taylor's obsession with cutting out any superfluous movement, the new trolley required operatives to lift and shelf in one motion, regardless of the height of the shelf, and of the weight of the item. It was designed from the perspective of one size fits all. Acknowledging these problems, management provided a foot-stool, however the stools were free standing and lacked the support designed into the old trolley, making lifting harder and more dangerous.

Over two weeks the issue of the new trolley reached a point of contestation between all three teams and shift management, when they demanded a meeting with the shop manager in order to demonstrate the design flaws. One of the members remonstrated with one of the night-shift managers asking her:

> Do you think they (more senior management) would use this thing (the new trolley) if they had to do the job?

While Jenni, another member inquired:
Surely M... (day manager) wasn't serious, I mean I know he might have to tell us about this, but surely, they are going to see sense.

The response from the shift manager was that she understood that this new trolley was to be *'rolled out, and the earlier people got used to it the better.'* From the RAs perspective, the new trolley slowed the pace of work, was impractical and dangerous. The teams also quickly realised that it would effectively end their notion of teamwork, the established custom and practice that defined their ways of working. Each team had, through their different ways of working, developed a sense of ownership over the labour process in their particular aisles. The new methodology required them to work all over the floor rather than on specific aisles, and held the prospect of reduced or restricted interaction between team members. The new process thereby introduced individualisation, undermining team solidarity and the idea of *'looking out for each other'*. The team talked about how they would respond. The more experienced workers argued:

> Denise: They can't force us to work in this way, I mean, I won't work all over the shop. I for one, will leave.

Sharon: Well, that is an option, but first, we must show them (the management) that this is not a practical idea.

Carol-Ann: I mean its (new trolley) ok to put out the 'overs', but not the deliveries.

Amelie: And what about this foot stool, I mean try lifting a board (six jars) of beetroot. I have, and it is just too unsteady. I found it difficult to stretch, and in the end, I had to put each jar on, one after the other.

Jenni: We just won't get the work out either.

Such comments underscored the limitations the staff experienced through the reorganisation of their work, and also their recognition of what it took to get their work done safely and efficiently. The new system forced the staff to abandon their tacit skills, slowing down the pace of work. Moreover it could not accommodate volume as it was small, and would hold fewer products than the old shelving trolley. Given that team productivity would be negatively affected it was subsequently easy for the teams to convince the two night-shift managers that the new trolley had limited use, and should be restricted for the storage of surplus stock. However, this example shows how shopfloor work practices and opinions can be ignored in the design of work instruments. The team leaders suggested that the evening teams would demonstrate to the Store Manager that the new trolley was not fit for the purpose of volume shelving and suggested:

Denise: The managers know full well it is useless, but they still have to insist we use it. But, if we get Phil (Store Manager), he will see that we are making sense.

This illustrates that there was a tacit understanding amongst the experienced workers that the obduracy of middle managers was rooted in the bureaucratic character of the industrial relations system and in the rigidity of the management culture at *ShopCo* at large. However, the Store Manager had a reputation for his personal and communication skills, and staff were also aware that he had the authority and autonomy to make a judgment with regard to the new trolley, and that he would not necessarily be bound by the bureaucracy.
For example,

Amelie: Phil will just want to know that the work will get done, he won't care either way.

The meeting with the store manager was subsequently organised, and the proposed changes were reversed. Management was unable to substantially reduce the numerical handling of deliveries and goods still had to be handled several times, although the back-room inventory was almost eliminated. The teams felt they had achieved a minor victory and continued to work in much the same way for the time being, but this was short-lived.

The timing of jobs

The next change came with the announcement that all the team members would be subject to time and motion studies. *ShopCo* management drew on a crude combination of two types of work measurement systems that included predetermined motion-time and stopwatch-derived systems (Wright and Lund, 1996). In the first case, management assumed that the RAs were capable of shelving a case per minute, without timing the different elements of the task, or counting the actual number of cases in a full holding crate. For instance, shift managers using a stop-watch took note of the starting and finishing shelving times of a full holding crate for each team member and then calculated individual performance times. The result of this was that there was considerable variation in performance amongst team members, who were differentiated by height, weight, gender, age and experience. Moreover, the number of cases a crate could hold also varied as did the time it took to prepare, organise and present the merchandise on the shelf. What was surprising was that although this was a critical productivity issue that challenged the teams' notions of a fair evening's work and set about establishing a new productivity norm, no union representative was present. The idea behind the timing seemed to be that it established an ideal performance standard, which every member should then compete to achieve. The measurement methods were crude and arbitrary, suggesting that the target of 60 cases could be achieved only in ideal environmental circumstances. As Wright and Lund (1996) remark:

> a problem with such systems is that elemental times derived may fail to take account of varying work methods or environmental conditions. Added to this, differences in performance rating of different industrial engineers may affect the supposed accuracy of the final time standard (p. 203).

The timing and the standardisation of the replenishment task effectively put an end to teamworking. Management took a number of further measures to enforce productivity. They required each worker to operate from a separate holding crate rendering individual performance more transparent to surveillance. They also put a renewed emphasis on customer service, and this additional work brought more pressure on the workers. During the early part of the evening shift, the RAs could be interrupted by customer requests for help, making the management of individual effort all the more difficult, since critical shelving time was lost.

In addition, the RAs were to be involved in the ordering process. For instance, at the start of each shift, they picked up strips of colour coded paper. Red strips indicated that a product was 'out of stock' and had to be inserted in the item slot on the shelf, while a green slip indicated that an item was overordered, and that stock remained. Since these new elements were not taken into account during the timing of the job, such additional jobs acted as a double-bind for the workers because they faced disciplinary measures if they neglected customer service or failed to sustain productivity targets.

The interviews with the managers reveal that the company's notion of the team was based on the idea that all store members form 'the team', sharply contrasting with shopfloor practice, where the team is more akin to organic group working. The logic of the management version of the team is underpinned by labour flexibility, whereby within constraints, workers can be allocated wherever and whenever necessary throughout the store. It does not seem that the staff's version of the teamworking was perceived as a challenge to the management, it is more the case that the logical consequences of the lean model is individualised working practices, the antipathy of the kind of solidarity, identity and meaning characterising the small group working at ShopCo.

One of the effects of the disbanding of teamworking was that team leaders lost their informal supervisory roles, while responsibility for productivity shifted to the evening shift management, who adopted a much more stringent line. They walked the aisles continually enforcing the pace of work shouting at workers they perceived to be slacking. This brought about new tensions between the shift supervision and staff. Lean staffing and the unreliability of the delivery of stock further exaggerated these tensions. As mentioned earlier, while the intention of the Transport Management System is to achieve a seamless joining between the arrival of deliveries and the start of the evening shifts and to enable real-time progress monitoring, the late arrival of deliveries made this largely ineffective.

Delayed deliveries created backlogs of work and had immediate negative effects for RAs, who previously were better able to regulate their effort. Shift management's response to this situation was to adopt an aggressive approach, and further enforce the speed-up of work. This was heightened towards the end of the shifts when team members were tired. While the lean gurus (Womack *et al.*, 1990) assume such incidents are eliminated by smart working, the reality, as experienced at ShopCo, is that management simply resort to intensifying the pace of work. Such circumstances increased the likelihood of injury particularly back, joint, muscle, and repetitive strain injuries due to sustained lifting, reaching, bending and stretching. I experienced painful muscle strain, which would have forced me to resign from the job, had this not coincided with the end of the ethnography. Injury was a common experience and formed a frequent conversation topic amongst the staff and the managers. This, and the climate of enforced work pacing through crude bullying, scolding and shouting alongside formalised disciplinary measures, while not malicious, was directly due to the constraints the lean model placed on management, and duly the workers. The withdrawal of overtime was another feature of the lean model and left management with fewer optional measures for the smooth running of the shifts, while also resulting in a loss of earnings for some workers. In this context, the shift managers' roles at ShopCo became comparable to the traditional foreman role characteristic of the factory system.

In order to inculcate a culture of responsibility the RAs were also required to fill in productivity sheets at the end of each shift giving details of the number of crates shelved and any 'overstock' sorted. Invariably, the staff did not comply with this requirement, and worked according to the rules set out in their contracts. The following typifies some of workers' response:

> Line manager: Sign this Marianne.
> Marianne: C..., I'm not signing that.
> Line manager: Why not? The new rule says it has to be done.
> Marianne: My contract does not say I have to sign that. It's not in my contract.
> Supervisor: I'm going to have to report you.
> Marianne: Do what you like C.... Well, as I say C..., my contract says nothing about signing.

Such exchanges contrast significantly with the absence of resistance suggestive in the work of Rosenthal, Hill and Peccie (1997). Rather than acceptance, they show rather sullen and tacit non-compliance amongst the workers within the context of a low trust industrial relations system, whereas Gregory and O 'Reilly (1996) insist that the unions have negotiated away their influence over the organisation of work at shopfloor level. This study would suggest that this vacuum is being strongly felt among front line workers.

Conclusions

This account of replenishment assistants' experiences of work and lean working in particular offers a glimpse into the realities of the supermarket work experience, and provides context for the destruction of team working, the extension of Taylorism, and the individualisation of the labour process within the food retail sector. The evidence of this case account is that the shift from quality competition to price competition at ShopCo ended in a deterioration in the working conditions for replenishment assistants. Contrary to Rosenthal, Hill and Peccie's (1997) argument that workers accept the flexibilisation of work, this research shows that the imbalance in the power relationship between the replenishment assistants and management provides a more succinct explanation. The teams resisted but were ultimately unable to forestall changes in their work organisation, and were adversely affected by increased work speed-up. The demise of teamworking was a bitter loss to the workers concerned, since they had attributed meaning and value to being able to work within a framework of limited autonomy that gave them some discretion over how the job was organised.

This case study also shows that the application of just-in-time systems is much more problematic than the prescriptive literature suggests. For instance, the aim *to eliminate unnecessary steps* (Lund and Wright, 2003: 106), which is a core feature of SCM, in this case translated into management's attempt to reduce the numerical handling of the dry grocery deliveries, failed. This failure resulted in the abandonment of one of management's cost saving strategies when they acquiesced to worker pressure for the retention of the existing trolleys, and the established work pattern. Nevertheless, it is difficult to assess whether 'better' technology would have improved the work exper- ience for the replenishment assistants, for as Wright and Lund (1996) argue, management do not necessarily choose technologies that are premised on the *high trust* principles advocated by Human Resource Management.

The study has also shown that ShopCo management, in order to retrieve the lost 'efficiency' in product handling, very readily resorted to traditional Taylorism and work speed-up, a finding consistent with Danford *et al.* (2005) and Rinehart *et al.*'s (2007) critique of the lean model. ShopCo showed little inclination for innovation, but rather adopted two crude measurement methods and simply imposed a predetermined productivity norm. The research has also shown that this was followed by further work reorganisation, when work was individualised, whereby workers operated separate aisles. This shift magnifies the significance of direct control and the role of line supervision (Friedman, 1977), suggesting that there is little that is new in management systems in the retail food sector. For the replenishment assistants the task was made more susceptible to traditional management surveillance and to demands for speed-up. In the case of ShopCo the workers paid the price. Arguably, given that there is no sign of any major departure from market economics and price competition, it is fair to suggest that supermarket workers generally will increasingly find themselves in the tyranny of the *bleak house* model of employment relations provided by the lean production model.

REFERENCES

Barrett, M. and McIntosh, M. (1982) *The Anti-Social Family,* London: New Left Books.

Benders, J. and Van Hootegem, G. (1999) 'Teams and Their Context: Moving the Team Discussion Beyond Existing Dichotomies', *Journal of Management Studies*, 36: 5, 609–28.

Burgess, R. (ed.) (1982) *Field Research,* London: George Allen and Unwin.

Clarke, S. (1990) 'What in the F...'s Name is Fordism', in Burroughs, R. Gilbert, A. and Pollert, A. (eds) *Fordism and Flexibility*, 13–30, Basingstoke: Macmillan.

Danford, A., Richardson, M., Stewart, P., Tailby, S. and Upchurch, M. (2005) *Partnership and the High Performance Workplace,* Basingstoke: Palgrave Macmillan.

Friedman, A. (1977) *Industry and Labour, Class Struggle at Work Monopoly Capitalism,* London: Macmillan.

Garraghan, P. and Stewart, P. (1992) *The Nissan Enigma,* London: Mansell.

Gregory, A. and O'Reilly, J. (1996) 'Checking out and cashing up: the prospects and paradoxes of regulating part-time work in Europe', in Crompton, R., Gallie, D. and Purcell, K. (eds) *Changing Forms of Employment: Organisations, Skills and Gender*, 207–34, London: Routledge.

Guest, D. and Hoque, K. (1994) 'The Good, the Bad and the Ugly: Employment Relations in Non-Union Workplaces', *Human Resource Management Journal*, 5: 1, 1–14.

Kenny, B. (2001) 'Selling Selves: Control, resistance and detachment on the South African shop floors', *19th Annual International Labour Process Conference,* School of Management, Royal Holloway, University of London.

Lund, J. and Wright, C. (2003) 'Integrating the supply chain: industrial relations implications in US grocery distribution', *New Technology, Work and Employment*, 18: 2, 101–15.

Marchington, M. and Harrison, E. (1991) 'Customers, competitors and choice: employee relations in food retailing', *Industrial Relations Journal*, 22: 4, 286–99.

Moody, K. (1997) *Workers in a Lean World, Unions in the International Economy,* London, New York: Verso.

Ogbonna, E. and Harris, Lloyd C. (2002) 'Organisational Culture: A Ten Year, Two-Phase Study of Change in the Food Retailing Sector', *Journal of Management Studies*, 39: 5, 673–706.

Phillips, A. (1983) *Hidden Hands,* London: Pluto Press.

Proctor, I. and Mueller, F. (2000) *Teamworking,* Basingstoke: Macmillan.

Rinehart, J., Huxley, C. and Robinson, D. (1997) *Just Another Car Factory? Lean Production and its Discontents,* Ithaca and London: ILP Press.

Rosenthal, P., Hill, S. and Peccie, R. (1997) 'Checking Out Service: Evaluating Excellence, HRM and QTM in Retailing', *Work, Employment & Society*, 11: 3, 481–503.

Thompson, P. and McHugh, D. (1995) *Work Organisations,* Basingstoke: Macmillan Press.

▶

Turnbull, P. and Wass, V. (1997) 'Markist management: sophisticated human relations in a high street retail store', *Industrial Relations Journal*, 29: 2, 98–111.

Williams, K., Haslam, C., Williams, C., Cutler, J., Adcroft, A. and Johal, S. (1992) 'Against Lean Production', *Economy and Society*, 21: 321–54.

Womack, J., Roos, D. and Jones, D. (1990) *The Machine that Changed the World*, New York: Rawson and Associates.

Wright, C. and Lund, J. (1996) 'Best-Practice Taylorism: "Yankee Speed-up", in Australian Grocery Distribution', *Journal of Industrial Relations*, 38: 2, 196–212.

Wright, C. and Lund, J. (2006) 'Variations on a lean theme: work restructuring in retail distribution', *New Technology Work and Employment*, 21: 1, 59–74.

Just 'Mothers Really'? Role Stretch and Low Pay Amongst Female Classroom Assistants

Chris Warhurst, Scott A. Hurrell, Kay Gilbert, Dennis Nickson, Johanna Commander and Isobel Calder

Introduction

Much is made by government in the UK about the need to stimulate high skill, high wage jobs – usually framed in public policy discourse in terms of the knowledge economy or its close cousin the creative economy (see for example Reich, 1993 and Florida, 2002 respectively). Critics point out that claims of such emergent economies sit ill-at-ease with labour market data showing a polarisation of what Goos and Manning (2007) term lovely and lousy jobs, the latter being typically low pay and low skill.

Whilst it is not uncommon during times of alleged economic shifts for academic discourse to focus on the lovely jobs (see Warhurst *et al.*, 2009), more nuanced accounts reveal blurred boundaries between the lovely and the lousy jobs. Recent research indicates that some of the lovely jobs are no longer so lovely. For example solicitors are dividing between those with good and bad pay, career opportunities and tasks (Muzio, 2004). Of the latter, some have little more than a 'proletarian role' according to Sommerland (cited in Bolton and Muzio, 2008: 286). Medical doctors feel buried by bureaucracy, constrained by managerial controls and fear that training opportunities for career progression are disappearing (Puttick, 2007). These developments have two dimensions. The first, and well researched, is the deprofessionalisation that is occurring as autonomy is eroded with steadily declining job control and task discretion amongst professionals (Felstead *et al.*, 2007). The second, less well noted and researched, is a complementary *downward role stretch*. This role stretch involves not just work intensification but also organisational deskilling as some professionals undertake additional and more routine tasks that might previously have been expected to have been done by other non-professional workers, usually secretaries and admin-istrative staff. In other words, those workers who have ascribed lovely jobs are now undertaking – and feeling swamped by – some relatively lousy tasks. Teaching is a prominent example. In Scotland, following the publication of what is called the McCrone Report (Scottish Executive, 2001), it was agreed that there was a need to minimise teachers undertaking of routine work 'not directly related to their key role in teaching and learning' (p. 16). Tasks to be removed include administration, for example filing and photocopying, and the supervision of pupils in the non-teaching areas of schools, such as corri-dors and cloakrooms.

Of course, such tasks are not eliminated, merely displaced to other workers, often creating new occupations. Thus, medical doctors are now supported by nursing practitioners (Dent, 2008), solicitors by para-legals (Muzio and Ackroyd, 2008) and, our focus in this chapter, teachers by assistants. Govern-ment in the UK has introduced teaching assistants in English schools and classroom assistants in Scottish schools. There is even some suggestion that dis-placing care and welfare duties to such assistants represents part of a profession-alisation project on the part of teachers (Bolton, 2007).

Although there have been support staff, both paid and unpaid, in class-rooms for many years, classroom assistants were introduced into Scottish primary schools by central government in 1998. The initiative was then expanded to 15,000 classroom assistants across all of the nearly 2,800 state schools by 2007. Exploratory research commissioned by the EOC revealed that classroom assistants are overwhelming female – typically older women with children – generally possess intermediate level qualifications, work part-time and are low paid, earning on average less than £11,000 per year. Although classroom assistant pay was found to be notionally between £10,000–£13,500 per year this calculation was based on a 35 hour working week for 52 weeks of the year. In reality, on the pro rata basis on which they worked, classroom assistants could earn as little as £5,500 per year (SCER, 2005).

What the research also revealed – and the focus of this chapter – is an *upward role stretch* as some of these classroom assistants take on the tasks of teachers. The problem, however, is that although the potential for this role stretch was foreseen by government, its subsequent practice has been under-appreciated. The outcome is a 'sticky floor' with an informal upskilling not reflected in increased pay. A key reason for this undervaluing, the research suggests, lies in perceptions of both the work of classroom assistants and the type of workers who are classroom assistants – 'mothers really', as one (female) parent in the research explained. So perceived, some classroom assistants are now doing duties of teachers but with neither formal recognition nor reward. Analysis of classroom assistants thus reveals how the emergence of new occupations, supportive of professionals, constitutes a not unproblematic development.

The next section of this chapter outlines the research methods used in the exploratory research. The findings centre on three issues: how the work of classroom assistants is perceived; the existence of an upward role stretch in that work; and that pay for classroom assistants remains low. The chapter argues that the gendered nature of the occupation, especially its association with working mothers and secondary income earners, institutionalises low pay. Classroom assistants seem to accept this pay because of the compensating satisfaction gained from working with children but also because the job's working patterns suit female workers with young children.

An outline of the research

The purpose of the EOC-commissioned[1] research was to examine whether the *actual* work of classroom assistants was consistent with the role *intended* by policy-makers in central government and that *stated* by the employing local authorities. To this end, two main stages of research were undertaken. The first stage involved desk research examining government policy documents and various local authority classroom assistant job descriptions and associated terms and conditions of employment. Occupation-specific statistics as well as materials from trade unions were also examined.

Given that there had been no examination of classroom assistants jobs since their introduction (see Wilson *et al.*, 2002), it was important that empirical research was undertaken. The second stage therefore involved fieldwork in nine primary schools in three different Scottish local authorities. These schools were selected for representative size, location and rural/urban mix. Both quantitative and qualitative data collection occurred. Tailored questionnaires were administered to head-teachers, teachers and classroom assistants. The questionnaires focused on classroom assistants' demographic details, terms and conditions of employment, work duties and respondents' views on wider issues associated with the classroom assistant role (for example the skills and qualifications needed to get and do the job, the attractiveness of the job). One hundred and sixty questionnaires were distributed with a good overall response rate of 48 percent (Saunders *et al.*, 2000). The response rate was disaggregated as 63 percent for classroom assistants and 43 percent for head-teachers and teachers. Interviews and focus groups were then conducted with classroom assistants, teachers and head-teachers in one school in each of the three authorities. In two of the schools, focus groups were conducted with parents and observations made of classroom assistants at work. All of these respondents were women. The in-school research was also complemented by further qualitative research with potential job entrants still at school and labour market gatekeepers. A focus group was conducted with college students undertaking a Professional Development Award (PDA)[2] intended as preparation for classroom assistants and interviews with two female returners, a careers adviser, a PDA course leader and a childcare work co-ordinator. The fieldwork was completed by two focus groups of B.Ed[3] students who would potentially become teachers, some of whom were also currently working as classroom assistants or had previously been classroom assistants.

Although reference is made in this chapter to the questionnaire data, the research findings mainly draw upon the qualitative material in order to give voice to those respondents at the chalk-face – head-teachers, teachers, parents and, of course, the classroom assistants themselves. It is to their perceptions and experience of the work and employment of classroom assistants in schools to which we now turn.

Being mothers really

Despite reported attempts to attract men, the typical classroom assistant was a working mother,[4] aged 31–50 years with school age children, working part-time (25 hours per week) and typically doing so during school hours (9a.m.–3.30p.m.). All worked 39 weeks per year on school term-time-only contracts. The majority (72 percent) of classroom assistants stated that the workings hours suited their family life and their childcare responsibilities. As one classroom assistant explained; 'I was a parent helper in here ... before I started, and my kids were younger at the time so it suited me because I didn't have anyone to watch them'. The desire for working patterns compatible with these responsibilities meant that, in the words of one classroom assistant 'there would be a mass exodus' if classroom assistants had to work during school holidays.

Only a third of classroom assistants possessed a childcare qualification. In fact, no Scottish local authority requires classroom assistants to have any relevant classroom assistant qualification. Classroom assistants did however possess a variety of other qualifications, with most having compulsory school leaving age Standard grade[5] qualifications but ranging through to HNDs and even first and post-graduate degrees. They also had a range of backgrounds, one, previously a human resource manager, chose the job also in part for a reduction in working hours; she said 'I was doing horrendous hours before and I wanted to do less hours.' However, almost all classroom assistants (92 percent) stated that they did the job because they liked working with children. Every surveyed classroom assistant reported at least one aspect of working with children amongst the most liked aspects of their work; most stated that they simply enjoyed working with children and just over half liked being part of a child's education, growth and development and watching children gain confidence: 'I think that you can see instant rewards for your work ... from the children ... There is a lot of personal satisfaction if you know you are helping kids', said one. None reported that they worked as classroom assistants because there was nothing else available or because they were looking to move into care work. In explaining how she came into the job one classroom assistant explained:

> ... it's a big change for me because I was a cleaner before but I ... had helped out with primary [school children] and I just really enjoyed it, you know working with the children so ... I thought I am just going to go for it.

Another similarly described her shift from parent helper to classroom assistant as a 'natural progression'. Indeed, a number of the classroom assistants had previous experience of working with children in schools by, for example, being volunteer parent helpers and playground supervisors.

It was noted that 'physical skills' were needed in the job, particularly for those classroom assistants who dealt with pupils with special learning needs and who, for example, might need physical restraint or toileting help. On one occasion two classroom assistants were observed physically restraining and calming a pupil with discipline problems as he bolted from the classroom. However the most important attributes for the job all respondents stated, were experience of working with children and the possession of related skills. Classroom assistants require patience, empathy and good communication skills. Interestingly, these qualities, what might in other circumstances be termed 'social skills' (Grugulis et al., 2004) were distilled by one parent into 'having a good knowledge of children ... – mothers really'. Similarly, one classroom assistant noted 'being a mother is the best training'. Not surprisingly, a recurring theme amongst the respondents was the extent to which the required skills were 'feminine'. One classroom assistant, recalling her experience working with a rare male assistant, firstly noted how he was very good at his job, before going on, 'I think [he] was a one off ... I think a lot of them are female skills'.

When pressed about the nature of such female skills, she continued; 'The listening, the patience, the negotiating'. Similarly a parent suggested that the best person for the job 'would probably more likely be female, because they are more understanding, I am not saying that men are not understanding but women are more in the family home doing everything with the kids.'

Relatedly, there was concern amongst some respondents about the perceived appropriateness of men wanting to work with young children, with one parent noting how 'There is a thing isn't there, about men working with young children ... I think it's difficult for the men ... because of what these kids could accuse them of.' In this respect, a male student on the B.Ed who had previously worked as both a nursery nurse and classroom assistant noted how he always felt that he had to ask his immediate supervisor or manager whether it was alright for children to sit on his knee because, as he explained, 'I just didn't want to take the risk, if a parent walked in that door and went "What are you doing?" So I felt pressured to ask, for my own safety.'

Despite these concerns and the emphasis on stated 'female skills', there was widespread belief that men could, in theory, do the job. Nevertheless there was recognition that men wouldn't do the job because of the low pay and poor prospects. 'A man wouldn't work for our money,' one classroom assistant said; 'there is no room for promotion or advancement so they are not going to get any further in the role. The money's bad [and] there would be no overtime for them,' said another. A typical point made by classroom assistants was that 'the salary is obviously going to put men off ... it's not something that you could support a family on'. In this instance the same respondent also recalled that a man had until recently been working as a classroom assistant in her school but had left for a better paying job: 'the chap that we had in really loved it and he loved working with kids. He came to see us the other week and he says he does miss the school but obviously in the job he's in [now] he's making treble what he was making here'. Thus, one head-teacher surmised, the reason why men usually did not apply for the job was because the job provided only a 'second salary ... It's not keeping a household going because they do not get paid enough ... it's not full-time, it's just term-time, it is pro-rata ... and I think most men ... don't see it as viable to be honest'.

Whilst a close association was made by all the women between being a classroom assistant and having perceived natural female skills, such associations should not mask the upskilling occurring within the job. The role had stretched upwards beyond routine tasks into more direct involvement with pupils' learning more normally associated with trained and accredited skills.

The emergent role stretch

It was clear from the research that classroom assistants were undertaking routine, non-teaching work intended to free 'teachers' time to teach' (SOEID, 1999, p. 1). Ninety-two percent of classroom assistants surveyed at least sometimes helped teachers with photocopying; 80 percent provided general administrative support to their schools by, for example, doing filing and typing; 84 percent always or frequently supervised pupils outwith lesson times.

The 1998 governmental Classroom Assistants Working Group never-theless assumed that classroom assistants would work 'at a range of levels' and subsequent policy documents signalled a number of duties for classroom assistants (SOEID, 1999; Scottish Executive, 2001; General Teaching Council Scotland, 2003),[6] with the formal guidelines outlining four such duties:

- The organisation and use of resources
- The care and welfare of pupils
- Contributing to learning and teaching in the classroom
- Attending to pupils' accessing of the curriculum

However, much of the policy prescription from central government, which was to be operationalised by local authorities as the employers, lacked clarity. The first two of the four duties involved 'more basic' tasks that could be undertaken with 'straightforward' guidance from teachers and neatly con-formed to classroom assistants undertaking routine tasks and not teaching. The latter two duties were recognised by the government to involve 'more complex' tasks (SOEID, 1999: Annex B). However the phrasing created ambi-guity about how classroom assistants might practically support pupil learn-ing and this ambiguity created the opportunity for role stretch.

Even at the outset classroom assistants were uncertain about their role: 'it was all new to them to define what they were and weren't supposed to do,' said one. Moreover, some teachers were uncomfortable having another member of staff in the classroom who had teaching related duties. The lack of planning and historical perceptions about what one head-teacher described as the 'hired help' compounded this uncertainty. Classroom assistants agreed, noting how there were tensions arising from mixed and uncertain expect-ations on the part of teachers and themselves, with one suggesting that 'there are some teachers who are willing to have you inside and let you do things and use your initiative whereas sometimes ... you just go in and you are given something to do and that's it'.

Compounding the lack of clarity, newly qualified teachers lacked training in how to work with classroom assistants. One B.Ed student reported that he 'had to ask my classroom assistant at my placement, "What do I do with you?" and she laughed. She's like, "Well, what do you want me to do?" I say, "Well, what can you do? What are you allowed to do for me?"'

After the initial adjustment problems, the role has become more planned, with more responsibility and more participation for classroom assistants in pupils' learning. For example, a head-teacher recognised how:

... three years ago, we didn't set aside planning ... they just came in and the teacher would say, 'Just now could you manage to do that for me?' ...

it wouldn't be planned, they wouldn't have any idea – they would go into the classroom and not know what they were going to do. There were some teachers who I would say saw them as 'Could you clean the paint pots out?' That doesn't happen [now] ... They are there really to support the learning of the children and the children come first. So I think it has changed since we initially started, very much so.

Consequently one deputy head said there was 'a better quality of teaching and interaction with the children within a class setting'. All teaching staff agreed that classroom assistants were now highly valued and a more comfortable relationship had emerged in the classroom. Parents too recognised the importance of classroom assistants and were very supportive of them; as one stated: 'I don't really see how a classroom can run without them.'

As this bedding-in occurred, the role of classroom assistant however changed from one of providing general support to one of working with children. In the survey, nearly 70 percent of classroom assistants and 76 percent of teachers believed that the role of supporting pupil learning had increased. Over 50 percent of classroom assistants and 60 percent of teachers reported an increase in the support given by classroom assistants to pupils in classroom activities. Teachers were clear that they were accountable for what happened in their classrooms and that the assistants worked under their direction: supporting, not being, a teacher. This work was normally phrased as 'extension' or 'consolidation' work. Some of this work, though supportive, was considered contextual to learning, for example the organisation of resources as directed by the teacher.

However, some work was intrinsic to learning, for example, literacy development, with teachers reporting that classroom assistants were hearing children's reading, and teaching simple phonics and language skills. Undertaking such work aligns with the more complex tasks outlined by the government. However classroom assistants were not only acquiring a more active role in pupils' learning, this role was commensurate with the requirement for skills and knowledge strongly associated with formal teacher training.

In some cases, therefore, classroom assistants were doing tasks normally seen as being exclusive to trained teachers and becoming proto-educators. As a consequence, in some instances, the boundary was blurring between supporting and doing teaching. The implication was noted by one head-teacher:

... we've caught out teachers who have given a reading group to a classroom assistant and have never seen the children and very discretely our classroom assistants have said 'You know that you [the head-teacher] said that we've not to ...?' and so in a round about way we've questioned the teacher and discovered that she's not taken the class and it might have happened for three weeks. And you know, teachers are doing themselves out of a job …

Of course, despite the blurring of their occupational boundaries, a major difference between these teachers and their classroom assistants was the level of pay of each occupation. Indeed, the pay for the job was perceived to be a real problem for classroom assistants.

The sticky floor

Whether undertaking basic or complex tasks, classroom assistant pay is low. In Scotland, classroom assistants are paid according to local government pay scales and, despite the absence of any job evaluation, the job was initially allocated to the lowest clerical grade. At the time of the research, hourly pay rates in a number of Scottish local authorities varied from £5.14–£7.80. The adult UK National Minimum Wage was £4.85 per hour and the Low Pay Threshold (the commonly accepted benchmark for low pay) was around £6.40.[7]

In the survey, the low pay was cited by most classroom assistants (64 percent) as what they least liked about the job: 'Do you know we were the lowest paid workers – it's a shocker!' said one. Moreover, classroom assistants complained about the increase in the volume of their work not being matched by increased pay and also the lack of paid overtime for their required liaising with teachers after classes to discuss, for example, the assessment of pupils. The upward role stretch of some classroom assistants, therefore, was not reflected in the receipt of any higher pay.

It was not uncommon for the classroom assistants to compare their pay with other workers, as one put it: 'I've got a friend who does three nights a week in Asda and she makes double what we make … you don't need qualifications to do this job, but you do have a lot of responsibilities.'. 'It is only 40 pence difference between [the] cleaning job in here and the [classroom assistant] job,' said another classroom assistant. Such comparisons were also made by a number of the head-teachers and teachers, with one head-teacher noting how 'none of them are in it for the money, because were they in it for the money they would be working in a call centre'. There was general consensus that classroom assistants should be paid more. Over half of the teachers surveyed suggested that the comparator group should be nursery nurses. However nursery nurses – also involved in child development and learning, and requiring the 'skills' of communication, empathy and patience with children – received £17,000–£20,000 per year or the equivalent of £9.58–£11.08 per hour at the time of the research (Findlay et al., 2005). One head-teacher said, 'I would certainly put them up with a nursery nurse because they do the planning with the teacher, they do the assessment even if it is a minor part and they certainly have an understanding of the learning process.'

That said, some teachers and parents did suggest that low pay was a trade-off for other attractive terms and conditions, with the hours and holidays for example being viewed as beneficial. One teacher suggested that 'they are having school hours and school holidays and they accept the lower wages because the hours suit them and they are not having to pay for childcare over the holidays'. Similarly a parent suggested that 'If I had a job nine to three and got £13,000 and all those holidays I would be delighted.' Indeed, this trade-off was also acknowledged by a number of classroom assistants as one that they were prepared to make and which compensated for the low pay, 'you are working when they [the children] are at school ... and you have the school holidays,' one explained. The outcome was that classroom assistants did not have to worry about the cost of childcare – an issue of some importance to low wage workers in a country with limited subsidised or state provided childcare (Grimshaw *et al.*, 2008; Mason *et al.*, 2008). Indeed, the evidence strongly indicated the job of a classroom assistant was one deemed attractive by potential applicants for this reason. For example, one school which had recently advertised a classroom assistant post had received over 300 applications, a response described as 'incredible' and 'unbelievable' by the head-teacher. Another school claimed to receive around 70 applicants for each classroom post advertised. Whilst satisfied with her work as a classroom assistant, one lamented this recruitment and its consequences: 'because we are mums ... they hook you on the line and pull you in,' she said poignantly.

The nature and consequences of this 'women's work'

Emerging from the need to relieve teachers from routine work, classroom assistants' jobs display the key features of what Goos and Manning (2007) describe as lousy jobs – low pay and low skill. Such an ascription however, masks a number of issues.

The job of classroom assistants emerged as a new occupation in response to a perceived need to free teachers' time to teach and quickly expanded. Contrary to Brygren and Kumlin (2005)'s findings that such expansion tends to feature atypical recruitment, the introduction and expansion of classroom assistants has been met, stereotypically, by women. More specifically it is an occupation carried out by a particular subset of women: mothers with young dependent children. Although available to men, few enter the occupation. Whilst there was some evidence to support Kmec's (2005) claim of male self-exclusion, the research reveals that the female respondents, whether parents or staff, raised concerns about men's perceived suitability for the role (see also Bolton, 2007).

All of the female respondents perceived similarities between the role of classroom assistants and mothers. Whilst nominally low skill and certainly not requiring formal qualifications, the work of classroom assistants is not unskilled. Instead the work requires what respondents described as natural 'female skills'. Witz and Wilson (1982) long ago noted that with services, women tend to cluster in jobs that seemingly replicate their unpaid domestic duties. Because of this association, these 'skills' are socially undervalued and so attract low pay (England, 2005; Grimshaw and Rubery, 2007; Bolton, 2007). Witz and Wilson also noted how employers can make further cost savings because they are able to utilise these women's already acquired skills by not having to provide training. This outcome is compounded by Guy and Newman's (2004) suggestion that emotional work – increasingly displaced to classroom assistants by the teaching professionalisation project (Bolton, 2007) – is often hidden in informal processes. The resulting low pay was recognised as such by all of the respondents and was certainly the least liked aspect of the job by classroom assistants.

This situation is exacerbated as the job has evolved and expanded as some classroom assistants become proto-educators, undertaking more complex duties requiring 'technical skills' related to pupil learning and associated with trained teachers. With ambiguous wording in the original policy guidelines, this role stretch lacks formal recognition and reward, even if it is a chalk-face reality noted by all of the respondents. The outcome is an effort-reward disjuncture, as classroom assistants fail to attract adequate payment for both basic and more complex duties.[8] The lack of adequate pay as the job expands and evolves creates a sticky floor that is recognised by classroom assistants. Moreover the upward role stretch has possible problematic ramifications for teachers. An occupation intended to provide professional support has the potential for displacing teachers; as one head-teacher noted, classroom assistants undertaking the more complex duties in this manner dilutes rather than reinforces teachers' jobs.

Given the lack of recognition and reward a question arises as to why these women are attracted to and remain in this job. One explanation might lie in a twist of habituation theory (Clark, 1999). The female classroom assistants regarded their jobs as an extension of unpaid mothering and/or unpaid volunteer work in the classroom. As such they did not see any effort-reward disjuncture because they were now being paid to do tasks that they undertook in the home anyway or had previously undertaken for no financial reward. This explanation however is unlikely as the classroom assistants *did* feel underpaid. It should also be noted that the classroom assistants and teachers self-defined comparator occupation, Scottish nursery nurses, had recently ended a very high profile and long strike over underpayment (Unison, 2003; BBC News, 2004).

Although similarly concerned about low pay, classroom assistants have not taken similar industrial action. From what the classroom assistants say, it is not the money that attracts them to the job but working with children. Recognition, therefore must go to some kind of 'psychic income' even if slightly different from England and Folbre's (2003: 73) 'appreciation of the care recipient'. In this respect is does appear that working with children is akin to the organised emotional care explored by Lopez (2006) in which care workers gained satisfaction from emotion work – a point also noted by Bolton (2007) for both teachers and learning support assistants[9] in England. Certainly it was very apparent that classroom assistants gained job satisfaction from working with pupils. Thus, despite Budig and England's (2001) rejection of the thesis, it does appear that compensating differentials (see Grimshaw and Rubery, 2007) exist for classroom assistants, with intrinsic job satisfaction at least partially recompensing for low pay. It has been suggested by Folbre (2001) that such intrinsic factors make workers such as classroom assistants 'prisoners of love', disinclined to protest and use industrial action to remove themselves from the sticky floor since any such protest would only hurt the pupils. (Though of course the nursery nurses' dispute would challenge this claim or at least require some further inquiry.)

What might be an uncomfortable explanation – that some women have a preference for part-time work with children despite some of its lousy job features because it fits with their chosen family lifestyles (see Hakim, 2000) – has, nevertheless, to be qualified by recognition that such choices are made within constraints. As Gash (2008) notes in a riposte to advocates of preference theory, compared to some other European countries, the UK, of which Scotland is part, has inadequate childcare arrangements (whether publicly or privately-provided), thus 'limit[ing] worker-carers' labour force participation' (p. 669). As the case of classroom assistants highlights, many women with young children work in jobs involving other people's young children because such jobs offer convenient working patterns that suit their own childcare needs. To reconfigure and so better conceptualise Folbre's (2001) terminology, such workers are thus not only 'slaves to love' – willingly working for low pay *because of liking children* – but also 'prisoners of love' – contingently locked into particular, often lousy, job types *because of having children* for whom they are the prime carers. Thus far from being entirely a matter of preference, institutional arrangements and normative pressures for women play their part in constraining women's choices (see also England, 2005; Grimshaw and Rubery, 2007).

Conclusion

Despite government proclamations of shifts towards an economy of what Goos and Manning (2007) term lovely jobs that are high wage and high skill, labour market data indicates a polarisation of lovely and lousy jobs in the UK economy. Moreover, awareness is increasing that the divide between these jobs can be overstated. Developments within existing occupations that might be termed 'lovely' – the professions most obviously – are creating a layer of new, intentionally supportive, occupations intended to relieve these professions of the more routine, lousy tasks said to be disabling the professions from their mission to heal, to counsel, to teach for example.

This chapter has examined one of these new support occupations – classroom assistants. It has revealed how, despite an original intention to relieve teachers of routine non-teaching tasks, an upward role stretch has occurred *into the residual work* of teaching professions. It has also highlighted how the overwhelming majority of classroom assistants are women and are low paid.

In this respect, the case of Scottish classroom assistants highlights how the nature of women's work, even in a new occupation, continues to be under appreciated in terms of both skill recognition and financial reward and so remains a lousy job by current accounts (Goos and Manning, 2007). A number of factors contribute to this situation. Societal norms and institutional arrangements constrain the choices of these workers so that the job is typically undertaken by mothers. The association of the work of the job with mothering and female skills results in a gendered undervaluing of their skills. The situation is maintained in part because these women derive job satisfaction and achievement from working with children. The example of the nursery nurses' strike indicates that there may be limits to the compensatory effect of working with children balanced against low pay. During the EOC investigation underpinning our research, the trade unions stepped up an organising campaign to stimulate activism amongst classroom assistants. Despite assumptions that clear demarcations exist between established occupations (in this case teaching) and new, supportive occupations, the case of classroom assistants reveals how the roles of certain support occupations are still evolving and in some instances expanding. As a consequence, it is likely that there will be pressure to improve these occupations' terms and conditions of employment. The new occupations therefore might present old problems around skill, pay and demarcation and which will challenge the current reward-effort bargain.

Acknowledgments

The authors gratefully acknowledge the research assistance provided by Kirsty Wallace, and Laura Hutchinson and Muriel Robison of the former EOC (Scotland) for permission to publish the empirical material included in this chapter.

Notes

1 Now part of the UK Equality and Human Rights Commission.
2 The PDA is a further education course providing classroom assistant training and generally perceived to be equivalent to SVQ level 2, with SVQs being similar to NVQs.
3 Bachelor of Education, a teacher-training degree in Scotland.
4 There are no precise figures for the ratio of female to male classroom assistants in Scotland (Schlapp et al., 2001).
5 Loosely equivalent to English 'O' Levels.
6 Until 1999, the Westminster-supported Scottish Office had administrative authority over Scottish education. From 1999 and the establishment of the Scottish Parliament, this authority was devolved to the Scottish Executive based in Edinburgh and the government in all but name (though since 2007 locally if not legally termed the 'Scottish Government').
7 The definition of the Low Pay Threshold varies and can be political (see Howarth and Kenway, 2004). Based on 60 percent of full-time median earnings, the UK figure would be £6.46 per hour for 2005; at two-thirds of the median hourly wage of all employees, £6.37 per hour. Figures calculated from ASHE data: https://www.nomisweb.co.uk/Default.asp.
8 Subsequent national surveys by the research team of classroom assistants, teachers and head-teachers in primary, secondary and special schools, and based on the findings of the pilot, confirmed that 57–67 percent of classroom assistants assess pupil learning, at least 26 percent set learning tasks and 10–13 percent plan the curriculum – the latter two certainly teachers' tasks (see EOC, 2007).
9 Encompassed by classroom assistants in Scotland.

REFERENCES

BBC News (2004) 'Nursery nurses in all-out action', 1 March, www.news.bbc.co.uk/go/pr/fr/-/1/hi/scotland/3496192.stm.

Bolton, S. (2007) 'Emotion work as human connection: Gendered emotion codes in teaching primary children with emotional and behavioural difficulties', in P. Lewis and R. Simpson (eds) Gendering Emotion in Organizations, London: Palgrave.

Bolton, S. and Muzio, D. (2008) 'The paradoxical processes of feminization in the professions: the case of established, aspiring and semi-professions', Work, Employment and Society, 22: 2, 281–300.

Brygren, M. and Kumlin, J. (2005) 'Mechanisms of Organisational Sex Segregation', Work and Occupations, 32: 1, 39–65.

Budig, M. J. and England, P. (2001) 'The wage penalty for motherhood', American Sociological Review, 66: 2, 204–25.

Clark, A. E. (1999) 'Are wages habit forming? Evidence from micro data', Journal of Economic Behaviour & Organisation, 39: 2, 179–200.

Dent, M. (2008) Medicine, Nursing and Changing Professional Jurisdictions in the UK, in D. Muzio, A. Ackroyd and J. F. Chanlat (eds) Redirections in the Study of Expert Labour, Basingstoke: Palgrave.

England, P. (2005) 'Emerging theories of care work', Annual Review of Sociology, 31: 381–99.

England, P. and Folbre, N. (2003) 'Contracting for care', in M. A. Ferber and J. A. Nelson (eds) Feminist Economics Today, Chicago: University of Chicago Press.

Equal Opportunities Scotland (2007) Valuable Assets: A General Formal Investigation into the Role and Status of Classroom Assistants in Scottish Schools, Glasgow: EOC.

Felstead, A., Gallie, D., Green, F. and Zhou, Y. (2007) Skills at Work 1986–2006, ESRC Centre for Skills, Knowledge and Organisational Performance, Universities of Oxford and Cardiff.

Findlay, P., Findlay, J. and Stewart, R. (2005) Nursery Nurses in Scotland 2005, Glasgow: Unison.

Florida, R. (2002) The Rise of the Creative Class, New York: Basic Books.

Folbre, N. (2001) The Invisible Heart: Economics and Family Values, New York: New York Press.

Gash, V. (2008) 'Preference or Constraint? Part-time Workers' Transitions in Denmark, France and the United Kingdom', Work, Employment and Society, 22: 655–74.

General Teaching Council Scotland (2003) Classroom Assistants: A GTC Position Paper, GTCS, Edinburgh.

Goos, M. and Manning, A. (2007) 'Lovely and lousy jobs: The rising polarisation of work in Britain', Review of Economics and Statistics, 89: 1, 118–33.

Grimshaw, D., Lloyd, C. and Warhurst, C. (2008) 'Low-Wage Work in the United Kingdom: Employment Practices, Institutional Effects and Policy Responses', in C. Lloyd, G. Mason and K. Mayhew (eds) Low-Wage Work in the United Kingdom, New York: Russell Sage Foundation.

▶

▶

Grimshaw, D. and Rubery, J. (2007) *Undervaluing Women's Work*, EOC Working Paper Series No. 53, Manchester: EOC.

Grugulis, I., Warhurst, C. and Keep, E. (2004) 'What's Happening to Skill?', in C. Warhurst, E. Keep and I. Grugulis (eds) *The Skills That Matter*, London: Palgrave.

Guy, M. E. and Newman, M. A. (2004) 'Women's Jobs, Men's Jobs: Sex Segregation and Emotional Labour', *Public Administration Review*, 64: 3, 289–98.

Hakim, C. (2000) *Work-lifestyle Choices in the 21st Century: Preference Theory*, Oxford: Oxford University Press.

Howarth, C. and Kenway, P. (2004) *Why Worry Any More About The Low Paid?*, London: New Policy Institute.

Kmec, J. A. (2005) 'Setting Occupational Sex Segregation in Motion', *Work and Occupations*, 32: 3, 322–54.

Lopez, S. H. (2006) 'Emotional labour and organised emotional care', *Work and Occupations*, 33: 2, 133–60.

Mason, G., Mayhew, K., Osborne, M. and Stevens, P. (2008) 'Low Pay, Labour Market Institutions, and Job Quality in the United Kingdom', in C. Lloyd, G. Mason and K. Mayhew (eds) *Low-Wage Work in the United Kingdom*, New York: Russell Sage Foundation.

Muzio, D. (2004) 'The Professional Project and the Contemporary Re-organization of the Legal Profession in England and Wales', *International Journal of the Legal Profession*, 11: 1–2, 33–50.

Muzio, D. and Ackroyd, S. (2008) 'Change in the Legal Profession: Professional Agency and the Legal Labour Process', in D. Muzio, A. Ackroyd and J. F. Chanlat (eds) *Redirections in the Study of Expert Labour*, Basingstoke: Palgrave.

Puttick, H. (2007) 'Doctors "feel under siege from culture of controls"', *The Herald*, 2 August, 1.

Reich, R. (1993) *The Work of Nations*, London: Simon & Schuster.

Saunders, M., Lewis, P. and Thornhill, A. (2000) *Research Methods for Business Students*, London: Pitman.

Schlapp, U., Wilson, V. and Davidson, J. (2001) *An Extra Pair of Hands? Evaluation of the Classroom Assistant Initiative: An Interim Report*, Edinburgh: Scottish Centre for Education Research.

Scottish Centre for Employment Research (SCER) (2005) Classroom Assistants in Scotland: A Pilot Study for the Equal Opportunities Commission (Scotland)', SCER Research Report 8, University of Strathclyde, Glasgow.

Scottish Executive (2001) *A Teaching Profession for the 21st Century*, Scottish Executive: Edinburgh.

SOEID (1999) *Classroom Assistants Implementation Guidance*, http://www.scotland.gov.uk/library/documents-w10/cag-00.htm, appendix B.

Unison (2003) Nursery nurse dispute briefing, 23 September, www.unison-scotland.org.uk/breifings/nurserynurse.html.

Warhurst, C., Thompson, P. and Nickson, D. (2009) 'Labour Process Theory: Putting the Materialism back into the Meaning of Services', in M. Korczynski and C. MacDonald (eds) *Service Work: Critical Perspectives*, London: Routledge.

▶

▶

Wilson, V., Schlapp, U. and Davidson, J. (2002) *Classroom Assistants: Key Issues from the National Evaluation*, Insight: Edinburgh.

Witz, A. and Wilson, F. (1982) 'Women's work in service industries', *Service Industries Review*, 2: 2, 40–55.

Vocabularies of Skill: The Case of Care and Support Workers

12

Anne Junor, Ian Hampson and Kaye Robyn Ogle

I was transferring a lady from a commode chair... across to her bed. And she arrested on me and died. I was holding her, and put her onto the bed and rang the emergency bell straight away. (Gail, Care Assistant)

I think that when somebody's dying, I definitely think that someone should be there to help them ...And when the patient's passed over and the room's left, ...I generally just bless the room and everybody that's on the ward and people that will be coming and going from there. (Kiri, Care Assistant)

These statements were made by Care Assistants, interviewed in New Zealand in 2006. There, as elsewhere, such staff, working in hospital wards and care homes, are low-paid, earning the equivalent of four and a half to seven UK pounds per hour. The quotations suggest why aspects of Care Assistants' work may be overlooked and its skills undervalued. Care Assistants do 'abject' (Kristeva, 1982) and 'dirty' (Bolton, 2005b) work for us, dealing with reminders of our mortality and frailty, and preventing disruptions to our busy time-frames. Physically or emotionally unpalatable work may be 'technicised' or avoided by medical and nursing staff, and at the caregiver level turned into the step-by-step technical competencies of 'personal hygiene assistance'. But this renders invisible the skills needed to integrate the physical and pyschosocial aspects of caregiving:

Care involves a constant tension between ... seeking to preserve an older person's dignity and exerting unaccustomed authority, overcoming resistance to care and fulfilling extravagant demands, reviving a relationship and transforming it (Abel, 1990, cited in Wellin, 2007, p. 1).

Nor do we yet have adequate names for the coordinating skills required to mesh the rhythms of caregiving into the time-frames of market-regulated bureaucratic hospitals and care homes (Davies, 1990).

This chapter looks at some of the skills needed to do care and support work, in hospital and community settings, working with vulnerable adults, very sick people, and frail elders. On the basis of pay levels and technical skills required by employers, much personal care work is seen as relatively low-skilled, whilst 'allied' health support roles occupy an intermediate skill category. Our central argument is that, regardless of the technical skills required to provide quality care and support, there is a range of social and coordinating skills still awaiting full codification (Bolton, 2004). It matters, both for workers and for the quality of care and support, that these skills be recognised.

We illustrate this argument by examining the social and organisational skills required in eight care and support jobs. These positions were amongst a much wider set of public sector jobs that we analysed in order to develop a taxonomy for naming the underrecognised social and organisational skills in any job. In the first half of the chapter, we describe this research and outline some key aspects of the eight care and support roles in question. In the second half of the chapter, we use the taxonomy to draw out some under-recognised skills in the eight jobs, focusing particularly on the work of low-paid Care Assistants. We analyse how the skills of Care Assistant work are described in a typical job advertisement, indicating how the advertisement underspecifies the range and level of social and organisational skills required, and extending this analysis to the other jobs we studied. Echoing the theme of this volume, we give voice to the experiences of care and support workers, showing how their skills contribute to the social life of the workplace – a workplace that coincides with the social world of some care recipients.

The research

The chapter is informed by interviews conducted in 2006 as part of a wider-ranging skills analysis project, funded by the Pay and Employment Equity Unit of the New Zealand Department of Labour. The views in this chapter are, however, our own. The authors are part of a team who in 2006 conducted 57 interviews in the public administration, health and education sectors. We developed from the results a tool designed to 'shine a spotlight' on unrecognised skills. Interview participants talked in an open-ended way about their work, and also completed a structured job analysis questionnaire designed to pinpoint unrecognised skills. We derived the questionnaire from a literature review in the fields of skill analysis and job evaluation (e.g. Spenner, 1995), studies of emotion work (Strauss *et al.*, 1985; Bolton, 2005b), articulation or coordination work (Strauss, 1993; Suchman, 2000); and debates about skill within labour process theory (e.g. Warhurst, Grugulis and Keep, 2004). The interviews were one-on-one and lasted up to two hours.

Some were conducted in workplaces, allowing observation of the visible context of the work process. Using NVivo software, we coded interview transcripts and cross-referenced them to 94 position descriptions. We also coded transcripts of four half-day meetings with our New Zealand reference group, whose members included training and job evaluation experts, service user advocacy groups and unions. The sets of skilled activities thus distilled were then cross-referenced to literature on workplace learning (Brown and Duguid, 1991; Engstrom, 2001; Boreham *et al.*, 2002). The outcome was a taxonomy for describing key underspecified skills at a range of levels (New Zealand Department of Labour, 2008).

Here we apply the taxonomy to care and support work skills, going back to transcripts of interviews with eight of the interview participants, working as health and rehabilitation staff employed or funded by a New Zealand regional District Health Board (DHB).

The Australian and New Zealand team members who conducted and analysed the interviews brought three different experiential perspectives to the task, either as givers or recipients of care and support services. One had intensively researched her own experiences as an intensive care nurse. A second was receiving regular inpatient treatment for a chronic condition. A third had interacted with care staff over a period of seven years, first as a family carer and then spending up to 20 hours a week visiting parents in a dementia unit and a succession of residential care homes and acute geriatric hospital wards. As Bolton and Houlihan (2005, pp. 690–1) have argued, naturalistic accounts of everyday experience such as these are traditional sources of insight in sociological research. Bolton (2008) has effectively illustrated the methodology in a study based on observations made as a hospital in-patient.

The background

The paid workforce in the New Zealand health and disability sector is divided, on the basis of training and qualifications, into a regulated and a non-regulated sector. In 2008, the regulated sector included doctors, 44,500 Registered Nurses with degree-level qualifications, 3,500 Enrolled Nurses with certificate-level credentials and 160 Nurse Assistants (a classification replacing Enrolled Nurse), as well as six 'allied' health occupations, such as 2,000 Medical Radiation Technologists. The non-regulated sector, where qualifications range from nil to postgraduate, has a paid workforce of 65,000, of whom about 30,000 work in residential care homes (Ministry of Health, 2007; New Zealand Nurses Organisation, 2008; Service and Food Workers Union, 2007).

Care and support services in the non-regulated sector include inpatient and outpatient care and rehabilitation; residential, community and home based assessment and assistance; and mental health and disability support (DHB Non-Regulated Workforce Strategy Group, 2005). Five of the eight workers in this chapter were in non-regulated public sector jobs. As we did not interview in care homes, which in New Zealand are outside the public sector, we draw on the Australian participant observation, described above, backed by secondary surveys of care home workers (Richardson and Martin, 2004; Moskos and Martin, 2005; Healy and Moskos, 2005).

In New Zealand, as in Australia, 'ageing-in-place' policies have meant that patients and residents entering care facilities are increasingly dependent on care. As a result, staff are increasingly required to have formal qualifications, typically at a level between that of a school leaver and a skilled tradesperson. Employers are thought to look for personal qualities such as empathy, and for basic 'employability 'or 'personal development' skills, and to be willing to support training in occupational safety and health, medication awareness, behaviour management, and the literacy skills required to do increasing amounts of paperwork (Booth *et al.*, 2005, pp. 5–6).

The argument

Skills hierarchies in health and disability work are based mainly on technical knowledge and qualifications. But in care and support work, other high-level skills are required:

> ...providing instrumental/bodily care, with knowledge and skill, is a necessary but not sufficient criterion for excellence in working with the chronically ill, of whatever age. Instead, ...we see greater demand for collaborative, person-centered, holistic treatment – a social model – throughout the health care system (Wellin, 2007, p. 46).

Our research has indicated that the skills required by this 'social' model include interactive or emotion management skills, cognitive skills of shaping awareness, skills used to shape long-term support relationships, and coordinating skills. These skills appear to be underspecified in qualifications and job descriptions. Firstly, they need to be recognised as skills, not as 'natural' attributes, and secondly there is a need to recognise how they develop to higher levels in the workplace, through a progressively deepening capacity for reflective problem-solving in shared activities.

The research has led us to challenge *a priori* definitions of social and organisational skills as 'soft', unspecialised or low-level. Formal qualifications are only one aspect of skill recognition. All skills – technical, social and organisational – are applied and honed in the context of work practice. The further in-service development of technical skills is well-recognised in parts of the health sector, and basic standards of social and organisational skills are being defined through generic competencies. But in the case of social and organisational skills, there are at present no mechanisms for recognising how they continue to develop in the workplace, and are used to bring both technical skills and core competencies to life. This is particularly the case in jobs requiring few technical qualifications. On investigation, some jobs requiring low levels of technical knowledge may turn out to require quite high levels of social or organisational competence (Bolton, 2004).

Skills are political constructs in the sense that they must be claimed, identified and valued before they are accepted as skills (Steinberg, 1990; National Research Council 2008, pp. 37–43). Nevertheless, skill claims must have a real foundation. It is early days in the use of our taxonomy to high-light underrecognised skills, but in this chapter we set out to illustrate the use of such skills in low-paid and middle-range jobs.

The way in which the skills of 'assistance' and 'support' are defined has an influence on the way the work processes are carried out. For example if Care Assistants are defined as providing 'clinical support', they are likely to be seen as subordinates providing services to more expert staff such as Nurses. If care recipients are defined as 'patients', they are likely to be seen as passive recipients of technical/clinical intervention, notwithstanding the active role they often play (Strauss *et al.*, 1985). If they are called 'clients' they may be seen to be the grateful dependents of experts. If they are seen as 'customers' they may be seen as purchasers of services, although, as Bolton and Houlihan (2005) have argued, humanity and moral agency can be key elements in the customer/provider relationship. Paid caregiving involves managing the contradictions of freely given emotion (Bolton, 2005a) within hierarchical and commodified or market-rationalised work processes (Diamond, 1992). Care and support may involve coercive giving, if the service is unwanted or has custodial elements. Daily support of people reacting to enforced dependence in catastrophic ways may for these reasons require subtle relationship skills, with a profound ethical dimension.

The work roles

All eight roles studied in this chapter had either care or support aspects, and required varying levels of technical knowledge. We focus most heavily on jobs seen as requiring the lowest level of technical skill – Hospital Care Assistants. Gail and Kiri worked in aged care, in medical and rehabilitation wards respectively. Sandra had moved from Care Assistant to the more specialised but less well paid role of Occupational Therapy Assistant, working in hospital and community settings with people aged 17 to 65 who had physical disabilities and mental health issues. She oversaw rehabilitation exercise sessions and visited clients' homes, customising mechanical and electronic aids and providing training in their use.

Ngaire was classed as an Enrolled Nurse, although since 2000, new entrants to this job have been called Nursing Assistants. Their certificate-level qualification has a greater technical component than that of Care Assistants, but is below that of Registered Nurses. Working in a hospital, Ngaire contributed to rehabilitation and assessed elderly patients' post-discharge support needs. Although using physical and psycho-geriatric assessment tools, she saw her role primarily as the interpersonal one of 'teaching' people to regain functionality. Sarah was a community-based psychogeriatric nurse, working with elderly people who had a combination of chronic physical illness or disability and mental illness.

Three allied health workers were in middle-level technical occu-pations whose status is still evolving. Fran, a hospital Pharmacy Tech-nician dispensed and monitored the medication of HIV positive outpatients. Jackie, an Anaesthetic Technician had responsibility for the safe man-agement of theatre equipment and teams, sometimes in emergency situations. Carmel, a Medical Radiation Technologist, led a team working in medical imaging, and part of her work had forensic aspects:

> We often do cases here for any Coroner's things, any murders, shot-guns, suicides, children who have possible non-accidental injuries, ... anywhere the police are involved and we have to x-ray the bodies ... There are cases where the mother is holding onto the baby and they arrive. Yes, you do feel – but you explain to them that we do have to do what we have to do and yes, just talk to them ... You try not to think of it too much as being a child or anything like that. It's you've got your job to do and you have to switch off for a bit ... [That's] ano-ther thing that people have no idea that we do (Carmel, radiography technician).

The issues

In both New Zealand and Australia, experienced Care Assistants earn very little more after ten years than on entry (Healy and Moskos, 2005, pp. 13–14). A large Australian survey of care home staff in 2003 suggested that, whilst many valued the intrinsic rewards and autonomy of the work and most felt highly skilled, 61 percent were dissatisfied or very dissatisfied with their pay. Turnover rates were high, with a quarter of staff having been in the job for less than a year (Richardson and Martin, 2004, pp. 28, 40, 58). A typical comment was:

> ... Twenty years' experience, six years of study and I could earn more as a barmaid ... with a lot less stress involved (cited in Richardson and Martin, 2004, pp. 26–7).

In similar vein, a member of our New Zealand reference group spoke of a looming recruitment and retention crisis in the health and disability sector, and a growing pay gap between the public and community/private sectors. The Government had responded in its 2007 budget by allocating 14 million UK pounds to help raise hourly rates for Care Assistants to a minimal 4.60 UK pounds and to support a restoration of collective bargaining in the sector (Service and Food Workers Union, 2007). A new career framework was under discussion, designed to bring Care Assistants into the regulated sector, by assimilating their role to that of Nursing Assistant and providing the possibility of progression through formal qualifications to registered nursing grades (Ministry of Health and DHBNZ Workforce Group, 2007).

Despite its benefits, this proposal focused not on recognising care skills, but purely on redefining the role in terms of technical support for Nurses, with the option of building on these skills to become a nurse. A reference group member affirmed, however, that it was also important to do what our research was attempting to foster:

> ...being honest about what kind of work is involved ... and just how involved and difficult it is (Reference Group member, 2006).

In New Zealand, the push to regulate Care Assistant qualifications is resulting in pressure for experienced staff to gain at least certificate level accreditation. Gail, one of the interview participants, was complying but felt that the formal training was based on an under-estimation of the technical competence of the job, as well as undervaluing its social and organisational skills, thereby reinforcing its low status:

> Just recently we've been asked to complete our educational books, which I don't think a lot of Care Assistants were doing ... You get a pay rise when you do your books ... But there's no incentive. Some of those questions are absolutely insulting ... silly things like cleaning a set of dentures for a patient ... It's just putting us down even more. It makes you feel like you are the underdog (Gail, Care Assistant).

On the other hand, Kiri welcomed the opportunity to update workplace knowledge through training in recent developments such as the use of 'slippery sheets' in lifting, and there was general enthusiasm for the skills gained in team meetings:

> On a Thursday we have a multidisciplinary team meeting and it takes up the whole morning. We discuss every client on the ward. That has been huge for my learning as well, hearing input from the whole team how to manage these people (Sarah, Community Psychiatric Nurse).

Thus the building of interactional skills was seen as an aid to managing patients and clients. Enrolled Nurse Ngaire, for example, commented that the accuracy of pre-discharge assessments increased if she was able to engage in genuine conversation with patients: 'They're more at ease to tell me about their problems and pains'. Aside from such instrumental uses, however, relationship-building is fundamental in caregiving, in its own right, as an aspect of the humanity and moral agency of the work (Bolton, 2008). Sarah expressed this view:

> I love talking to elderly people and hearing their stories: they just delight so much. And having someone to listen to them talk about things that happened years ago, yes (Sarah, Psychogeriatric Nurse).

Bolton (2005a) has identified the 'gift' aspect of emotion work. In care work, it is a key element of quality. But if it is to be more than a gift to the employer, provided by people with the right 'attitude' or personality, its skill elements need to be identified. It is a skill to sit and listen to reminiscences, in a focused and non-condescending way, with an ability to learn from what elderly clients have to tell (Moskos and Martin, 2005, pp. 10–12). The skill of trained and reflective attention lies in its use of memory and narrative to support identity. It certainly matters that this social skill, and the organisational capacity to fit it into a work schedule, be defined and valued in jobs located at various levels of the technical hierarchy in the health and disability sector. In the next section, we suggest that even when employers recognise the need for social and organisational skills, they are hampered by lack of a vocabulary for specifying the higher-level skills that explain quality care.

Why caregiving skills are hidden

This chapter opened with examples suggesting that some caregiving skills are hidden because they are deployed 'behind screens' (Lawler, 1991), as a result of social and cultural taboos, whilst others are tactfully carried out 'behind the scenes' to preserve care recipients' sense of independence. A third reason is the tacit nature of much awareness-sharing among team members. Kiri's unobtrusive ritual of blessing the bed and room whenever a patient died illustrates a dignified informal leadership skill in freeing the work team to return to normal routines without blunting their humanity.

Some skills are hard to define, because they are what Strauss (1985, 1993) called 'supra' or second-order integrative skills, 'oiling the wheels' of individual and group activity. In carrying out an activity smoothly, it is necessary to have learned to do some things automatically so as to focus on solving problems. For example, solving the problem of manoeuvring a hoist and using it with a frightened patient, requires automatic skill in operating it. At the collective level, 'supra' skills involve fitting together 'discrete and conflicting bits of accomplished work' (Strauss *et al.*, 1985, p. 189). This capability is captured in our taxonomy's coordinating skills. We are now ready to test whether the taxonomy can shed light on underrecognised skills.

Naming and valuing hidden care and support skills

Figure 12.1 is a 'mocked up' advertisement for a Care Assistant, assembling phrases used in a range of actual position descriptions and web-based person specifications. The job in question has two main roles and purposes. The first is to provide unspecified assistance to nurses, in order to ensure high quality care. The second involves general duties, some in 'complex situations', in order to maintain the smooth running of the ward. We shall see that combining these two roles is not easy, and calls for unrecognised higher-order skills.

Care Assistant
You will work closely with nursing staff to provide clinical and non-clinical assistance to patients, ensuring a consistently high quality of care. In addition, responsibilities include general duties to ensure the smooth and efficient functioning of the ward, dealing with routine and complex situations.
You will be:
– Enthusiastic, professional, self motivating, and able to work autonomously
– Strongly committed to providing patient focused care, with a natural empathy towards patients
– A team player with strong organisational and time management skills
– Adaptable, able to multi task and to prioritise your own work in a busy environment
– Tactful and diplomatic
You will:
– Relate well to people from a variety of backgrounds and cultures
– Have a sense of humour
– Make decisions by considering the pros and cons of an approach
Essential
– Excellent communication and interpersonal skills, with good command of English
– Health Care Assistant Certificate or equivalent
Desirable
– Experience working in a hospital or care home environment

Figure 12.1 Typical job advertisement – Care Assistant

The advertisement lists several broadly-defined activities: working closely with nurses; relating to diverse people; and making decisions, described in terms of conscious deliberation ('considering pros and cons'). Contexts include 'complex situations', so these skills will be needed at above entry-level. Knowledge is required at health certificate level, and previous experience is desirable, again suggesting requirements above entry-level. But the listed skills – time management; tact and diplomacy; interpersonal, communication and language; teamwork; and laborious decision-making – are described very generically. Attempts at more specific skill definition rely on personal traits and attitudes, individualising and naturalising the skills ('commitment', 'enthusiasm', 'sense of humour').

The lack of clarity about skills and skill levels in this typical advertisement helps to explain the flat pay structures in care work. The one precise element is the qualification. There does not seem to be a vocabulary for defining the growth of expertise in social and organisational skills beyond base level, so terms like 'good', 'excellent' and 'strong' are used. Further clues to the required skill level are the abilities to work autonomously; to multitask, and to contribute to team-work levels 2, 3 and 4 respectively in our taxonomy (Figure 12.2). So let us test whether the taxonomy can shed light on some of

---

Skill Sets and their Elements
A. Shaping awareness
A1.Sensing contexts or situations: Capacity to see significance of wider contexts or changing situations
A2. Monitoring and guiding reactions: Capacity to monitor your own and others' reactions; and to manage situations where awareness levels vary
A3. Judging impacts: Capacity to evaluate impacts of your or the work group's actions
B. Interacting and relating
B1. Negotiating boundaries: Capacity to set your own boundaries and respect those of others; and to influence or negotiate within and across authority lines
B2. Communicating: Capacity to respond to and use non-verbal and verbal communication adaptively
B3. Connecting across cultures: Capacity to deepen your understanding of diverse cultures and of your own cultural impact, or to build intercultural relations
C. Coordinating
C1. Sequencing and combining your own activities: Capacity to prioritise, switch and refocus attention, and to interlink your own activities
C2. Interweaving activities collectively: Capacity to follow up and follow through
C3. Maintaining or restoring workflow: Capacity to maintain workflow; and to address contingencies, overcome obstacles, or help put things back on track
Skill Levels
1. Familiarisation: Building experience by listening, practice & reflection
2. Automatic fluency: Applying experience automatically
3. Proficient problem-solving: Using automatic proficiency while solving new problems
4. Creative solution sharing: Creating new approaches by exchanging solutions
5. Expert system–shaping: Helping embed expertise in an ongoing work system

Figure 12.2   Taxonomy of under-recognised skills and skill levels

the skills which the framers of this advertisement were seeking. We do this by providing examples of how these skills were used, at different levels, in various caregiving jobs, and showing how terms in the advertisement attempt to describe these skills.

The first group of skills in Figure 12.2 – those of shaping awareness – is barely mentioned in the position description. Yet certainly the skills of sensing contexts and situations were key aspects of work performance. At the most basic level, both Care Assistants were constantly scanning the work environment for risks, without interrupting other tasks. Kiri explained that checking the safety of power points, bathroom fittings and bed rails was '... just something that you don't really pay much attention to. You just automatically do it'. As Gail said,

> You're always watching out behind your back to who's moving around and walking on their own ... So you're not only just doing your own work, you're looking out for anything.

This example of 'multitasking' – the experienced capacity to focus attention intently on a range of things at once – is a skill vital to the safety of frail and confused people, which some interviewees referred to as *vigilance*.

Care Assistants were also using another awareness-focusing skill – the capacity to pick up the significance of small early warning signs of any change in patients' condition. Kiri felt that their closer and more continual association with patients, combined with longer years of experience, meant they were using this skill at a higher level than more clinically trained nurses:

> And I generally can read the signs if somebody's going to die ...And on more than a few occasions ...I've been able to let the Nurse know and they've been able to call the family to get them in. And a lot of the time, new grad nurses don't have any idea of what a patient looks like when they're about to sort of...(Kiri)

This very profound level of awareness was not valued as a skill. It was seen only as incident-reporting. Yet Kiri talked with anger of the lack of awareness skills in a nurse who insisted on carrying out observations on a patient who was in the throes of dying. Care Assistants' awareness-shaping skills are used in the procedure of 'specialling', where they give one-on-one attention to a person who is very sick, confused or aggressive. In such cases, negotiation skills are also required.

Occupational Therapy Assistant Sandra also used situational awareness and negotiating skills, when accompanying therapists in home visits to unpredictable clients. Here too, techniques for de-escalating aggression were based on step-by-step monitoring of the client's reactions, and of the care workers' coping capacity and impact on an unpredictable situation:

> Like now it can be a real volatile situation and I can just stay as calm as anything really... It's just a skill that you learn I think, along the way...You never really know but a lot of the time you do become very tuned in to reading the situation...(Sarah, Psychogeriatric Nurse).

Certainly, such skills are taught in the behavioural management unit of the Certificate course, and it is obvious why care home managers prefer staff to study such units on-the-job. But it is one thing to learn the techniques, and another to put them into practice smoothly in the midst of a work situation. The higher-level capacity of self-monitoring and staying calm whilst 'being very tuned in to reading' a threatening situation is one that Sarah had learned the hard way, over time, after being beaten up by a client. It is a multitasked problem-solving skill.

Jackie, the Anaesthetic Technologist, described a situation where she was called on to use an even higher level of awareness-shaping skills to coordinate fast-moving team work:

> I just have a way of knowing if something's happening in the department, and they hadn't paged me, but I knew – because they paged other people to this particular theatre, that we were going to be doing an emergency Caesarean Section, and it was a placental abruption. So that means that the patient comes up on the trolley and the midwife is ...putting her hand in a place that the baby can't be delivered ...So about two minutes warning. So what did I do? I assisted and coordinated the staff ... The anaesthetist that was on call was actually out of the department and so I organised another anaesthetist to be there. I had absolutely nothing ready like IV fluids or anything out, I just asked a colleague of mine ...to just do this, do this. And then we – together really, got everything in time so that she could go off to sleep straightaway and the baby got delivered within a matter of minutes and ... the outcome was a live baby (Jackie, Anaesthetic Technician).

The tacit awareness-focusing skills illustrated here involved a rapid collective registering of situational cues. Interestingly, Jackie described her role as one of both 'assisting and coordinating'. This is an instance of middle-level technical skills being combined with higher-level coordinating skills. In less dramatic circumstances, Jackie regularly used awareness-focusing skills, following and anticipating each step of a procedure to be able to hand instruments to the anaesthetist before being asked. When asked if this meant that she knew as much as the anaesthetist, she said. 'No! hell, no!' and cited the latter job's ten years of knowledge-based training. Yet the job's awareness-shaping and coordinating skills need to be assessed independently of technical skills.

Next, we unpack the job advertisement's requirements for 'strong' to 'excellent' 'communication' and 'interpersonal' skills, and turn 'enthusiasm' 'empathy' and 'sense of humour' into learned skills and claimable work value. Caregivers, even in medical wards, but more so in other settings, are working in the space where care recipients live. This gives importance to the skills of respecting the boundaries of small private worlds, and enhancing the 'feel' and 'look of the workplace. Just as Bolton and Houlihan (2005) draw attention to the moral agency in customer service, so we argue that 'aesthetic labour' skills go well beyond 'looking good and sounding right' (Warhurst and Nickson, 2007). In the case of Care Assistants, these skills included providing sources of joy in a way that was appropriate and authentic:

> I'm there contributing all the harmony. No, I'm more the fun. No, I like to try and be happy for people ... The one thing I get said [to me], is everybody likes to see my smiling face in the morning. (Kiri).

Fun was neither synthetic nor superficial:

> I have a certain standard with the patients and if that patient wants to talk and have a bit of fun, that's fine, I'll do that because it cheers them up. But if a patient wants to be serious and get on with the job, you know. I read the patient, yes, and staff members (Gail).

Negotiation skills were also required to manage people over whom Care Assistants had no authority. Kiri described the need to manage visitor aggression. Gail outlined the networking skills needed to ensure timely delivery of supplies. Her use of banter was a skilled strategy, not the natural 'sense of humour' of the position description:

> I know how to get things out of people that other people don't know how to get things out of. Like the engineers and getting extra supplies brought down to the wards. You get to know who brings the things and delivers the things to the ward and how to get hold of them fast. You've got to know who's in the know (Gail).

Communication skills involved the capacity to respond to and use non-verbal and verbal communication adaptively. We can turn the concept of 'empathy' into a set of skills by noting the interplay of awareness-focusing and expressive behaviour involved:

> I think you do need to be able to be quite onto interpreting patient's body language, especially if they've had a stroke. If they can't speak, ... it's quite handy to sort of have some idea of how to be ... able to communicate with them, to speak with them and go by their body language. And when you've got something right, that you can understand what they're saying back to you (Kiri).

Judging when to use silence rather than words, when 'someone needs a cuddle', what forms of touch are *tapu*, and how to pace communications so that patients could assimilate information, were not techniques to be learned in a training course, but skills requiring judgment and honed by practice. Kiri described how she and colleagues had learned by trial and error to communicate interactively with a cognitively-delayed woman in her 50s, relying on non-verbal cues:

> If you tried to speak to her ... she got upset ... You had to be able to – I don't know, coax her along to do things in daily life. Like, she had a doll that she was really close to, and everything you did for the patient, you had to do for the doll ... To be able to have a shower, to take her meds, to have her oxygen on, it was sort of you did one for her, you did it for the doll as well (Kiri).

Boundary negotiation is an underrecognised skill of interaction. It includes the ability to say 'no' gracefully. Whilst it was accepted that Care Assistants should decline, for safety reasons, to do things about which they did not feel confident, Gail had to learn by experience where to draw the line, when asked to do things that were within her competence:

> At first ... I just pushed myself ragged and I tried to keep everybody happy and put my own work behind. But now I just say 'No, I'm doing something else, sorry.' ... I don't like doing that.... It's probably a daily thing actually. Having to say no doesn't always go down well (Gail).

Gail had also solved the problem of saying 'no' to patients, when their requests threatened to become too disruptive to her work schedules. She managed to transform 'no' from being experienced as a rejection, to being a way of including patients in her work process, and giving them back some control over the situation, in a way that provided reassurance and gained cooperation:

> If I'm having a really bad day or something terrible has happened, I'll always say to my patients, 'Look, I might not be back for a while because we're having a few problems. But I'll try and keep an eye out for your bell', or 'I ask that you be patient, because there's a really sick lady down the corridor ...' (Gail).

Intercultural skills are mentioned in the job advertisement, and are an element of the taxonomy. However, they require a more extended treatment than can be given here. This is because in NZ such skills are deployed within a bicultural service delivery framework based on negotiated partnership with Māori, as well as within a broader multiracial context. They are rightly the topic of another paper.

Finally, we use concepts of coordinating skills to tease out the capabilities embedded in 'flexibility', 'time management' and 'prioritisation'. For the two Care Assistants, coordination meant meshing together the two halves of the job – assisting nurses and ensuring the smooth running of the work unit. Each Care Assistant interacted with 30 patients, up to six nurses, family members, supply orderlies and the telephone, weaving predictable and unpredictable activities together. The skill lay, less in the sometimes prosaic details of activities, than in the way they were coordinated without undermining the humanity of patients and working relationships with colleagues. Care Assistants were 'on demand from the patients, the staff and their own work':

> You've got to get your work done by a certain time, or else other things can't happen (Gail).

The predictable part of the morning shift began with a hand-over, updating each patient's needs. Then Care Assistants began their rounds of the rooms, waking patients, putting them in a good mood, providing a warm flannel and having them sitting up with a cup of tea by the time the orderlies arrived, then distributing breakfasts, cross-checking them against the dietary requirement list. This round was overlapped or followed by helping some patients with showering, changing and toileting; and bed-making. Next came work in the sluice room to empty the sanitiser and ensure safe bundling of linen, another round of tea, another round in the sluice room, fitting in a ten minute break, and then setting up and distributing lunch.

Into these rounds they fitted a further longer-term schedule of tasks to do 'every second day, when there is time', such as the important work of maintaining supplies, and ordering new stock within budget:

> Yes, that's my day, a mental map of how to get through my day ...what needs to be done first and what can wait till later (Gail).

The mental map was constantly readjusted, as the Care Assistants also paid intermittent attention to admissions, discharges, and internal patient movements, and to interactions with orderlies, volunteers and visitors. Interwoven with these more or less predictable lines of work, there were two unpredictable aspects of the job. One was the constant presence of the call button that could be used at any moment by a patient for needs ranging from toileting to emotional support. The other related to the second aspect of the job defined in the position description – assistance to nurses. Nurses too could at any moment call for help, for example with lifts or two-person sponges. 'Flexibility' does not quite spell out the coordinating skills involved in maintaining one's own lines of work, whilst interweaving them with those of nurses. Nor does 'initiative' quite cover the constant decision-making that was required:

> So you're good at knowing when you can drop something and go and do something else, and come back to what you were doing. And in between anything, a Nurse can call you and you've got to choose whether you go with her and do what she wants, or you say 'No, I can't come' (Gail).

The job advertisement spoke of 'evaluating the pros and cons of alternative solutions'. But the decision-making needed to switch among lines of work involved a more rapid and fluent skill of problem-solving in the midst of activity. The advertised requirement, 'proven ability to work effectively in a team' was a coordination skill involving constant interweaving: 'I have to fit what I'm doing with other people, a lot of the time'. Kiri had acquired the negotiating skills to try and book the Nurses up for a particular time to do the more predictable two-person tasks – a skill of managing up. But many of the Nurses' calls for help were in contingency situations, when prioritising correctly was 'absolutely' important: 'it could mean a life'.

Conclusion

Recognising the skills of care and support workers matters for two sets of reasons. For the workers themselves, there are issues of pay and employment equity, and also of job design. We have noted a widespread grievance, on both sides of the Tasman, about the gap between the value of care work and the way it is perceived and paid. We have traced this gap, not so much to the underspecification of technical skills, as to a failure to recognise social and organisational skills, particularly as these acquire depth and subtlety through experience.

The reason the skills have been hard to 'pin down' is that they are enacted through the improvisation that is needed in caring for often unpredictable people whose routines of daily living need to be maintained in the face of disintegration and loss. One Care Assistant felt that 'no two days are ever the same'; the other felt that routines dominated and needed to be humanised. This is work where managing contingency has been routinised, and as the Anaesthetic Technology example showed, the skill of enacting well-oiled routines underpins an effective response to contingency.

The knowledge assessed in qualifications will become increasingly important as an ongoing element of the work, particularly as it brings together explanatory theory and a sharing of congealed wisdom derived from experiences of effective practice, for example in managing challenging behaviour. But what is still missing is a framework for identifying deepening levels of skill through the experiences in which knowledge is applied. In the case of Care Assistants, we have not made exaggerated claims for these skills, and have demonstrated even higher levels of the skills of situational awareness, negotiation and coordination in the jobs of 'allied' health workers. Nevertheless, we have shown that Care Assistants' higher-level skills are real, and have explained why experienced Care Assistants feel underremunerated.

Within the economically-rationalised health sector, the routines that manage chaos and maintain quality of life lend themselves to the work intensification of an efficiency-driven labour process. Failure to recognise the coordinating skills behind the routines and the awareness-shaping skills that humanise them has meant a misrecognition of the size of the personal care job. Work intensity is not something to be recognised in work value claims, but through the collective negotiation of more reasonable working conditions. Nevertheless, documentation of the hidden dimensions of the job can assist work reorganisation arguments. We have hinted that part of Care Assistants' workload problem lies in their dual role of supporting nurses and maintaining the ward. Ambiguity over their role in multidisciplinary teams results from the devaluation of their social and organisational skills, relative to clinical knowledge. Whilst the opportunity for a career path through the acquisition of clinical skills may be welcomed by some, it does not address the issue of undervaluation of current non-clinical skills.

As Appelbaum has commented, the skill demands of care work jobs can shrink or grow, depending on 'what we want to say about the quality of services' (cited in National Research Council, 2008, p. 40). Recognition of skills involving awareness, relationships, and the maintenance of effective routines, matter profoundly to care recipients and to the peace of mind of their families. These skills are amongst the foundations of quality care.

REFERENCES

Bolton, S. (2004) 'Conceptual Confusions: Emotion Work as Skilled Work', in Warhurst, C., Keep, E. and Grugulis, I. (eds) *The Skills that Matter*, pp. 19–37, London: Palgrave.

Bolton, S. (2005a) *Emotion Management in the Workplace*, Basingstoke: Palgrave Macmillan.

Bolton, S. (2005b) Women's Work, Dirty Work: The Gynaecology Nurse as 'Other', *Gender, Work and Organisation*, 12(2): 169–86.

Bolton, S. (2008) 'Me, Morphine and Humanity: Eight Days on Ward 8', in Fineman, S. (ed.) *The Emotional Organisation: Passions and Power*, 13–26, Oxford: Blackwell.

Bolton, S. and Houlihan, M. (2005) 'The (Mis)representation of Customer Service', *Work, Employment and Society*, 19(4): 685–703.

Booth, R., Roy, S., Jenkins, H. *et al.* (2005) *Workplace Training Practices in the Residential Aged Care Sector*, Adelaide: NCVER.

Boreham, N., Samurçay, R. and Fischer, R. (2002) (eds) *Work Process Knowledge*. London: Routledge.

Brown, J. and Duguid, P. (1991) 'Organisational Learning and Communities of Practice: Towards a Unified View of Working, Learning and Innovation', *Organisation, Science*, 2(1): 40–57.

Davies, K. (1990) *Women, Time and the Weaving of the Strands of Everyday Life*, Aldershot: Avebury.

Diamond, T. (1992) *Making Gray Gold*, Chicago: University of Chicago Press.

District Health Board Non-Regulated Workforce Strategy Group (2005) (homepage) www.moh.govt.nz, date accessed 15 July, 2008.

Engstrom, Y. (2001) 'Expansive Learning at Work: Towards an Activity-Theoretical Reconceptualisation', *Journal of Education and Work*, 14(1): 133–56.

Healy, J. and Moskos, M. (2005) *How Do Aged Care Workers Compare With Other Australian Workers?* Adelaide: National Institute of Labour Studies, Flinders University.

Kristeva, J. (1982) *Powers of Horror: An Essay on Abjection*, transl. L. Roudiez, New York: Columbia University Press.

Lawler, J. (1991) *Behind the Screens: Nursing, Somology and the Problem of the Body*, Melbourne: Churchill Livingstone.

Ministry of Health New Zealand (2007) Health and Independence Report (homepage) http://www.moh.govt.nz/moh.nsf/, date accessed 28 July, 2008.

Ministry of Health and District Health Board New Zealand (DHBNZ) Workforce Group (2007) *A Career Framework for the Health Workforce in New Zealand*, Wellington: Ministry of Health and District Health Board New Zealand.

Moskos, M. and Martin, B. (2005) *What's Best, What's Worst? Direct Carers' Work in their Own Words*, The National Institute of Labour Studies, Flinders University, Adelaide.

▶

▶

National Research Council (2008) *Research on Future Skill Demands: A Workshop Summary,* Hilton, M. Rapporteur, Center for Education, Division of Behavioural and Social Sciences and Education, Washington, DC: The National Academies Press.

New Zealand Department of Labour (2008) *Spotlight: A Skills Recognition Tool,* Wellington: Pay and Employment Equity Unit, Department of Labour Te Tari Mahi.

New Zealand Nurses Organisation (2008) Clinical Workforce to Support Registered Nurses, Draft: 10 July (home page) http://www.nzno.org.nz/, date accessed 28 July 2008.

Richardson, S. and Martin, B. (2004) *The Care of Older Australians: A Picture of the Residential Aged Care Workforce,* National Institute of Labour Studies, Flinders University, Adelaide.

Service and Food Workers Union (2007) Fair Share for Aged Care, http://www.sfwu.org.nz (home page), date accessed 12 July, 2008.

Spenner, K. (1995) 'Technological Change, Skill Requirements, and Education: The Case for Uncertainty', in Bills, D. (ed.) *The New Modern Times: Factors Shaping the World of Work,* Albany: State University of New York Press, 81–137.

Steinberg, R. (1990) 'The Social Construction of Skill: Gender, Power and Comparable Worth', *Work and Occupations,* 17(4): 449–82.

Strauss, A. (1993) *Continual Permutations of Action,* New York: Aldine de Gruyter.

Strauss, A., Fagerhaugh, S., Suczek, B. and Wiener, C. (1985) *The Social Organisation of Medical Work,* Chicago: University of Chicago Press.

Suchman, L. (2000) 'Making a Case: "Knowledge" and "Routine" Work in Document Production', in P. Luff, J. Hindmarsh and C. Heath (eds), *Workplace Studies: Recovering Work Practice and Informing System Design,* Cambridge: Cambridge University Press, 29–45.

Warhurst, C., Grugulis, I. and Keep, E. (2004) *The Skills that Matter,* London: Palgrave Macmillan.

Warhurst, C. and Nickson, D. (2007) 'A New Labour Aristocracy? Aesthetic Labour and Routine Interactive Services', *Work, Employment and Society,* 21(4): 785–98.

Wellin, C. (2007) Paid Care-Giving for Older Adults with Serious or Chronic Illness: Ethnographic Perspectives, Evidence, and Implications for Training. Paper prepared for the National Academies Workshop on Research Evidence Related to Future Skill Demands, homepage http://www7.national-academies.org/cfe, date accessed 1 July, 2008.

The Emotional Socialisation of Junior Doctors: Accumulating an Emotional Debt

13

Carol Boyd-Quinn

Introduction

What is it like to be a junior doctor, and how does a doctor 'become'? Recent changes to UK doctors working hours contained in the European Working Time Directive, along with the reorganisation of training of junior doctors set out in *Modernising Medical Careers* (http://www.mmc.nhs.uk/), support the ongoing emphasis on the structural aspects of doctors' physical work. The emotional dimension of doctors' work is, however, equally important and this chapter seeks to address the gap in the literature. With the broader concept of the professional socialisation of doctors covered elsewhere (see for example, Becker *et al.*, 1961; Bloom, 1979; Fox, 1989; Light, 1979; Merton *et al.*, 1957; Mumford, 1970), this chapter focuses on the emotion work and emotional socialisation of junior doctors through their training years, during which time they may encounter an array of frightening, upsetting and morally challenging socialisation experiences.

In the process of emotional socialisation, it is proposed that doctors-in-training may accumulate an 'emotional debt', whereby there is a shortfall in available emotional resources to manage given situations. It is postulated that this bank of emotional resources, or 'emotional bank', may be credited by individual factors such as life experience, coping strategies and personality traits, along with a range of social and structural factors such as working relationships and training. At the same time, the subjective experience of emotionally-charged situations will also be dependent on this range of individual, social and structural factors, consequently influencing the extent of 'emotional spending'. Where spending is in excess of banked emotional resources, the accumulation of an emotional debt may occur. The chapter also considers how such a debt can be mitigated through, for example, the development of coping strategies, as well as possible consequences of any such debt, such as psychological and physiological outcomes.

In understanding the process of the emotional socialisation of doctors, it is important to appreciate that 'doctors-in-training'/medical students, particularly in the penultimate and final years, work alongside experienced doctors acquiring a range of practical skills whilst attending daily ward rounds and surgical theatres. Usually assigned to different consultants and wards, medical students may find themselves working alongside a new and unfamiliar set of doctors and nurses every few weeks, making it difficult to become an accepted member of the team, and they may instead feel more like a 'spare part'. In addition, groups of medical students are often split up and shared between wards meaning they are often the only medical student in a given team, and different ward, theatre and break times can make it difficult to meet up with peers during 'working hours'. Excluded from the tight support cliques of the nurses and doctors, it is pertinent to ask how the potentially estranged medical student learns to cope with, and respond to, an array of emotionally challenging situations?

Conceptualising 'emotional debt'

Emotional labour, emotion work and emotion management embody the concepts of the 'commercialisation of feeling' (Hochschild, 1979, 1983) and the 'scaling up of institutional privilege over the ownership of emotion' (Fineman, 2000), where employees become increasingly expected to manage their emotions in an organisationally-prescribed manner that is regulated as part of the labour process (James, 1989, 1992; Smith, 1992; Sturdy, 1998; Taylor, 1998; Warhurst and Thompson, 1998). The complex and dynamic nature of emotional labour has been presented in a typology of emotional self-management (Bolton, 2005; Bolton and Boyd, 2003), highlighting the flaws in earlier deterministic perspectives. The medical profession illustrates the applicability of this typology and its deployment of emotional labour in the context of 'pecuniary', 'prescriptive', 'presentational' and 'philanthropic' emotion management (Bolton, 2005; Bolton and Boyd, 2003: 295). For example, pecuniary emotion management is evident in the organisation's focus on achieving patient satisfaction with treatment received in order to meet hospital targets; prescriptive emotion management, in terms of doctors adhering to organisational behavioural rules about patient dignity and respect, for example by requesting a chaperone for intimate examinations; presentational emotion management is observed in those doctors showing empathy and patience towards patients; whilst philanthropic emotion management refers to those human emotions which are 'gifted' in addition to any organisationally-prescribed emotions and which lie within the personal realm of an individual doctor.

According to this typology of emotion management, actors operate fluidly within organisational constraints, applying different sets of feeling rules to complement given situations. In doing so, they maintain ownership of their emotions and emotional identities, as evidenced by their awareness of the contradictions in what they say and do with how they actually feel (Bolton and Boyd, 2003). Achieving this high level of emotional dexterity is, however, likely to require practice through repeated exposure to emotionally-challenging situations. This point highlights an important gap in the literature – what happens in between first undertaking emotion work as a novice in hospitals and potentially becoming a 'skilled emotion manager', and to what extent is an emotional debt accumulated during this time?

The concept of 'emotional debt' is also informed by Frost's (2004) concept of 'toxic emotions' in organisations, which in a medical context could be demonstrated by the potential toxicity of emotionally-challenging situations encountered by novice doctors. The author describes how various actions and situations (organised into 'seven deadly Ins', namely INtention, INcompetence, INfidelity, INsensitivity, INtrusion, INstitiutional forces and INevitability) can produce 'poisonous situations' that can 'strip people of their confidence and self-esteem' leading them to 'disconnect from their work and its demands...and withdraw their commitment and loyalty to the company' (Frost 2004: 112).

For doctors-in-training, the array of early experiences involving, for example, vulnerable children and adults in hospitals, is compounded by working relationships with peers, nursing staff and senior doctors. In Frost's (2004: 112) empirical work of practising managers he describes how emotional toxicity can result from 'Intention', whereby some managers act to humiliate others in front of colleagues, fitting with some senior doctors' approach towards medical students and junior doctors. Frost's category of Incompetence finds resonance in those senior doctors who are technically highly skilled but who have little or no people management and/or poor communication skills. Other comparisons with Frost's seven deadly Ins include Intrusion where 'charismatic leaders seduce their followers into striving for high accomplishment...(and) such intensive work routines that an unhealthy balance is created' (Frost, 2004: 114). As some of the nation's brightest and most highly motivated students, doctors-in-training may be easily led into accepting intensive work regimes. Even with the protection of the European Working Time Directive (EWTD), one survey of 3,460 UK junior doctors reports that 24 percent of medical junior doctors and 25 percent of surgical junior doctors lied about (understated) the number of hours they worked when submitting records of their hours in an audit of EWTD compliance (PTEMB, 2007). These figures are, however, an improvement on 2001 figures which showed 60 percent of UK junior doctors were exceeding working limits (Scallan, 2003).

The concept of 'toxic emotion' is reasonably useful in demonstrating the potential for a 'toxic ecology' (Frost, 2004) within hospitals, as well as contributing to the concept of an 'emotional debt' that may accumulate as a consequence of exposure to this environment. This debt may in turn trigger the development of coping strategies, as well as having implications for doctors' performance, health and wellbeing. One caveat is that in different organisational contexts the occurrence of 'toxic emotions' form a fundamental aspect of the job and in some cases, such emotions can lead to positive, healing feelings. Bolton (2007) illustrates this with a study of a pupil referral unit (PRU), which deals with children with emotional or behavioural difficulties, where teachers described strong positive, nurturing feelings for those very children who launched daily verbally and/or physically abusive assaults upon them. In the context of the medical profession, doctors-in-training may also find themselves caring about the welfare and health of the verbally/physically abusive patient, rationalising the patient's behaviour into the relevant context of head injury or dementia, for example. The 'toxic emotions' created by a challenging workplace such as a PRU or hospital may in certain cases therefore, nurture a more caring, understanding and empathetic approach towards vulnerable people, as well as prompting the development of particular coping strategies for given situations. Frost's (2004: 124) remedy to rid the organisational environment of these toxins is clearly untenable in such settings, and the burden to manage these situations falls upon the medical staff, again bringing into focus the concept of an 'emotional debt'.

'Emotional debt' is, therefore, conceptualised as a shortfall in an individual's emotional bank or resources following exposure to given emotionally-demanding social experiences. This chapter explores a collection of those experiences and doctors' responses to, and reflections on, these.

Methodology

My background in academic research primed me to notice interesting themes and tensions within the medical profession during my training to become a medical doctor. Consequently, every opportunity was seized to collect and record data from peers and medical staff between 2006 and 2008. The data presented in this chapter is sourced from a series of interviews conducted with senior and junior doctors, and final year medical students, along with the results from a small questionnaire survey of medical staff in two Scottish Accident and Emergency departments carried out between June and August 2006. The content and structure of the self-administered, semi-structured questionnaire was modified from a similar study I carried out in the transport industry (Boyd, 2003). Personal reflections on my experiences as a doctor-in-training also contribute to this account of frontline medicine.

Baby doctors in training: practical and emotional skills learning experiences

The term 'baby doctor' was regularly used during my five years of medical train-ing; a term that carried with it connotations of nurturing and support. Developing practical skills such as taking blood, inserting urinary catheters and performing physical examinations all featured strongly in clinical teaching and in the final two years of training, medical students are expected to perform these tasks alongside junior doctors on a day-to-day basis. Whilst the mantra 'watch one, do one, teach one' was not common in practice, medical students are expected to learn quickly and a steep learning curve is encountered from day one. In my experience, doctors-in-training relished these opportunities and challenges, and building a practical skills set was enthusiastically embraced, despite the difficult situations our inevitable mistakes created. I recall an early attempt at inserting a venflon/cannula into a patient's arm during a five week teaching block in an Accident and Emergency department. All went well until the final stage in the process when the end cap of the cannula would not stay on due to the pressure of blood gushing out. The patient panicked, sending streams of blood up the wall beside her bed, I panicked, as there was no nurse or doctor helping me, and her mother started screaming. Just before I thought about blacking out, a helpful doctor walked calmly into the cubicle, swiftly released the tourniquet on the patient's arm and the bloodbath stopped. The event caused much amusement at the doctors' station and it was the first of many valuable practical 'learning experiences' for me.

Emotional learning is, in contrast to practical skills learning, a far more informal and implicit process in medical training. For example, Saunderson and Ridsdale (1999: 293) report from a qualitative study of UK general practitioners, that techniques developed by doctors to cope with patient deaths stemmed from personal experience rather than medical training. Despite this gap in training, management are just as keen to exert a level of control over the emotion work of doctors. For example, certain aspects of pecuniary, prescriptive and presentational emotion management are evident in the 'tick-box com-petency' themes contained within recently introduced foundation training for junior doctors, but there is a continued reliance on informal learning in emotion management skills. Patients' Charters and auditing practices within hospitals further support management's (and government's) attempt to control both the physical and emotional aspects of work. However, tensions and con-tradictions exist in any organisational attempts to gain control over a doctor's emotions. As one junior doctor told me:

Treating patients can never be a straightforward transaction-type process. Remember, many patients feel scared and deeply vulnerable. They need the doctor to be caring, patient and understanding. Sometimes a little humour can break the ice too. All of this requires the doctor to manage their own emotions as well as tuning into the patient's emotional state. Caring about the patient is central to this. I can't see how the doctor-patient human exchange could be distilled into a tick-box competency (Junior Doctor interview, 16 July, 2007).

Whilst doctors-in-training may understand what is expected of them in terms of emotion management, no formal training or support is provided, consequently putting the onus on the individual to find their own way through the emotional jungle of hospital life. As in the aforementioned PRU example (Bolton, 2007), one obvious response is the development of coping strategies and the prompts to cultivate these are, at times, compelling. As one final year medical student explains:

I was working in a palliative care hospital and became friendly with one of the patients who was about my age and was suffering from breast cancer. We talked about her son who was about to start school and she was devastated that she was not well enough to go out with him to shop for his new uniform and birthday present. One day just before she passed away, her son visited with his early birthday present (a bicycle) and he was dressed in his school uniform so that his mum could see him before she died. It was heartbreaking and I just didn't know how to act towards her husband. I couldn't even look him in the eyes. It's an experience I'll never forget and I wish I could have dealt with it better (final medical student interview, 3 June 2008).

Learning detachment: emotion work in medicine

Everyday training as a doctor brings with it some form of an emotionally stirring event. Ostensibly, young doctors may be considered so keen to learn about medical practice, some might assume that difficult situations are simply rebuffed and 'dealt with'. This can, however, lead to a failure to acknowledge the personal feelings and attitudes of young doctors who may encounter (potentially toxic) situations which they would have rather avoided. As one final year medical student explains:

I was in the obs and gyn theatre to practise vaginal examinations on patients under general anaesthetic immediately before their operations. I had previously consented all the patients to do this but wasn't sure what operations they were actually having. It wasn't until I had done my third examination that I realised this patient and the next one were having terminations of pregnancy. I couldn't leave the theatre for fear of looking stupid or weak, so I stayed. That night I cried in bed upset at being the last person to feel those little babies alive. I also feel guilty about being there and I pray about it in mass. I feel I should have been told in advance and given the chance to consider the implications of being complicit in these procedures (Final Year Medical Student interview, 3 June 2008).

For young doctors, the impetus to capture every learning opportunity that is available on the ward and in the operating theatres – regardless of any emotional consequences – appears as the prevailing culture in (some) hospitals. Learning to detach oneself from the immediate situation whilst simultaneously translating the experience into one of value and importance, as opposed to one of emotionally disturbing and toxic content, may be a common response from many doctors-in-training. According to Frost's (2004) concept of toxic emotion, the insensitivity shown towards trainee doctors could undermine their self-esteem and confidence and/or cause them to emotionally disconnect from work. An example from my personal experience provides support to this position.

During my first week on an obstetrics and gynaecology block I attended an emergency caesarean section operation on a young pregnant Pakistani woman who was visiting relatives in Glasgow. She had woken up that morning with her baby's foot protruding from her vagina. As the woman spoke no English, her sister-in-law tried, albeit clumsily, to translate during the history-taking consultation. The patient was unsure of her last menstrual period and so it was difficult to estimate how far she was into her pregnancy. An ultrasound scan identified two heartbeats and measurements strongly suggested that this twin birth was borderline viable, that is, of at least 24 weeks gestation. Faced with the woman's condition and the uncertainty of the gestation date, the doctors had to quickly decide whether to accept that a spontaneous abortion was underway, or to perform an emergency caesarean section to try to save the babies. The young woman was understandably terrified and cried throughout the consultation. A decision was made and she was rushed to theatre.

I waited with the team of doctors and specialist nurses from the neonatal ward while the patient was anaesthetised and the operation began. Silence fell on the crowded operating theatre as the first baby was pulled from a gaping uterus – blue and lifeless. The neonatal nurses attempted in earnest to resuscitate the child while the second baby was being delivered, small and pink, and then to everyone's surprise, a third tiny baby appeared. The patient was in fact expecting triplets and one was already dead when she arrived in hospital. Her measurements were therefore inaccurate and she was actually less than 24 weeks pregnant, meaning the infants had only a very small chance of survival. Two hours and three dead babies later, the patient wept inconsolably as we attended to her dressings and pain medications. It was a thoroughly heartbreaking experience for all involved and as one midwife commented later:

> This job just doesn't get easier. That was the worst thing I've seen in a good while.

From my perspective, having personally suffered two recent miscarriages, standing beside the first dead triplet wrapped in a clean white blanket and the cots of her tiny doll-like siblings who would also soon be dead was utterly horrific. Excluded from the supportive networks of the midwives and doctors, I drove home later that night feeling numb from the day's effort of controlling the intense sadness I felt for myself and for the patient. Total detachment from what was happening and a determined focus on 'being professional' had allowed me to make it through the day. Adhering to prescriptive emotion management rules maintained the professional face of solemnity for the patient's and the other staff's benefit. However, the attempt to ignore the internal tempest of emotions was exhausting leaving me questioning why I should want to be a doctor at all, and more importantly, was I up to the challenge. In short, the toxicity of the day's events drained my emotional bank, created an emotional debt and (temporarily) stripped any confidence I had regarding my suitability for a career in medicine.

This example highlights how individual factors in the form of my personal experience of miscarriage influenced the subsequent haemorrhaging of my emotional bank and the creation of an emotional debt of lost confidence and emotional exhaustion. Mitigating that debt involved talking to my partner, as well as rationalising the incident into an important learning experience. We now turn to a further aspect of doctors' work, namely organisational violence, where original data from a small research project is presented.

Biting the hand that heals: patient-led violence and emotion work

> The cost of violence against (NHS) staff is great. Victims can suffer physical and psychological pain. Confidence can be irrevocably dented and stress levels rise (John Denham, Health Minister, BBC News, 18 November 1999).

Patient-led violence in hospitals, particularly prevalent in accident and emergency departments (see for example, James et al., 2006; Jenkins et al., 1998; Knott et al., 2005), may be a contributory factor in creating a 'toxic ecology' (Frost, 2004) in some hospitals. For doctors-in-training, aggressive patients may present as much of an emotional challenge as vulnerable, placid patients, requiring many forms of emotion management; leading to a potential drain on emotional resources and the acquisition of an emotional debt.

The link between emotion work and occupational violence has been discussed elsewhere (Boyd, 2003), where the organisation's need for 'friendly, customer-friendly' workers can mean, particularly in the service, transport and health sectors, employees act as emotional punch bags when angry customers vent their frustrations on to staff. In the first national survey of 572 NHS-affiliated organisations, more than one-third (37 percent) of surveyed NHS staff had experienced harassment, bullying or abuse at work in the previous year, most of which was perpetrated by patients, clients or their relatives (NHS, 2004). In addition, 15 percent of respondents experienced physical violence in the previous year.

In a small research study undertaken during a nine-week period in two Scottish Accident and Emergency departments, a spectrum of patient-led violence was recorded with almost three-quarters of staff (72 percent) experiencing verbal abuse at work at least once a week (Boyd-Quinn, 2007). Work-related violence can take a number of forms including verbal abuse (e.g. swearing, racial or sexual insults), threats of violence, physical assault (e.g. biting, pushing, punching, spitting, attack with an object), unwanted physical or sexual contact, interfering with equipment or assault with a weapon (Chappell and Di Martino, 1999; Knott et al., 2005). Behaviours that inflict fear and anxiety are also considered within workplace violence definitions (Knott et al., 2005: 354). Indeed, as Flannery et al. (1995: 451) report, some verbal threats from patients provoked as much psychological distress for staff victims as did some physical assault. Patients with mental illnesses present a particular problem for staff safety where their illness excuses their violent behaviour. As one respondent explains:

> I feel I've been very lucky that I've only been physically assaulted by a patient with dementia. I was kicked, which I didn't do anything about because of her illness (Female Nurse, hospital A).

Low levels of reporting patient-led violence attributed to factors such as a lack of support from management and/or police – a finding reflected in the wider literature (see for example, Barlow and Rizzo, 1997: 77) – suggest that some medical staff may accept the risk and occurrence of patient violence as simply part of the job. As one respondent explains:

> Lip service only is paid to zero tolerance policy by local police. I have been coerced by police in an attempt to dissuade me from making a report to police. There is an unwillingness to arrest verbally abusive

drunks. The impression we get is the police think we should accept this as part of the job (Female Doctor, hospital B).

The survey data provided, however, limited evidence of this toxic environment creating 'positive, healing feelings' (Bolton, 2007) with respondents describing how patient-led violence made them feel angry (60 percent) and intimidated (37 percent), as well as experiencing reduced job satisfaction (40 percent). Only 14 percent of respondents believed that verbal abuse had no effect on them and similar results were reported for physical abuse. From these experiences, patient-led violence is a further possible contributory factor to the creation of a 'toxic ecology' (Frost, 2004) in accident and emergency departments, which can lead to negative psychological outcomes for some affected individuals.

My personal experience of patient-led violence occurred when I was pushed off my chair by an agitated patient. This patient was passed on to me to have sutures in her arm which had been injured with a kitchen knife during a domestic argument. This was my first time suturing something other than a banana skin, orange or dummy arm. The young woman was crying quietly as I entered the room with my equipment and her mother sat silently at the other side of the room staring at her hands. Neither acknowledged my introduction. While I was explaining what I was about to do to her arm (leaving out the part about her being my first victim/patient), she began arguing with her mother: 'you knew all the time. I told you and you wouldn't listen. Why didn't you ever confront him?' Her mother said nothing and kept her head bowed. Aware that I had three more patients waiting for me to take bloods, I carried on and managed to get her consent for the procedure. Hands shaking I began and was surprised at how tough real skin is to penetrate with a needle. Absorbed in my suturing, I hardly noticed the patient had started sobbing: 'I hate you. Look what you've done to me and him as well. He's a bastard and you've done nothing'. Just then, she stood up, pushed me out of the way (and off my chair) and ran out of the room with the needle and thread swinging loosely from her half-stitched up arm. I went after her but she was running out of the department. One of the doctors came up to me and told me to forget it. It was Friday night and the 'fun was just beginning'. I dutifully went on to attend to my waiting patients (remembering to remove the tourniquet each time) and even managed to take blood on a first attempt! Later, walking out of a patient's room, I could hear some commotion at the doctors' desk. The young woman I'd seen earlier had reappeared, sutures ripped out and arm bleeding on to the floor. I thought about ducking into one of the cubicles beside me but it was too late, she was running towards me. Brace yourself, I thought, afraid of what was coming. Instead of receiving the punch in the face that I was expecting from this angry, upset young woman who had endured my clumsy suturing, she threw her arms around me and began sobbing into my neck. 'He abused me since I was a wee girl and no-one would believe me', she cried. Two of the doctors came up and untangled her from my frozen body and led her away into a room. 'Better get cleaned up and changed', one said as I noticed the blood from the young woman's arm was in my hair and on my clothes. I moved seamlessly to my next patient, an intravenous drug user who was handcuffed to a prison guard. 'Hiya doll', he said cheerily as I entered his cubicle with my tray for taking bloods. I was relieved he was at least sober, friendly and handcuffed.

This example highlights the benefits of my previous experience in working with the public. Earlier in my career, I worked as cabin crew in the airline industry and regularly encountered frightening, upset, drunk and abusive passengers. The key point is, however, at age 40, I have many more years of life/work experience and potentially a greater variety of individual coping strategies invested in my emotional bank than, for example, the average 22 year old medical student or junior doctor in their early years of training. Continuing with the monetary metaphor, my experiences as an apprentice doctor, along with my responses to those experiences are likely to be subjectively different from that of any one of my peers based on the individual nature of resources in my personal emotional bank. This will also be true for the rate of my 'emotional spending' during exposure to difficult situations. As such, we can appreciate how structural, individual and social factors, such as the extent of training, previous experience and supportive working relationships, may influence an individual doctor's subjective experience of patient-led violence, highlighting the possible differences in emotional bank balances, the extent of emotional spending and the accumulation of an emotional debt between individuals.

Building an emotional debt

The potential costs or implications of an emotional debt leads us to consider Hochschild's (1983) description of emotional labour as a combination of 'surface acting' and 'deep acting', which results in the alienation from one's true self. Despite this being a simplistic and absolutist account of emotion work, my experience of medical training left me at times feeling emotionally numb and at pains to block out feelings that I found too upsetting or disturbing to acknowledge. It is at this point coping strategies began to take shape and for me, and taking on a different persona that had in-built 'force-field' became my life-line. Breathe through my mouth to block out the offensive smells on early morning ward rounds, focus on the patient's dilemma then leave the cubicle and move on to the next patient with a metaphorical shaking off of any emotional debris. However, as one psychiatrist told me, as humans we are not impenetrable and upsetting experiences stay with us and if not acknowledged, can manifest themselves in a variety of ways – for example, physical and psychological symptoms such as insomnia, depression and alcohol dependence.

The emotional debt: possible health implications

Emotion work, like physical work, often requires 'patience, tolerance and stamina' (Callaghan and Thompson, 2002). As with physical work, emotion work could equally be an important variable in employee health and wellbeing. One survey of 790 junior doctor reports that one in five junior doctors report suicidal thoughts, while an astonishing 86 percent reported psychological anxiety symptoms (e.g. insomnia, loss of appetite, fatigue, irritability) (BMA, 2007). In addition, almost one in three felt they had made more mistakes at work, while almost half said they cared less about patient care. We can link this finding to Frost's (2004) proposition that toxic ecologies can lead to reduced employee performance. Reduced job performance can also be related to problems with employee health and wellbeing, such as alcohol dependence.

There is already a comprehensive literature on the poor state of doctors' health, with a variety of studies reporting junior doctors as having an increased prevalence of depression, suicide, alcohol dependence, job stress, physical illness, pregnancy-related complications and suicide (Brooke, 1997; Firth-Cozens, 1997; Finch, 2003; Flaherty and Richman, 1993; Gabbe *et al.*, 2003; Girard *et al.*, 1991; Hawton *et al.*, 2004; Hsu and Marshall, 1997; Lindeman *et al.*, 1996; Osburn *et al.*, 1990; Phelan, 1998, Tempelaar, 1997). For example, Hawton *et al.* (2004: 1) report that doctors are at higher risk of suicide than many other occupational groups. Tempelaar (1997) reports that more problems with addiction were found among doctors in the UK than in the general population, whilst Brookes (1997) reports how doctors and lawyers were among the occupational groups with higher than average mortality from alcohol-related diseases.

Whilst much of the literature attributes these findings to long working hours, work intensity, job stress and poor leadership or poor working relationships, dealing with emotionally challenging or 'toxic' situations while carrying an emotional debt could be a further contributory factor to negative psychological and physiological outcomes for doctors. As such, the relationship between emotion work and workers' health remains an important gap in the literature.

Conclusions

This chapter has presented a discussion of the emotion work of doctors-in-training. In doing so, a range of personal reflections, interviews and questionnaire data is presented. A key assertion is that the emotional burden of doctors' work has not been fully integrated into the literature, with particular attention being given to the potential emotional debt that may accumulate as a consequence of exposure to a range of 'toxic' work experiences for doctors whose formal training equips them mainly only for the physical aspects of work. Medical students and newly qualified doctors are likely to respond to these experiences according to a range of individual, social and structural factors and a common emergent theme from the data presented was the active development of individual coping strategies, such as detachment and the rationalisation of upsetting situations as 'valuable learning experiences'. The discussion also highlights the range of morally challenging and upsetting situations apprentice doctors may find themselves in with little understanding or support from colleagues or management. For Frost (2004: 112), such toxic emotions may lead to the 'stripping of confidence' and/or reduced performance. Equally, continued exposure to toxic emotions may lead to depleted emotional resources, which in turn could be manifested in negative health outcomes. As such the balance of an individual's 'emotional bank', the pattern of 'emotional spending' and the accumulation of an 'emotional debt' are all areas for further research and debate.

Overall, the emotionally demanding nature of doctors' work should not be underestimated and more emphasis in preparing medical students and junior doctors for the potentially traumatic aspects of dealing with the inevitable range of emotionally challenging situations in hospitals should form a significant part of the teaching curriculum. The emotion work of doctors is, however, still woefully underacknowledged, as reflected in the recently introduced UK competency-based training programmes for new doctors and the author's experience of medical school. This oversight may remain until the bottom-line is affected through, for example, unmet performance targets or doctors' leaving the profession prematurely due to ill-health or disillusionment.

REFERENCES

Barlow, C. B. and Rizzo, A. G. (1997) 'Violence against surgical residents', *West Journal of Medicine*, August, 167: 74–78.

Becker, H. S., Geer, B., Strauss, A. L. and Hughes, E. C. (1961) *Boys in White: Student Culture in Medical School*, Chicago: University of Chicago Press.

Bloom, S. W. (1979) 'Socialization for the physician's role: A review of some of the contributions of research to theory', in Shapiro, E. and Lowenstein, L. (eds) *Becoming a Physician*, Cambridge, MA: Ballinger Publishing Company.

Bolton, S. (2005) *Emotion Management in the Workplace*, London: Palgrave.

▶

▶

Bolton, S. (2007) 'Emotion Work as Human Connection: Gendered Emotion Codes in Teaching Primary Children with Emotional and Behavioural Difficulties', in Ruth Simpson (ed.). *Gender and Emotions*, 17–34, London: Palgrave.

Bolton, S. and Boyd, C. (2003) 'Trolley dolly or skilled emotion manager', *Work, Employment and Society*, 17(2): 289–308.

Boyd, C. (2003) 'Customer violence and employee health and safety', *Work, Employment and Society*, 16(1): 151–69.

Boyd-Quinn, C. (2007) 'Biting the hand that heals: Patient-led violence in two Scottish Accident and Emergency Departments', Paper presented at the Work, Employment and Society Conference, 12–14 September, University of Aberdeen.

BMA (2007) *Cohort Study 2006 Medical Graduates: First Report*. BMA: London.

Brooke, D. (1997) 'Impairment in the medical and legal professions', *Journal of Psychosomatic Research*, 43: 27–34.

Brookes, J. G. (1997) 'The incidence, severity and nature of violent incidents in the emergency department', *Emergency Medicine*, 9: 5–9.

Callaghan, G. and Thompson, P. (2002) 'We recruit attitude: The selection and shaping of routine call centre labour', *Journal of Management Studies*, 39(2): 233–53.

Chappell, D. and Di Martino, V. (1999) *Violence at Work*, International Labour Organisation: Geneva.

Fineman, S. (2000) *Emotion in Organizations*, 2nd edition, London: Sage.

Firth-Cozens, J. (1997) 'Depression in doctors', in Robertson, M. M., Kantona, E. (eds) *Depression and Physical Illness*, New York: John Wiley.

Flaherty, J. A. and Richman, J. A. (1993) 'Substance use and addiction among medical students, residents, and physicians', *Psychiatry Clin N Am*, 16: 189–97.

Flannery, Jr. R. B., Hanson, M. A. and Penk, W. (1995) 'Patients' threats: Expanded definitions of assault', *General Hospital Psychiatry*, 17(96): 451–53.

Finch, S. J. (2003) 'Pregnancy during Residency: A Literature Review', *Academic Medicine*, 78(4): 418–28.

Fox, R. (1989) *The Sociology of Medicine*. Englewood Cliffs: Prentice Hall.

Frost, P. (2004) 'Handing toxic emotions: New challenges for leaders and their organization', *Organizational Dynamics*, 33(2): 111–27.

Gabbe, S. G., Morgan, M. A., Power, M. L., Schulkin, J. and Williams, S. B. (2003) 'Duty hours and pregnancy outcomes among residents in obstetrics and gynecology', *Obstetrics and Gynecology*, 102:948–51.

Girard, D. E., Hickman, D. H., Gordon, G. and Robinson, R. O. (1991) 'A prospective study of internal residents' emotions and attitudes throughout their training', *Acad Med*, 66: 111–14.

Hawton, K., Malmberg, A. and Simkin, S. (2004) 'Suicide in doctors: A psychological autopsy study', *Journal of Psychosomatic Research*, 57(1): 1–4.

Hochschild, A. (1979) 'Emotion work, feeling rules and social structure', *American Journal of Sociology*, 85(3): 551–75.

Hochschild, A. (1983) *The Managed Heart: The Commercialisation of Human Feeling*. Berkeley: University of California Press.

▶

▶

Hsu, K. and Marshall, V. (1997) 'Prevalence of depression and distress in a large sample of Canadian residents, interns and fellows', *American Journal of Psychiatry*, 144: 1561–6.

James, N. (1989) 'Emotional labour: skill and work in the social regulation of feeling', *Sociological Review*, 37(1): 15–42.

James, N. (1992) 'Care = Organization + Physical Labour + Emotional Labour', *Sociology of Health and Illness*, 14(4): 488–509.

James, A., Madeley, R. and Dove, A. (2006) 'Violence and aggression in the emergency department', *Emergency Medicine Journal*, 23: 431–34.

Jenkins, M. G., Rocke, L. G., McNicholl, B. P. and Hughes, D. M. (1998) 'Violence and verbal abuse against staff in accident and emergency departments: A survey of consultants in the UK and the Republic of Ireland', *Journal of Accident and Emergency Medicine*, 15: 262–5.

Knott, J. C., Bennett, D., Rawet, J. and Taylor, D. (2005) 'Epidemiology of unarmed threats in the emergency department', *Emergency Medicine Australasia*, 17(4): 351–58.

Light, D. (1979) 'Uncertainty and Control in Professional Training', *Journal of Health and Social Behavior*, 20: 310–22.

Lindeman, S., Läärä, E., Hakko, H. and Lönnqvist, J. (1996) 'A systematic review on gender-specific suicide mortality in medical doctors', *British Journal of Psychiatry*, 168: 274–9.

Merton, R. K., Reader, G. G. and Kendall, P. L. (1957) *The Sociology of Science*, Chicago: Chicago University Press.

Mumford, E. (1970) *Interns: From Students to Physicians*, Cambridge: Harvard University Press.

NHS Staff Survey (2004) Commission for Health Improvement, London, http://www.healthcarecommission.org.uk/_db/_documents/04007747.pdf

Osburn, L. M., Harris, D. L., Reading, J. C. and Prather, M. B. (1990) 'Outcomes of pregnancies experienced during residency', *Journal of Family Practitioners*, 31: 618–22.

Phelan, S. T. (1998) 'Pregnancy during residency II: Obstetric complications', *Obstetrics and Gynaecology*, 72(3): 431–6.

Postgraduate Medical Education and Training Board (PTEMB) (2007) *National Trainee Survey 2006 key findings* www.pmetb.org.uk/trainee-survey

Saunderson, E. M. and Ridsdale, L. (1999) 'General practitioners beliefs and attitudes about how to respond to death and bereavement: Qualitative study', *British Medical Journal*, 319 (7205): 293–96.

Scallan, S. (2003) 'Education and the working patterns of junior doctors in the UK: A review of the literature', *Medical Education*, 37: 907–13.

Smith, P. (1992) *The Emotional Labour of Nursing*, London: Macmillan.

Sturdy, A. (1998) 'Customer care in a consumer society: Smiling and sometimes meaning it? *Organization*, 5(1): 27–53.

Taylor, S. (1998) 'Emotional labour and the new workplace', in P. Thompson and C. Warhurst (eds) *Workplaces of the Future*, Basingstoke: Macmillan.

▶

▶

Tempelaar, A. F. (1997) 'The problem doctor as an iatrogenic factor: Risks, errors, malfunctioning and outcomes', in Lens, P. and van der Wal, G. (eds) *Problem Doctors*, Amsterdam: IOS Press.

Warhurst, C. and Thompson, P. (1998) 'Hands, hearts and minds: Changing work and workers at the end of the century', in P. Thompson and C. Warhurst (eds) *Workplaces of the Future*, Basingstoke: Macmillan.

Who's Driving Now? GPS and the Restructuring of Taxi Work

14

Carolin Grampp, Maeve Houlihan and Paul McGrath

Are you talkin' to me...?

Well I'm the only one here

'Travis Bickle' (Robert De Niro) addresses himself in a mirror in 'Taxi Driver', directed by Martin Scorsese (1976)

The story of this chapter began with a taxi journey taken by one of the authors, with a driver who was visibly frustrated by an onboard computer at which he was tapping away. He explained that the newly installed mobile data terminal (MDT) used global positioning systems (GPS)[1] to track his specific location, and that of every driver in the company, and combined the information with incoming bookings to automatically offer work to drivers according to their location and status. The system generally eliminated the need for him to communicate verbally with the taxi company office, replacing the more familiar dispatch radio with silence and potentially, greater efficiency and productivity.

The encounter made us want to know more about the realties of taxi work, and wonder about the dynamics of working with such systems of work allocation. Clearly, GPS had the potential to radically alter a taxi company's fleet management capability, work intensity, and implicitly its control over drivers. Familiarised by urban folklore with taxi drivers' independent and idiosyncratic work practices, we were curious about how this technology would work out. How would GPS dispatch affect the culture and work organisation of taxi work? Would drivers reject the potential intrusion into their privacy and independence? What effects would the new system have on their skills, and those of dispatchers? What would the taxi company do with this additional control capacity?

In this chapter, we explore the culture, relationships and changing context of taxi work, based on case research with a large Dublin taxi company,

'*TaxiCo*'. The Irish taxi driver operates nominally (if not in effect) as an independent contractor and sole trader. However, as this case will make clear, external parties (including regulatory bodies, the taxi company, the individual dispatcher, the customer and technologies such as GPS) greatly influence the taxi labour process and, just as many other workers, taxi drivers struggle to retain control over their work effort.

Beginning with a description of the culture of taxi work, followed by an account of method and introduction to TaxiCo, we then discuss in detail the work processes of job allocation and network communication, before and after GPS. The story presented here features the daily lived reality of dealing with new technology for two key stakeholders: driver and dispatcher. We detail the reactions of these parties to their changing work organisation and discuss the emerging implications. In effect, this is a story of technological innovation, an autonomous (and precarious) occupation and the marriage of the two.

The culture and organisation of the taxi work

Taxi driving is an occupation that bears a number of universal hallmarks. First, it is mobile work, in which the driver, as a sole trader or as part of a wider network, operates in isolation, separated from co-workers. Second, the majority of taxi drivers operate a two-way radio which affiliates them with a taxi company. Where that is the case, they pay radio rental to the taxi company, and a fee on each job received from the base. Third, taxi work is unpredictable, and unplanned. Drivers wait at ranks or circulate in the pursuit of customers and the plying of their trade. Drivers 'do not know from one call to the next where they will be going; there is always the possibility of a "road trip" or a call which takes them out of the city, county, or province...' (Berry, 1997). Fundamentally, taxi driving is isolated work, heightened by the 'fleeting nature of his [SIC] relationship with the customer' (Davis, 1959). And yet, taxi drivers bear witness to society in all its forms: from the tourist to the brusque business client, and from late nights drunks to the elderly hospital patient being transferred home.

In Ireland, as many other countries, taxi drivers operate on the basis of a taxi licence, a 'taxi plate', which they must personally qualify for and purchase. Clearly, the car itself is a taxi drivers' means of production, and drivers variously lease from fleet owners, pay rental to a taxi company, timeshare with an owner-driver ('cosying') or, as is now generally the case in Ireland, personally purchase their car. For most drivers, this involves undertaking a substantial loan under security of earnings: prior to deregulation in 2000, taxi plates were scare and prohibitively expensive at a cost of up to €114,000 (Barrett, 2003).[2] However, deregulation cut the plate cost to €6,300 (*ibid*) and made licences freely available, greatly reducing the barriers to entering the trade. Since 2000, the number of taxi plates in Dublin has increased from 2,700 to well over 10,000 (*ibid*).

As sole traders, taxi drivers are in direct competition with each other for their income, and so for individual jobs. An associated culture of individualism is commented on by Trudel (1996) arising from the 'tyranny of the trip', expressly a short-termist, anti-cohesive mentality. The stereotype of taxi drivers as verbose individuals is reflected perhaps in the comment of one TaxiCo manager*:*

> Taxi drivers are a peculiar kind of people and have their own way of dealing with things.

Despite these isolating dimensions of taxi work (portrayed vividly in Scorsese's 1976 film) there is some evidence of a community culture among taxi drivers, reinforced by common experience and evident in certain work norms, rituals and specialised language. Community practice involves tipping each other off about work and problematic 'fares', looking out for each other's safety, and confronting transgressions of informal 'rules', including an etiquette for queuing and accepting jobs at ranks. While there is no formal induction process, taxi drivers learn and reinforce these cultural containers by gathering to talk while parked at a rank, through the sharing of breaks at mutually recognised gathering points (usually standing, as if to stress the fleeting nature of the encounter), and informally through off-duty socialising. All these are occasions of rich storytelling and the exchange of experiences enables drivers to constitute, negotiate and enact an effective occupational community (Orr, 1990; Brown and Duguid, 1991). Unlike many occupations, however, such meetings are unpredictable and snatched, as interaction is suspended by the arrival of a customer.

With few opportunities to meet formally, a key means of connectivity for drivers working for the same company is the virtual community created by a two-way radio network. By this means, drivers can 'hear' the organisation into being, listen to the pattern of jobs, read nuances, discover who is doing what, and where the trouble spots are. The centrality of radio interaction is similarly illustrated by John van Maanen's field research of mobile police work (1988).

The vast majority of taxi drivers are male. Cultural and public expectations conform to this; while TaxiCo customers can request a female driver, they rarely do. Drivers work long hours, and while regulations specify a 40 hour week this is not enforced and most build their hours around demand and income targets: 'there's no going home until I've made enough to pay the bills' is a common refrain. Drivers operate at all hours of the day, but peak activity periods are office opening and closing times, and particularly night shifts when the majority of other transport sources cease. Daytime traffic congestion means that many find themselves forced into night-time work, despite a general preference for more sociable hours (Boland, 2001). To add to this, taxi driving is clearly a risk-laden occupation. The International Labour Organisation lists taxi driving as the solo occupation at greatest risk of violence (Chappell and Di Martino, 1998). The fact drivers are alone and presumed to be carrying a day's earnings makes them especially vulnerable, and robbery at knife or needle point is common. Local practices emerge to deal with this threat: pulling up at police stations or radioing in their movements if they sense trouble, and alerting fellow drivers of suspicious passengers.

On the other hand, taxi drivers themselves endure a troubled reputation in some respects. Some commentators suggest this may relate to historic associations with bootlegging and even prostitution (Berry, 1997). More common lore tactics such as fumbling with change to encourage tips, 'taking the long way around', holding out for longer fares and fare inflation, although likely to be the practice of only a minority, paint the taxi driver as a 'cowboy' in public imagination (Davis, 1959, p. 163). Schlosberg (1980) has described the taxi industry as a class system: working class drivers, 'exploited' by taxi companies, fleet owners and dispatchers. This exploitation, he argues, is 'transferred into his own exploitation of his passengers' (1980, p. 79). In Dublin, dialogue on radio phone-ins and media commentary is notably unsympathetic towards taxi drivers, both influenced by and reinforcing stereotypes.

Economic and political environments are pertinent to taxi work and there have been changes in both in recent years: customers with money to spend; the appointment of a taxi regulator with a strong passenger serving ethos, and a market-based outlook. Despite an image of entrenchment, we found a strong narrative of professionalism and modernising among sectors of the taxi community, particularly within TaxiCo, and among the industry representative bodies. Union or association membership is high among Irish drivers (75 percent at TaxiCo, spread across three unions). Organising became extremely active around deregulation: lobbying, campaigning on safety and customer service issues, and seeking to influence government plans for the future of the sector. Interestingly, the tone of this influence has been criticised as one of 'demands rather than dialogue' (Trudel, 1996), an interpretation shaped perhaps by the series of strikes and demonstrations among taxi drivers around the period of deregulation. Pre-2000 taxi drivers are generally united in their criticism of reduced entry barriers having paid exceptionally high prices for their plates and now finding their earning potential challenged by the ready supply of additional drivers who have had to pay so much less. Indeed, even post regulation drivers criticise what they describe as a 'flooded market', saying it is a challenge to earn a consistent week's wages. The ease of getting a license since deregulation has also seen many new drivers take up taxi work as a second job, although part-timers are resented for absorbing lucrative cash work during high demands hours and weekend evenings; a factor increasing dependence on dispatch companies to ensure steady income. It is common to hear established drivers criticise the values and professionalism of more recent drivers. All of this highlights the competitive, fragmented and contentious nature of the industry and a picture emerges of an occupation that is not only isolated, but in many senses alienated (Berry, 1997).

Having related this somewhat negative account of taxi culture and work organisation, it is important to add that drivers do speak highly of the positive aspects of their work: its endless variety of people and places, but most especially its independence and flexibility. It is for this reason that these characteristics deserve particular scrutiny when considering the implications of GPS technologies.

TaxiCo: an introduction

We studied TaxiCo (one of only two Dublin firms using such systems), during the period of their introduction of GPS tracking and computerised dispatch. Data collection took place primarily in the summers of 2001 and 2002, and periodically continues. Our initial research phase involved indepth interviews with three members of TaxiCo's owner-management team, five TaxiCo drivers, and five 'base' staff (two dispatchers, two tele-operators and an administrator), supplemented by short observation periods of dispatch operations. Subsequently, we spoke more informally with more than 30 TaxiCo drivers on 'pay day', the sole occasion when drivers visit the company premises. We also gathered accounts from the regulating body (initially Dublin Corporation which is now replaced by the national Taxi Regulator), the National Taxi Drivers Union, and all taxi drivers encountered during the period of this research.

TaxiCo was established in the 1950s, and having for a time traded as a cooperative, became a public limited company with share capital in 1999. It grew rapidly from that time through the help of radio technology that allowed it to increase its customer management capacity, and consequently its taxi fleet. Today it declares itself *'Dublin's leading and largest taxi company... at the cutting edge in the industry'*. At the start of the study in 2001, the fleet consisted of 350 taxis with an average of 170 on the road. It currently operates a fleet of over 800 taxis, including those linked to TaxiCo through its bureauing function, with an average of 400 cars on the road at any time.

TaxiCo specialises in the provision of account taxi services, mostly for large companies, institutions and government offices. Acting as a broker,

TaxiCo owns and operates an office, provides branding identity and manages the recruitment and coordination of drivers, and the distribution of work. Drivers are self-employed, and pay weekly rent for their MDT system in addition to a substantial 12 month deposit as security, and a fee for each job they receive from TaxiCo. In the case of contract work, TaxiCo finances the credit and charges the customer accordingly. Account customers amount to approximately 75 percent of TaxiCo's business while the rest consists of non-regular cash customers. With account work, TaxiCo invoices clients on a fixed basis and pays a weekly cheque to the driver reflecting the fares earned, minus deductions for fees and equipment rental. While cash work may thus be more lucrative as no fee is payable, account work is valued for its dependability and regularity, and has other advantages such as guaranteed payment in the case of a 'banger' (a no-show).

The work process of taxi dispatching – past and present

The main parties involved in providing a taxi service are the drivers and the dispatcher. In a more indirect manner, management, tele-operators and the administrative staff are important players. The way in which those parties interact has considerably changed since the introduction of GPS dispatch and MDTs.

The dispatch system pre GPS

The traditional way of dispatching a taxi vehicle to a pick-up was a paper and radio-based system. Tele-operators recorded fare requests on specially designed paper dockets, recording customer details, the time of the fare request, the pick-up location and destination and any additional requests. The completed slips were sorted in pigeonholes – one for every 15 minutes, right through the 24 hour clock.

Once due, an overseeing dispatcher sent out a call stating the general location of the customer over the radio, which all drivers could hear. Drivers identifying themselves as free and in the vicinity radioed the base to request the call and at the dispatcher's discretion would then be issued the specific location. Dispatchers obtained information on the drivers' location and dispatched customer fares via constant radio contact over two channels. To minimise the need for the dispatcher to repeat information, drivers were expected to record these details. Nonetheless, drivers often contacted the base to obtain job clarification. Additionally, drivers were required to contact the base to convey the charge accrued, after job completion. All this communication was transmitted to every active radio in the fleet, reflecting an 'open' or multi-way radio system. In addition to enabling drivers to bid for jobs and hear where work was going, this also allowed those 'parked up' at ranks to gather socially in one car while waiting, yet still remain alert to jobs coming in. Hearing the organisation at work in this way was a continual and dynamic knowledge base:

> You picked up where the best areas for radio work were, where to be at particular hours of the day or night ... (Driver).

With the later introduction of closed radio systems, drivers heard only the voice of the operator, but not the replies of co-workers responding to the dispatcher. Frequently the dispatcher broadcasted messages from a driver to the fleet regarding traffic disruptions or matters of global relevance. The switch to closed radio introduced a partial barrier to communication across the virtual community ('it was a one side conversation'), although drivers nevertheless became adept at reading and inferring the movements of colleagues from dispatcher comments.

> ... with the old systems, the talk systems, everybody had a code number, you would hear the code numbers being given out, you would know your friends' code numbers and that (Driver).

A driver's situation and location created a priority system that influenced the assignment of jobs. Jobs went first to the vehicle longest parked, and closest to the pick-up location. Parking was therefore rewarded and often essential, especially in less busy periods. However, when the fleet was busy and no vehicles were parked, jobs went out on a first-come first-served basis. Depending on the amount of work and time of the day, the dispatcher would put outstanding jobs out to the whole fleet to bid for, or directly assign them to certain drivers.

Dependence on dispatchers for 'quality' jobs nurtured a certain level of politics and strategic behaviour. Dispatchers claimed it was common for drivers to falsely identify their location, to increase their chance of getting a job. Equally, drivers described much suspicion that dispatchers favoured certain people with certain jobs. Just as Berry (1997) found in his ethnography, drivers felt dispatchers would for example send them on a dummy call or 'banger' in order to allocate a lucrative job to a preferred driver. A culture of mutual distrust is evident in the comments of both dispatchers and drivers, and fed a wider sense of 'misbehaviour' around competition for jobs. For example, though strongly disapproved of, drivers regularly described practices such as queue jumping, fobbing off short runs, and contriving to steal jobs.

These dynamics, coupled with the time consuming nature of dispatch work, had implications for the overall efficiency at TaxiCo. As one manager put it: 'we were barely able to maintain the customer base.... we could never think of expanding'. The shortage of taxis in Dublin meant customer demand was continually growing, and simply left unmet. This undersupply was to be addressed by deregulation in 2000 however, bringing huge numbers of new drivers on stream very quickly. For taxi companies, this was both a threat and an opportunity.

The rationale behind GPS implementation

In late 2000, TaxiCo's management team decided to invest in new technology to enhance operational efficiency and pursue a growth and development strategy in order to secure a lead position in the newly deregulated environment. Following research on international practice, TaxiCo selected and installed a Raywood computer-based taxi dispatch platform. This offered GPS driver tracking, plus the capacity to integrate and enhance its dispatch systems. By linking individual meters to the system via mobile data terminals, they could eliminate dependence on drivers identifying their status and location. TaxiCo management described their goals explicitly: increased work efficiency, improved customer service, expanded control over drivers, enhanced organisational data and the capacity to expand the customer base and provide service offers. They further expressed the wish to reduce central office's interaction with drivers. Raywood systems can be purchased in a variety of configurations depending on the individual needs of the company. The revolutionary characteristic of the system installed at TaxiCo, was its complete replacement of closed radio systems with automatic dispatch.

The new work system under GPS

The new dispatch process consists of a single integrated system that actively processes incoming data. Each driver carries a MDT in the car that registers their current activity status and position via satellite signals, automatically transmitting both to the base. At the base, a tele-operator takes customer calls, entering 'jobs' into the system, while cross-references to previous data enables input-short cuts. Customer locations are translated by the system into coordinates on the 71 grid zones in which Dublin is divided. The system either immediately attempts to dispatch the job or stores and automatically dispatches it at a later time as required. It 'queues' free vehicles in each grid zone, and automatically sends a job to a car via the MDT screen. The driver acknowledges acceptance of the job via a key code, and on completion, client fare details are sent electronically to TaxiCo's accounting department. Thus driver interaction with the base is now principally indirect.

The dispatcher supervises electronic dispatch, resending outstanding jobs no driver has acknowledged, and dealing with problems. These are handled via a 'query' voice channel which replaces the radio system and is used only at the dispatcher's discretion in response to a request for communication coded by the driver into the MDT. It is not heard by the fleet.

Analysis

The 'objectivity' of the new system suggests a more fair and equitable distribution of jobs, and cuts dispatch time by at least half relative to voice channels. A by-product of the objectivity of the new system, however, is a definite alternation in the flow and direction of information within TaxiCo. As researchers, we observed this to have consequences for the relationship between drivers and the firm, with drivers now apparently holding less control over their work process than previously. We wondered how this would be felt. In the following sections, we review responses of drivers and dispatch operators to this new situation and discuss the implications.

A changed communication climate

Under the old system TaxiCo's radio link allowed drivers to identify regularities and patterns in fares, to profit from the experience of other drivers and to dialogue with the base and each other. Now there is 'no more listening all the time' as one driver put it. GPS dispatch has altered interaction from a network to a hub-and-spoke from base to driver, eliminating the direct link between drivers. Receiving only preselected information, now drivers have less access to potentially valuable information about conditions or certain job experiences:

> You are losing a lot of the feel for work as you don't hear where places are working on the system ... you wouldn't know who is giving a lot of work, what companies are giving a lot of jobs ... you only know what you are doing (Driver).

In addition, the removal of the traditional voice channel has regulated driver communication. This significantly reduced query volume, to the pleasure of dispatchers who voiced antagonism towards the previous system:

> The query channel used to get terrible abuse ... 60 to 70 percent was irrelevant to the working situation – just muck, useless repetition, all job

related but useless in efficiency. Stuff like 'What was that job again?'
(Dispatcher).

In addition to such concerns, a more practical reason for dispatchers' evident
dislike was the reality of noise levels arising from working with the radio
system. At the base, operators had to cope with continual incoming driver
responses on the radios, with one having to shout louder than the other to be
heard. This made it difficult to hear incoming customer calls too, and customers often had to be 'asked repeatedly for information'. The dispatch room
was visibly stressful and staff described how they were 'physically exhausted'
after a day's work. Some drivers also welcomed the end of their 'radio days' for
similar reasons:

> Now I can listen to my music in peace, you get used to the radio but
> sometimes the noise of it would give you a pain in the head. I was glad to
> see the back of it (Driver).

However, more commonly, drivers are conscious of 'no more listening all
the time' and how this has changed the experience of their working day.
They can no longer hear the company at work as they drive, nor participate
vocally in its virtual network and this is felt keenly by some:

> You miss the bit of banter on the radio (Driver).

This social dimension is especially relevant considering the isolated nature of
taxi work, however losing the voice network has broader consequences for
drivers, and they tangibly described the implications:

> You don't know who the drivers are anymore ... you'd know so and so
> had such and such a number ... all the numbers have changed as well
> with the new system. I have lost contact with who is who since the
> system's came... you don't hear people called to jobs (Driver).

> Less, you meet less now ... I believe TaxiCo has about 400 drivers, I would
> know probably ten, fifteen at most and the same, very few would know me
> ... we are all working away, doing a couple of thousand jobs a day (Driver).

> It is a lonelier job now ... you don't hear anything anymore, even though
> you only had the one-sided conversation before (Driver).

Now the only means of contact with fellow drivers is through personal mobile
phone, or per prearranged gatherings. Waiting periods can no longer be shared

without losing out on fares as differences in vehicles can lead to different job offers from the system. In very real ways, this has diluted the level of affiliation between drivers and heightened the individualistic nature of their work:

> You have to stay in your car ... that would cut down on the time you can spend talking to others for the simple reason that each car is designated its own number ... four or five people in one place from the same company, they have to stay in their car (Driver).

> ... if three drivers are sitting in a fourth car talking, the fourth car gets the job ... In the old days with the radio system, I could be sitting in the other guy's car and I could be accepting a job on his radio (Driver).

Decreased self determination and the end of old ploys?

The new system has made job allocation both more transparent and more opaque. Fares are automatically allocated to the driver closest to the job or first in the queue. When drivers had full access to information about the dispatch operations, they could use this information to ensure one job after the other and to 'cherry-pick' jobs without wasting time. It was also possible for drivers to hold back information or to give inaccurate details of their whereabouts. Dispatchers described the way they would instinctively get a feel for and sanction 'messing': on becoming aware of inconsistencies of driver's statements in terms of their location or vacancy, they could act upon it by not assigning jobs, whether their assumptions were correct or not. Now, the dispatcher is in a position of much greater oversight and control:

> Every meter movement he makes is recorded, every entry to the database is recorded for you (Dispatcher).

The dispatcher can use this information to guide the driver to the pick-up location or to update customers on the location of the taxi and expected pick-up time. From the dispatcher's perspective, GPS enables clarity and eliminates the 'fudge-factor':

> He is not lying, I am not lying, we are not fabricating our details whereas before drivers would be saying 'I will be with him in a couple of minutes' and you'd never know. The driver could tell you he is anywhere and sometimes he would (Dispatcher).

With the new system, new controls have also emerged. Drivers prefer certain jobs (airport runs for example, with the prospect of better tips), and dislike others (problematic social services runs for example, or jobs that take them to areas it will be difficult to get a return journey from). Whereas previously drivers could selectively choose to avoid certain work types and this choice was hidden, now they must register their rejection and in doing so risk attracting the attention of the dispatcher:

> There is no more picking and choosing – the system gives you the job. You take it or you don't take it. You don't take it, you get penalised (Driver).

As drivers are contracted to provide their services, dispatchers can now sanction such behaviour with penalties, such as being sent to the 'back of the [GPS dispatch] queue', or logging them out of system for short periods, thus denying them work. In the past, drivers might avoid undesired jobs by feigning being temporarily out of radio range, or out of the car. If the driver switches off the MDT, he cannot be allocated any jobs and simply loses work. Nor can he claim being unable to find a customer as a reason for abandoning a job, as the location coordinates are given exactly:

> The work is there in front of you. With the old system people could cheat and the company got the blame [if a taxi did not arrive] ... with this system it is the driver and the system, and the driver would be at fault more times (Driver).

A safer, more equitable work environment?

Despite some misgivings, when probed about their opinions of the new system drivers repeatedly emphasised certain direct advantages including better security arising from their location being known at all times and an emergency button on the MDT, less vehicle wear and tear due to shorter distances to pickup, and, generally speaking, a sense of more equitable work distribution. As one of the drivers reflected, '... *it cuts out the messing*'. While drivers acknowledged the 'surveillance' aspect of GPS, they were generally pragmatic:

> I don't mind that. We are all self-employed, it is not like we are running away from our employer... you are not getting paid when you are not working and that is that (Driver).

Not everyone was so accepting. One driver who left TaxiCo subsequent to the changes raised an aspect of MDT usage that receives little comment: road safety.

> I used to use that system but stopped. First of all, having it beeping at you all the time would drive you mad, and anyway its lethal trying to stab at

buttons when you are driving – I've seen many a near miss. I'd prefer the radio any day (Former TaxiCo Driver).

While retail GPS vendors are beginning to react to such concerns by modifying in-car-unit accessibility, taxi systems retain a highly technical interface that requires significant deftness and concentration to navigate while driving. Since undertaking this research we have repeatedly asked drivers to explain the MDT and GPS dispatch to us while taking taxis, and the distraction caused by having to read the screen and insert codes while driving is readily observable.

A more regulated and formalised relationship between firm and driver?

Earlier sections have indicated that the relationship between drivers and taxi company contains many elements of tension. Ostensibly, drivers are self-employed, in a contracting relationship with the taxi company, and inevitably both parties seek to maximise their self-interest. The emphasis on Account work at TaxiCo means the company is accountable for the reliability of its service to clients, and with deregulation came renewed emphasis on customer service. Driver commitment is key to this, but in practice there was little to ensure it, and TaxiCo had struggled at times to retain its clients.

Now 'objective' computer allocation means that most job allocation is unmediated by the dispatcher. This has eased the sense of suspicion that drivers often felt about job allocation, something which dispatchers in particular, welcome:

> You were either trying to please someone or you aren't pleasing – and you can't please all the people all the time. So sometimes you are seen as the devil itself but now you are not the protagonist at all. That is the good thing. You want to work? There is the work. Whereas before it was 'Why are you doing that?' – you were questioned for doing it, even when you were doing it the right way, because they didn't like the way you were doing it (Dispatcher).

However, the old mistrust still rears its head, and things are not quite so clear from the driver's point of view:

> I trust it [GPS dispatch] less... because with the old system I was hearing the same jobs going out night after night, day after day. Certain jobs you knew, say half one in the morning in certain areas, four jobs or five jobs at that, and you knew one of them was going local, one was a midrange,

and one was a good job and so on and so forth. I don't know whether those jobs are going out now over the satellite system or whether they are going out with the mobile phone ... in fact I think there is more scope for carry on than there ever was, I know people would disagree with that but that's my opinion (Driver).

This speaks to the strength of preoccupation with perceived preferential treatment from dispatchers and exploitation by other drivers, and flags an embedded sense of antagonism and distrust running through relations between driver and firm, and in lesser ways, among drivers themselves.

A changed role for the dispatcher

GPS dispatch has also had implications for the work carried out in the TaxiCo office, particularly the work of the dispatcher. Prior to GPS, his main responsibility was to issue jobs and to answer queries. The new system has substantially reframed the structure of the role and direct dispatch is no longer his primary activity. Instead, his main responsibility now is to ensure smooth overall operation. This pleased the dispatchers we spoke to and one described the fundamental culture shift succinctly:

> You were selling your work all the time over the radio. You were waiting on them (drivers) to pick and choose. They were responding but they were also picking and choosing, 'cause they had the pick up points and the destinations. So the customer really wasn't getting any service ... now everything is completely different, we manage the fleet. Before that they were managing us because they could do what they wanted to – it changed the whole outlook, the whole operation changed as such (Dispatcher).

The introduction of GPS dispatch has created a new level of calculability and control in TaxiCo's operations. With just a few keystrokes, managers and dispatchers can instantly review the activities of the firm as a whole, or of individual drivers or jobs, and translate this 'objective' information into action. It is now possible to identify undesired driver behaviours and sanction them if they do not adhere to the implicit rules. The result is a perception of much greater efficiency, and these gains were felt in the organisation of the office too:

> Now you have the same amount of people but they are better employed for it. They are not doing tedious work – they are doing specific work. We do not have them there editing work which shouldn't be edited in the

first place as we have it all streamlined... it is ten times more efficient (Dispatcher).

Despite these efficiency gains, it is striking that TaxiCo drivers report that their earnings have not increased since GPS introduction, although this was promised at the outset. Both the drivers and TaxiCo attributed this to the radically increased numbers of taxi operators subsequent to deregulation, which, while negatively impacting the drivers had improved customer responsiveness.

The new system is more customer friendly but not driver friendly (Driver).

However, outcomes are rather more clear for TaxiCo. The scale and efficiencies of the new system paved the way for expansion of the fleet and number of accounts. Significantly, TaxiCo radically expanded its revenue generation by contracting to supply GPS dispatch bureau services to three further taxi companies. This led to a doubling of the fleet at minimal investment. There is currently a waiting list to join TaxiCo as a driver.

Discussion

Like all service industries, the taxi business faces increasing consumer demands for quality, reliability and accountability. Indeed, deregulation has ensured that market forces make this even more pressing. It is evident that the perceived individualism and autonomy of drivers was seen as a problem at TaxiCo.

The objectives reflected in the design and implementation of any technology come into sharp focus when exploring its impacts. GPS technology in itself offers only the core capacity to trace object location. Indeed, authorities in Australia, Germany and Canada advocate GPS use in taxis as a safety device (Mayhew, 2000; Pelham, 2001). However, for TaxiCo, the adoption of a more elaborate integrated management control system was a deliberate choice. Further, the secondary goal of eliminating driver dialogue was activated by removal of voice channels and full automation of dispatches.

This is a comment of the political context of technology, and the key interaction of design and implementation decisions. GPS vendors are cognisant of its dual potential and have reconstructed it from a locating device to a control device through the development of 'added value' applications. Sales material from Trimble Navigation Ltd, a GPS applications reseller articulates a sales pitch that will make this duality palatable to users: *'Companies ... adopted the new tracking technology for efficiency and service. The drivers, however, were sold on the safety angle'*. Their sales pitch goes on to add *'They can now get jobs more appropriate to their location, arrive more quickly, and serve happier customers (who give better tips). And this adds up to better service and more passenger miles for lower overall cost'* (Trimble Sales Brochure, 2001).

Tellingly, despite TaxiCo's objectives of reducing interaction with drivers and increasing influence over them through the new systems, its pitch to drivers merely emphasised the safety angle. This strategy appears to have made the introduction of the system easier, as reflected by one manager's comment that:

> 95 percent of the drivers are happy with the system ... some drivers had difficulties at the start in dealing with the silence but only a very few chose to leave (Manager).

Indeed, drivers were largely positive about GPS dispatch, despite many of the issues they raised. Their strongest concerns related to the lack of income improvement it had brought, which they explained through deregulation and the increased numbers of cars on the streets. Not everyone has adapted well however, and some TaxiCo drivers did leave for other firms.

Conclusion

Despite several apparent issues, drivers at TaxiCo are broadly stoic about the benefits of GPS dispatch technology to them. Our argument is not that these benefits are unreal, or that drivers are wrong to be convinced by them. In many ways the goals of the driver and the company are the same – to max-imise yield. This is a unique feature of the status of drivers as independent contractors and sole traders.

And yet, some things are clear: The new system of GPS dispatch dictates the majority of their movements, and subtly limits their autonomy and choices. It has diluted community interaction and restricted drivers from hearing the virtual work of the organisation, from bantering with the base, from arranging meetings and from reading the 'nuances'. All of this deepens their dependence on TaxiCo and indeed the electronic dispatch system over time. In addition a number of more explicit outcomes are evident: TaxiCo drivers now incur significant extra costs to hire the mandatory MDT. Its sur-veillance capacity can then be used against them to 'punish' uncooperative behaviour. It has reduced their capacity to 'hide', to steal jobs, or to bluff about location or activity, and predisposed drivers to cooperation. In all these ways, the new GPS dispatch system has fundamentally redefined the power relationship between drivers and the firm. Thus, a lot has changed and the self employed driver's role is shifting to something new.

It is also clear from the foregoing that the support drivers receive from their supervisors and managers is tinted by an embedded antagonism, with mistrust in both directions. Dialogue with TaxiCo base staff shows that an image of the taxi driver as 'maverick', if not 'cowboy', prevailed: *'they'd tell you any porkies, just to get the work'*. Like all control systems, the new technology at TaxiCo makes possible new ways to monitor and extract feedback on performance, and to analyse and benchmark this performance against others, past trends and objectives. Codes of practice, productivity norms, quality control initiatives and performance appraisal are likely to follow. It will perhaps not be until such expanded control capacity is activated by TaxiCo that we will fully discover the extent of drivers' changed agency within this changing power relationship.

Notes

1 GPS is a navigation system devised by the US Department of Defence, which uses Earth-orbiting satellites to pinpoint at the exact location of a GPS receiver through longitude and latitude grid coordinates.
2 Prior to 2000 an alternative was to drive under a cheaper hackney licence. However hackney services can only be used for private hire, cannot be hailed from the street and cannot use bus lanes, unlike taxis, so that post-deregulation, the prevalence of hackney drivers is significantly declining.

REFERENCES

Barrett, S. (2003) 'Regulatory Capture, Property Rights and Taxi Deregulation: A Case Study', *Economic Affairs*, 23(9): 34–40.
Berry, K. (1997) The Last Cowboy (unpublished Masters Dissertation, Saint Mary's University, Halifax, Nov Scotia, Canada), http://www.taxi-l.org/cowboy.htm date accessed 30 July 2008.
Boland, R. (2001) Taxis aren't so cosy any more, http://www.taxi.ie/not-socosy.shtml date accessed 30 July 2008.
Brown, J. S. and Duguid, P. (1991) 'Organisational Learning and Communities-of-Practice: Towards a Unified View of Working, Learning and Innovation', *Organizational Science*, 2(1): 40–57.
Chappell, D. and Di Martino, V. (1998) *Violence at Work*, Geneva: International Labour Organisation.
Davis, F. (1959) 'The Cab-Driver and His Fare: Facets of a Fleeting Relationship', *American Journal of Sociology*, 65(2): 158–65.
Mayhew, C. (2000) 'Preventing Assaults on Taxi Drivers in Australia', Australian Institute of Criminology Trends and Issues in Crime and Criminal Justice No. 179, Canberra, November, www.aic.gov.au date accessed 30 July 2008.

▶

▶

Orr, J. (1990) 'Sharing Knowledge, Celebrating Identity: Community Memory in a Service Culture', in D. Middleton and D. Edwards (eds) *Collective Remembering*, London: Sage.

Pelham, M. (2001) 'Toronto Cab Rides Safer Than Ever', Toronto Observer, November 15, www.bccc.comm/Observer.online/features/taxi111401.htm date accessed March 2003.

Schlosberg, R. (1980) 'Taxi Driving: A Study of Occupational Tension', unpublished Doctoral dissertation, City University of New York.

Trimble Navigation Limited (2001) 'Putting GPS to Work: Tracking – Taxis Down Under', Product information catalogue.

Trudel, M. (1996) 'The Future of Transportation by Taxi', paper given at the first *European Conference of International Association of Transportation Regulators*, Strasbourg, France, October.

Van Maanen, J. (1988) *Tales of the Field: On Writing Ethnography*, Chicago: University of Chicago Press.

Creating, Connecting and Correcting: Motivations and Meanings of Work-Blogging Amongst Public Service Workers?

15

Vaughan Ellis and James Richards

Whooooo boy, the avalanche of preparation of teaching materials has hit. It is days like these that you get to experience the rich variety of metaphors (old clichés and older) that sum up this situation, by trading with colleagues: 'I'm submerged', 'I'm drowning'...Today's winner is Jeremy, with 'I'm trying to have my nervous breakdown but I'm having great difficulty finding the time.' Worked 57.5 hours last week (that's 164% compared to so called normal working hours) and 61.5 (175%) the week before. There must be a life raft around here somewhere (blog extract – UniSpeak Lossy – University Lecturer, September 28th 2007).

I'm...watching a patient in his 70s with severe Alzheimer's disease and a feisty temperament. Sadly he doesn't take too kindly to being told what to do...He swears, punches and falls regularly...I find it frustrating working in an environment where I can be kicked and punched and have to take it...yet equally I can't imagine how difficult and confusing it must be for this gentleman to not have a clue where he is or what's going on, and be asked to do things by a woman young enough to be his grandchild (blog extract – I am Not a Drain on Society – Casual auxiliary nurse – January 2nd 2008).

Introduction

Writers within the labour process tradition have long recognised that paid work is a central defining feature of people's lives (Baldry *et al.*, 2007). Work is motivated by economic and moral necessity (Noon and Blyton, 2007), offers economic rewards and the potential to realise self-potential. Work also provides an increasingly important means of meeting social needs (Hochschild, 2001; Pahl, 2000; Pettinger, 2005). Work then, carries many individual significances and meanings. However, it remains the case that in many important respects knowledge of the actual work that people do, and their experiences of it, remains largely 'hidden' from almost all apart from those that directly witness it. Although industrial sociology has made important contributions to our understanding of the nature and experience of contemporary work, this knowledge rarely reaches non-academic audiences. In short, much of what is known about work has arisen from third-party accounts in which workers' testimony is analysed and reproduced by 'outsiders' for consumption by narrow sections of society. As Edwards and Wajcman (2005: 1) presciently note '...Karl Marx used the now famous phrase "the hidden abode" to refer to what went on inside the production process. This abode is now in some ways more hidden than it was then'.

Building on this anomaly this chapter investigates the very recent and growing phenomenon of workers keeping publicly accessible online diaries (i.e. blogs or weblogs) which typically reveal candid although, generally anonymous accounts of personal experiences at work. The chapter seeks to answer why workers, independent of third parties such as employers or trade unions, are turning to new forms of Web communication technology to explore work-related matters and what they hope to achieve by doing so. Drawing on qualitative data sets, including nine in-depth semi-structured interviews with workbloggers and 'content analysis' of their blogs, this chapter investigates the meanings of and motives for keeping a workblog.

We suggest that such workblogs potentially offer a new means of uncovering insider primary accounts of contemporary work. More generally, we believe that creative use of emerging Web communication technologies can open up a much wider and potentially more attentive council for the individual worker than is achievable through the workplace itself, or even close family and friends. Having a wider and more attentive council enables individuals to share details of what they do at work and how they experience it. Keeping a blog allows the worker to reflect on work-related matters and seek advice from others. Furthermore, blogging offers the individual actor a voice free of hierarchy or the usual trappings of the workplace that generally render the ordinary employee silent.

Blogging about work

Recently, blogging, and in particular, workblogs have attracted growing media attention. Some have even attracted significant notoriety following media coverage, such as the television dramatisation of the blog *Belle de Jour: The Diary of a London Call Girl* (http://belledejour-uk.blogspot.com/), *Salam*

Pax the so-called 'Baghdad blogger' (http://dear_raed.blogspot.com/), and the publication of edited collections of work entries in book form (Blachman, 2007; Sticker, 2007; Chalk, 2006; Copperfield, 2007; Reynolds, 2006; Simonetti, 2006). The fact that public sector workers are authors of a significant proportion of workblogs has drawn further media coverage, with notable examples suggesting 'the truth about school life' (Wallace, 2007), 'exposing the everyday reality of modern-day policing' (*BBC One*, 2007), and disclosing the 'daily chaos of the Labour government machine while lampooning ministers and highlighting the idiocy of mandarin colleagues' (Oliver, 2008). The controversy surrounding public sector workers writing so publicly about their work is lucidly expressed by one broadsheet journalist:

> Web technology has changed the relationship between authority, employee and citizen. In the past, it was relatively easy for public authorities to control the 'authorised' version of events. Conversations about practice and policy were moderated by official spokespersons, speaking to the public through the approved traditional media of newspapers, radio and TV. Every now and then, a fly-on-the-wall documentary would open a window on how public services really operated. The odd whistleblower would bravely expose malpractice. But, on the whole, the views of public services – often restricted by 'gagging' clauses in the employment contract – were relatively easily policed (Butler, 2007).

Media representations of public servant workblogs are of course influenced by sectional interests and commercial imperatives to sensationalise the phenomenon to make it more newsworthy. Such accounts pay scant attention to what role blogging plays in the life of the workblogger. Academic attention on this phenomenon, so far, has also been limited, but where it has been conducted suggests workblogs are a forum for a creative, yet individualised form of employee resistance (Schoneboom, 2007) and extend the possibilities for expressing conflict at work (Richards, 2008). A common feature of these research projects has been the tendency to narrowly interpret the meaning and purpose of workblogs as a form of resistance to corporate ideologies through the adoption of individual coping strategies and promotion of countercultural values. Although Richards (2008: 101) recognised it would be wrong to stereotype *all* workblogs as a forum exclusively for the expression of conflict, instead preferring to characterise blogs as '...being a record of how workers experience[d] their jobs over time' the survey based methodology adopted was only able to offer limited insights into alternative meanings of, and motivations for, blogging.

This chapter builds upon and extends these earlier studies and is as much about allowing the many 'voices' of workbloggers to be heard above the cacophony of media interest, as it is about locating such activities in any recognised theoretical frameworks or debates. We believe that sensationalised media accounts of workblogs fail to reveal their true meaning and purpose and inaccurately assign disruptive intentions to their authors. We seek in part to address this unsatisfactory representation and reveal the full range of motivations for maintaining online accounts of work and the meaning derived from doing so.

'You're Dooced': the potential consequences of blogging about work

Since workblogs first entered public consciousness in the early part of this decade the rights of bloggers to produce publicly accessible diaries detailing the minutiae of their working lives has been contested by many employers and professional bodies (CIPD, 2008; Schoneboom, 2007b; Spencer, 2005). A number of bloggers have been dismissed from their jobs as a consequence of their online activities, which in the main have been conducted outside work hours, off premises and using their own resources. As one blogger who was dismissed commented, such dismissals raise challenging questions surrounding '...freedom of speech...and the intrusion of the corporate world into the personal; how far should a company have influence over the life of staff? Where do you draw the line? How much of your life is your life?' (Gordon, 2005).

Over recent years a number of individuals dismissed for blogging have gained considerable notoriety, largely due to considerable support, discussion and online protest by fellow bloggers and the resulting media attention it attracted. For example, in February 2002 Heather Hamilton, the author of a blog named 'Dooce' (http://www.dooce.com) was dismissed due to comments about her employer and her colleagues recorded in her blog. Her dismissal gained such notoriety that the term 'dooced' emerged to describe bloggers getting fired for their activities. In January 2005, Joe Gordon a senior bookseller at Waterstone's in Edinburgh was dismissed for entries on his blog that referred to the company as 'Bastardstone's', nicknamed his manager as 'Evil Boss' and called him a 'cheeky smegger' for asking him to work on a Bank holiday (Gordon, 2004 cited in Schoneboom, 2007b). The Guardian newspaper quickly questioned the company's actions in articles covering the dismissal, accusing them of failing to live up to their self-promoted image of a 'bastion of free speech' (Barkham, 2005). The consequences of Waterstone's decision to dismiss Gordon unleashed global condemnation.

These 'dooced' bloggers are by no means alone. A list maintained by the author of a blog titled Morpheme Tales provides a list of bloggers who have been fired for their activities (available at www.morphemetales.wordpress.com/2006/10/09/statistics-on-fired-bloggers/) and highlights the heavy price that a significant number of bloggers have paid for writing about their experience of work. Such draconian responses to workblogging suggest considerable levels of corporate insecurity and determination to ensure that what goes on behind the polished, glass fronted facades of contemporary workplaces remains hidden. Although we would stop short of accepting Schoneboom's (2007) argument that workbloggers are '...in many ways the intellectual descendants of writers such as Albert Camus, Henry Miller, Franz Kafka, T. S. Eliot, Charles Dickens and Nikolai Gogol' we do believe they fulfil an important social function, whether intentionally or not, and warrant greater scholarly attention.

The content and style of workblogs varies considerably and given the discipline of length and constraints of structure it is not possible to reproduce extracts from each of our participants here. However, in order to locate our subsequent discussion in context, the extracts at the start of this chapter are included as 'typical' examples of workblog entries and further extracts are included throughout the chapter. By including them our intention is to provide a flavour of our participants' writing styles, the topics they write about and offer a window into their experience of work. We do so for purposes of illustration, rather than making claims that these extracts are representative of *all* blog entries posted by a particular author or of the approach taken by all the bloggers in our sample.

Methods and sources

A sample of prolific and established workbloggers was drawn from a database of nearly 1,000 workblogs (maintained, updated and available at http://work-blogging. blogspot.com), originating primarily from the USA and UK and asked to take part in the study. Given the exploratory nature of this research we felt a purposive sample was appropriate and maximised the likelihood of 'gaining access' and capturing the voices of some of the most prolific or well established bloggers. For convenience we restricted our attention to UK bloggers and given the significant number of public sector bloggers, we decided to draw our sample from this group. Initial communication regarding the research aims and objectives was made with public sector bloggers who had well established, and 'live' blogs, via email, where contact details were available, or through posting entries on their blogs where they were not. Thirty workbloggers were approached and 12 responded, of which three subsequently declined a request to be interviewed. From these efforts we conducted in-depth, semi-structured interviews with nine individuals. The comparatively small sample is evidence of the difficulty of researching groups which value anonymity. Even nine interviews may not have been possible were it not for one of the author's ongoing attempts to sustain an 'insider status' amongst workbloggers by maintaining his own publicly accessible blog.

Each interview was free-flowing, but rooted in the goal of gaining an understanding of their purpose for starting and importance of keeping a blog going. After all, the participant is best placed to describe *their* experiences of employment and explain how *they* derive importance from a given employment experience (Ellis and Taylor, 2006). The interviews explored bloggers' motives for blogging and the factors shaping which facets of work experience are discussed in their blogs.

The preference for many workbloggers to maintain anonymity, even from the researchers, combined with their geographical dispersion influenced the use of telephone, instant messaging and asynchronous email interviews (see Table 15.1). Telephone and instant messenger interviews typically lasted for an hour each, whilst those conducted via email took place over a period of a week. All interviews were conducted between November 2007 and February 2008.

Although broader issues surrounding the use of e-interviews, whether through instant messenger platforms or email, are beyond the scope of this chapter, it is nonetheless appropriate to briefly comment on the relative merits of such approaches in order that the validity and reliability of our data can be assessed. Although these approaches do not offer the same opportunities to assess and respond to non-verbal cues or build verbal rapport as face to face interviews, and may lack spontaneity (Murray and Sixsmith, 1998; Selwyn and Robson, 1998) they do afford a number of unique advantages (McCoyd and Kerson, 2006). Asynchronous email interviews can be more convenient for both parties, maintain confidentiality for the participant (Bampton and Cowton, 2002), allow participants time to consider responses, often leading to greater depth of answers (McCoyd and Kerson, 2006), removing the need for time consuming transcription (Hamilton and Bowers, 2006) and avoiding the loss of expressed data (Mann and Stewart, 2000). Instant messenger platforms also provide a written record of discussions, maintain anonymity for participants and are cheaper than telephone interviews when dealing with geographically remote participants (Mann and Stewart, 2000). Although our approach to data collection may be considered unconventional (or as we prefer to describe it, innovative!) and was influenced by situational factors, rather than conscious design, we believe it to be apposite given our objectives and no less reliable or valid than more traditional qualitative approaches.

In order to gain further insights into the motives and meanings of workblogging we also analysed our participants' blog posts. In total 861 blog entries were read and a breakdown is shown in Table 15.2.

We read all blog entries posted by our participants between August 2007 and March 2008 and their content was analysed using an appropriate coding

Table 15.1 Data collection and work bloggers

Name of blog and URL	Gender	Age	Occupation	Employer	Blogging since	Interview method	Interview date	Details of readership (provided by blogger)
1. Random Act of Reality – http://randomreality.blogware.com/	Male	Mid 30s	Emergency medical technician	NHS – London Ambulance Service	September 2004 to present	Telephone	22nd November 2007	About 30,000 people per day
2. Trauma Queen – http://www.traumaqueen.net/	Male	Mid 20s	Emergency medical technician	NHS – Scotland Ambulance Service	September 2004 to present	Telephone	19th February 2008	1,500 to 2,000 unique readers
3. Purple Plus – http://kingmagic.wordpress.com/	Male	Late 30s	Emergency medical technician	NHS – unknown ambulance service	October 2006 to present	Telephone	15th November 2007	About 300 hits per day
4. Walking the Streets – http://parkingattendant.blogspot.com/	Male	Late 40s	Parking attendant	Unknown local authority	January 2005 to November	Instant messenger	14th November 2007	150-250 visitors a day
5. Bus Driving – http://busdriving.blogspot.com/	Male	Mid 60s	Bus driver	Stagecoach	April 2004 to present	Telephone	17th January 2008	About 250 per day or 1750 a week

Table 15.1 Data collection and work bloggers – *continued*

Name of blog and URL	Gender	Age	Occupation	Employer	Blogging since	Interview method	Interview date	Details of readership (provided by blogger)
6. I'm Not a Drain on society – http://bloodystudents.blogspot.com/	Female	Mid-20s	Casual auxiliary nurse	NHS Professionals	February 2005 to present	Telephone	9th January 2008	Normally about 250–300 per day, but can rise to 2–3,000
7. London Underground Life – http://londonundergroundlife.blogspot.com/	Male	Early 40s	Station security manager	Transport for London	April 2005 to present	Telephone	6th February 2008	About 100–130 hits per day
8. UniSpeak Lossy – http://unispeak.blogspot.com/	Male	Age not known	University lecturer – computing	Unknown UK university	September 2004 to present	Email	2nd November 2007 (received final email)	Not known
9. Dr Grumble – http://drgrumble.blogspot.com/	Male	Mid 50s	Teaching consultant	NHS – unknown region	October 2007 to present	Email	4th November 2007 (received final email)	Not known

Table 15.2 The number of blog entries posted by each blogger between 1st August 2007 and 1st March 2008

Blog Title	Number of posts
Dr Grumble	18
Walking the Streets	62
UniSpeakLossy	34
London Underground	127
I am not a drain on society	97
Purpleplus	50
Random Acts of Reality	168
Trauma Queen	148
Busdriving	157

frame. The vagaries of qualitative analysis are well documented (Boulton and Hammersley, 1996; Cassell and Symon, 1994) and careful consideration was given to ensure that codes were allowed to emerge from the data itself. In doing so our intention was to be able to reproduce an account of reality that our participants would recognise.

While workblogs may be viewed by many as being in the public domain we recognised there remains questions over whether technical accessibility equates to 'publicness' (Berry, 2004). Although bloggers publish their entries on an open, worldwide network, this will go largely unnoticed by most that use the Internet (Richards, 2008). Consequently, in reproducing blog extracts in a domain other than which they were intended has the potential to be intrusive and cause harm to their authors. In order to maintain appropriate ethical standards and be courteous, civil and respectful of the privacy and dignity of research participants (Jones, 1994) we obtained explicit permission to reproduce blog extracts from all research participants and provided a full explanation of intended use and likely audience.

Research findings

A creative outlet for underutilised skills

Writing at length about work is unlikely to be an end in itself. What makes such activity worthwhile must also serve an innate purpose – for example creative writing involves talents that individuals may find rewarding, and skill perhaps not required in their work life. Moreover, making one's writing publicly accessible may offer feedback, a sense of voice and the opportunity for it to be heard. For some of our respondents, wanting to express themselves through writing predated their employment in their present occupation and their blogging activity simply incorporated their (new) work over time. For others, there was a particular catharsis in sharing their experiences of pressure situations. For inexperienced employees in particular, it seems such writing offers a particular means of navigating early experiences of work and sharing personal perspectives:

> I started blogging before I joined the ambulance service. I did a lot for the Red Cross as a First Aider. It was luck that brought it all together. I'd been thinking for a while of keeping a blog; I'd done a lot of writing at school and I really enjoyed it. Between leaving school and starting work – between 18 and 22 – I didn't write at all. Around about this time I started writing again, in the form of a journal. I started to blog because I wanted to share what I was writing with other people – except I wanted people reading and discussing it... (interview with author of Trauma Queen – Emergency Medical Technician).

Writing about work, however, is by no means confined to new or indeed young employees. A bus driver less than 12 months from the state retirement age indicated how he began blogging as a means to offer 'insiders' and 'outsiders' a window into his daily working routine and experiences:

> When I came across blogs I'd never heard of them. I came across one that was to do with the American election – the last time Mr. Bush came in. I suddenly discovered there were so many more. I thought this is a great idea, you can just go online so easily and I think that, basically, it was so easy to do, and I'm interested in my job and I like my job, and it just seemed the natural thing to do. So, basically, I haven't gone into it to become a hard hitting blogger who slags off managers and other people and tells the world how bad it is to work for, etc. etc. I just thought I'd tell people stories about what happens to me while I'm working (interview with author of Bus Driving – Bus Driver).

Once employees discover, or perhaps rediscover, their hidden talents, blogging appears to develop into a further means by which feelings and insights about work can be communicated:

> When I write a blog some of them flow. They're there and then they're gone; they just flow. People who know me know the way that I think and they know the way that I talk. And as Barry [a similarly qualified colleague] says: I can read your blog and hear your voice. He can tell when I'm angry from the words that I am using. He can tell when I'm pissed off

at work by the words that I use (interview with author of London Underground Life – Station Security Manager).

Writing about employment is a major commitment and many bloggers regularly contemplate abandoning their habits. Yet, for some employees, experimenting with an innate form of expression develops into a habit that is difficult to shake off:

> There have been times when I've become disillusioned. I just think to myself: I can't be bothered with this anymore. And I think about it for a while and always come back to it. The thing is, even if I sometimes get disillusioned, I still love blogging. It's strange; it's like a bug to me, I like blogging and I love writing about my life. Just different things, things that I find funny as well and other things that I find very serious… (interview with author of Purple Plus – Emergency Medical Technician).

'I'm gonna get myself connected'

Bloggers also cited instrumental motivations for creating and maintaining their blogs. It is evident that creating a rich web of contacts through blogging is a real possibility and can deliver benefits to its members. An interesting question however, is who does the blogger consider their audience to be: to whom is a blog addressed? For one respondent, blogging offers a rather novel way of communicating with, about, and in some respects, on behalf of colleagues:

> Everyone at my work, for instance, knows who I am. They know of the blog and a number of them read the blog [sic]… My colleagues influence me to a certain extent about what gets written. There's a constant competition at work to see who can get a blog name. All my colleagues have pseudonyms that I write about them under. And I've been petitioned by people – 'why haven't I got a name yet?' So, occasionally I have written in a way so that they are mentioned more and play more of a role in my writing… (interview with author of Trauma Queen – Emergency Medical Technician).

The openness of Trauma Queen's writing about his work is rare, as is its 'internal' readership. It was more common for workbloggers to comment on how they use blogging to communicate and set up networks between people who worked in the same or related occupations but in *different* workplaces:

> There are lots of bus drivers who read it. A couple of people who work for the council read it. The guy who has an office job in Brisbane who reads

it. I know of at least two or three readers in America (interview with author of Bus Driving – Bus Driver).

The reasons why bloggers wished to connect with employees from similar occupational backgrounds varied, but included gaining a better understanding of each others' roles and making useful contacts that may prove valuable in the execution of their duties. The Internet has also facilitated networks of workbloggers and blog readers reaching beyond the narrow confines of occupation. For instance, interviews revealed how workblogging speaks to broader occupational themes, especially where bloggers share a common purpose or a common employer, such as the National Health Service or a local authority:

> ...we're all supposed to be working for the NHS, but we all work in our own little kingdoms. So, you get lots of interesting nurse bloggers. There's police and doctor bloggers and we're all in the same field, but we don't really ever cross over anywhere, or if we do it's very brief. So, how I see it is, by reading other professionals' blogs I get an idea how they work and I can help the police out a bit more than I could otherwise. Likewise people can read my blog and they can help me out occasionally (interview with author of Random Acts of Reality – Emergency Medical Technician).

The nature of the interaction, moreover, suggests a level of non-hierarchical communication or egalitarianism between professions and occupations that may not be possible on work time. For instance, a casually employed auxiliary nurse and aspiring medic outlines how networks built around and from workblogging can provide invaluable career assistance:

> It's making me more of a rounded individual. I mean, I get a better insight into the medical field by reading related blogs...I always ask the junior doctors at work how they find something and they're usually too busy to stop and talk. What better way of finding out about the future job that I'm going into, and the future profession I'm going to, than reading a blog about other peoples' recollections of it? It's like reading someone else's diary, it's like having a foot in someone else's life...I've gone and got more experience through these bloggers; I've been out on a shift observing with MacWitch [the online name of an ex-work blogger], who's a psychiatric practitioner (interview with author of I'm Not a Drain on Society – Casual Auxiliary Nurse).

Workblogging is by no means an activity performed by introverted and insular individuals disconnected from the 'real' world. Writing their blogs clearly opens up the potential for social connections and friendships to emerge from both insider and outsider curiosity about their work. It also offers a counterbalance to some of the pressures that can inhibit collegiality and social connection at work. A teaching consultant explains:

> Years ago I heard that people were marrying having met online. I thought that was mad at the time. Maybe it is. But you can get to know people quite well from an online contact. Some of the bloggers write in a very blunt manner. I write things I would be wary of saying in another forum. So in a way you see more of people and can therefore get closer to them in an online relationship that you do in real life. Concealed by anonymity they reveal their innermost thoughts. That may be very healthy (interview with author of Dr Grumble – Teaching Consultant).

The quotes presented here suggest that the motivation for writing a work-blog seems broader than simply 'sounding off in Cyberspace'. Furthermore, the outcomes of doing so are greater than a feeling of relief. They are best seen in the connections formed by bloggers and their readers who have common occupations or professions, but do not work with, and in most cases, have never met, yet via the internet, may end up having closer relations with than they do with work colleagues. It seems that first hand, candid and vivid accounts of work represent a vibrant potential ingredient in the formation of employee networks and may make potential contributions to the formation of distinct collective identities.

Blogging as occupational public relations

Ignorance of the minutiae of others' work may make us prone to forming false conclusions about the complexity, intensity and experience of particular jobs. This may be particularly true of roles within the public sector where exaggerated portrayals of workers as inefficient, 'work-shy' individuals protected by militant trade unions and enjoying privileged terms and conditions denied to others periodically feature in tabloid news-papers. The arrival of the 'social Web' however, has allowed workers the opportunity to provide unmediated accounts of their work content, how they perform their roles and their experience of them. In doing so, the potential exists to make some contribution to controlling their public relations, however limited, and regardless of whether such an aim is a deliberate intention.

The ways in which workbloggers go about shaping outsider perceptions of their work and the weight they put on this as a goal varies, but one example involved providing 'insider information' to readers seeking similar work:

> If someone sends me an email and asks for information about the blog...I give information. If someone asks for information about the job – 'I'm applying for that job' – I'll give them information like that. I don't mind. I'll give them information about the underground. If they're applying for the job I'll say this is how you do it...I don't mind doing that because it's part of my job.... And people have put down [using Internet search engines] things like 'vacancies on London Underground' and it'll come through [to my blog]...I've actually done a blog post last year on this sort of thing, and I was getting a few emails about this...I'll try and tell it the best way as possible, but I won't hold back the horror stuff, if they ask (interview with author of London Underground Life – Station Security Manager).

In another case the process of shaping outsider perceptions of occupations was a more explicit motivation for blogging about their work. Driven by the desire to correct misconceptions of their profession and seeing their blog as a powerful means of overcoming ignorance regarding the importance of their role, one blogger commented:

> ...I think it's very important that we have an efficient view of the emergency service...if you hear of a car crash through the media – four people were hurt and they were removed from the scene by fire crews, and given life-saving treatment from the fire crews before being taken to hospital by ambulance. [it's as if...] we're 'white van man' who just arrives to take people to hospital and that's all that we do. [...] we have a press department who ends up running around saying they can't comment on something, and you end up with a situation where no one really knows what we do and how we work. Because of that we have that public relations perspective...to an extent there's a community of education out there...so I write about what it's like to be an ambulance driver and hopefully someone will read that and next time will know that view will probably upset an ambulance diver...(interview with author of Trauma Queen – Emergency Medical Technician).

Another was motivated by the desire to provide an insider account of what he perceived to be the ongoing destruction of the National Health Service. The political intent of his writings is clear in the following extract that lucidly explains the reasons for starting his blog:

> What has gone wrong with our health service? All this talk of teamworking but nurses do not seem to be prepared to liaise with the doctors anymore.

There was a time when the ward sister was valued, revered even. But all the nurses want to do is leave the wards and work for NHS Direct – or become a specialist nurse or a nurse consultant. The ward sister is no longer valued. Life on the wards for a nurse is now so grim they can't be blamed. But it is sad, very sad. [That's why] Dr Grumble decided to start this blog. A blog to vent his wrath and tell the people of the UK how bad things have become in the health service they still cherish. The events [discussed on the blog] will not identify him because this sort of thing is happening in NHS hospitals throughout the country – every day (blog extract – Dr Grumble – Teaching Consultant, first published 3rd April 2006, reproduced 1st March 2008).

Dealing with day-to-day annoyances

Issues that are largely unpredictable or irremovable aspects of the labour process, such as an unexpected deluge of customers, 'illogical' management decision making or the death of patients, understandably rarely feature in trade union bargaining agendas, and yet for many workers, it is these events that form the core of their daily experience of work. Blogging can afford an opportunity to fill this vacuum and a space for venting such frustrations. One workblogger – a parking attendant – outlined how sounding off in cyberspace allowed him to cope with his first year in a rather frustrating and tightly disciplined job:

> I would have gone under in the first year, had I not been able to express my concerns… [on my blog]. There was no other forum [for my griev-ances]. Those who disagreed with the spreadsheet driven view [of man-agement] tended to get disciplinary notices… (interview with author of Walking the Streets – Parking Attendant).

Another workblogger saw such activities as an alternative to self-destruction:

> …I mean like, some bloggers use blogs as a way of getting something off their chests, and that does happen from time to time. It is a good medium for getting things off your chest. Instead of drinking ten pints of Guinness, or hitting the wall, it's sometimes just good to vent your spleen via your blog (interview with author of Purple Plus – Emergency Medical Technician).

Feeling unable or unwilling to articulate feelings of despair at employer actions whilst at work, some took the opportunity to vent their anger in cyberspace. The following extract is typical:

> There seems to be a concerted campaign to blame doctors for MRSA and C.difficile. But how much is the government to blame? Who took away

the ready provision of clean white coats? Surely contaminated clothes should stay in the hospital and be washed there and not taken out into the community? And who forced doctors to do safari ward rounds trekking to accommodate patients on the right ward? And who shoe-horned extra beds into already crowded wards? And who is responsible for there being too few side rooms so that patently infectious cases cannot be easily isolated? And who is responsible for Dr Davey having to change in the toilet and wearing his suit trousers while dealing with faeces? And who is responsible for bed occupancy being so high that many beds have more than one occupant in 24 hours? If you were looking for a way to spread infection you couldn't find a better one. Skimping and cost cutting is costing us and our patients dear (blog extract – Dr Grumble – Teaching Consultant, originally published on 29th September, 2007, republished on Thursday 28th February 2008).

Aside, from sounding off about their employers, there was also ample evidence of workers expressing grievances against their co-workers, customers and those in occupations that work alongside them. Such extracts confirm that although employees' experience of work is significantly shaped by the actions of their employers, colleagues and workers from related occupations also influence the individual experience of work, and capacity to do one's job as one would wish. Anger expressed at the actions of peers and other workers is colourfully expressed in the following blog extract:

After two weeks of being off on annual leave and the last week being very strenuous and exhausting, I arrived at work feeling totally and utterly knackered...what pissed me off most [though] was my late turn colleague said that the meal relief SS [Station Supervisor] has asked for me to look up the times for the N18 bus to get my late turn CSA home. Why am I pissed off by this you might wonder, two simple reasons: both of my colleagues could have done this quite easily by just picking up the office phone and ringing the Information Assistant at Broadway so why should I have to find out the information myself (blog extract – London Underground Life – Station Security Manager, Sunday 2nd December 2007).

Information from the interviews does not reveal whether workblogging has true therapeutic benefits but does suggest that airing frustrations and revealing the grim and haunting reality of some public service roles in cyberspace represents a new way of relieving some of the tensions and pressures of work. While such tensions will not be permanently resolved by blogging alone, the practice does seem to offer a positive and empowering way to attain a degree of temporary relief.

Conclusions

In this chapter we have looked at one way in which employees have begun to utilise new Internet communication technologies to reflect on employment-related matters and share their experiences with others. Through an analysis of blog entries and semi structured interviews with their authors our contribution has been to shed light on some of the motives for and meanings of workblogging. At the most basic level our data has reaffirmed insights gathered from previous research that blogging can in the short term help fulfil basic work-related needs (Richards, 2007). However, given the scant scholarly attention paid to workblogs so far, there is much still to reveal about this emergent practice. Future research could usefully look at the reactions and interactions of blog readers to gain a greater understanding of how blogs are used and interpreted, but also to examine what, if any, impact or significance they have for readers' own experience and understanding of work. Silent parties to blogging such as bloggers' colleagues, management and customers could also have useful contributions to make in understanding the significance and impact of blogs. Finally, given the interactive nature of blogs and the significant readership that many attract, questions remain over their latent potential as a tool to mobilise support for struggles both inside and outside the workplace.

Our findings have suggested that determined and creative approaches to maintaining blogs, and the popularity it can attract, allows workers to derive a sense of belonging and status beyond that often afforded through their employment. Moreover, in some instances, workers claim a sense of personal achievement and fulfilment by having a part of their working life – revealing their interpretation of workplace events – firmly in their control, unlike the experience of work itself. The variety of motivations and meanings of workblogs suggest the phenomenon is more complex and dynamic than previously believed.

The use of blogs mirrors and extends more familiar strategies to make sense of, or cope with, the experience of work, such as discussing experiences with partners and friends. We do not deny that much of what workers reveal on their blogs has probably always been shared with friends, family and other interested parties. Rather than leading to new activities *per se* the Internet has provided a relatively low cost platform for extending the reach of traditional discussions about work and has made such testimony publicly accessible. For those of us interested in the changing contours of work and seeking primary insider accounts of life on the front line there is no doubt workblogs can provide a valuable source of data and open up new possibilities in the study of contemporary employment.

REFERENCES

Baldry, C., Bain, P., Taylor, P., Hyman, J., Scholarios, D., Marks, A., Watson, A., Gilbert, K., Gall, G. and Bunzel, D. (2007) *The Meaning of Work in the New Economy (Future of Work)*, Basingstoke: Palgrave Macmillan.

Bampton, R. and Cowton, C. J. (2002) 'The E-Interview', *Forum: Qualitative Social Research*, Vol. 3: 2, Article 9.

Barkham, P. (2005) 'Waterstone's says bookseller brought firm into disrepute', *The Guardian*, January 12.

BBC One (2007) 'Wasting police time', *Panorama*, Broadcast 17 September.

Berry, D. (2004) 'Privacy, Ethics And Alienation: An Open Source Approach', *Internet Research*, 14(4): 323–32.

Blachman, J. (2007) *Anonymous Lawyer*, London: Henry Holt & Company.

Boulton, D. and Hammersley, M. (1996) 'Analysis of Unstructured Data', in Sapsford, R. and Jupp, V. (eds) *Data Collection and Analysis*, London; Sage.

Butler, P. (2007) 'The Power of the secret policeman's blog', *The Guardian*: Society, April 11, p. 12.

Cassell, C. and Symon, G. (1994) *Qualitative Methods in Organisational Research*, London: Sage.

Chalk, F. (2006) *It's Your Time You're Wasting: A Teacher's Tales of Classroom Hell*, Reading: Monday.

CIPD (2008) 'Recruitment, retention and turnover survey', cited in *CIPD Web 2.0 and HR*, Accessed 15th June, from http://www.cipd.co.uk/subjects/hrpract/general/web20hr.htm

Copperfield, D. (2007) *Wasting Police Time: The Crazy World of the War on Crime*, London: Monday Books.

Edwards, P. and Wajcman, J. (2005) *The Politics of Working Life*, Oxford: University Press.

Ellis, V. and Taylor, P. (2006) 'You don't know what you've got 'till its gone': Re-contextualising the origins, development and impact of the call centre, *New Technology, Work and Employment*, 21: 2, 107–22.

Gordon, J. (2005) 'Busy Day', January 12th, *The Woolamore Gazette*, Accessed 30th June 2008, from http://www.woolamaloo.org.uk/2005_01_01_archive. htm

Hamilton, R. J. and Bowers, B. J. (2006) 'Internet Recruitment and E-Mail Interviews in Qualitative Studies', *Qualitative Health Research*, 16: 6, 821–35.

Hochschild, A. (2001) *The Time Blind: When Work Becomes Home and Home Becomes Work*, New York: Owl Books.

Jones, R. (1994) 'The Ethics of Research in Cyberspace', *Internet Research*, 4: 3, 30–8.

Mann, C. and Stewart, F. (2000) *Internet Communication and Qualitative Research: A Handbook for Researching Online*, London: Sage.

McCoyd, J. L. M. and Kerson, T. S. (2006) 'Conducting Intensive Interviews Using Email: A Serendipitous Comparative Opportunity', *Qualitative Social Work*, 5: 3, 389–406.

Murray, C. D. and Sixsmith, J. (1998) 'Email: A qualitative research medium for interviewing?', *International Journal of Social Research Methodology*, 1: 2, 103–21.

▶

▶

Noon, M. and Blyton, P. (2007) *The Realities of Work*, Basingstoke: Macmillan.

Oliver, J. (2008), 'Hunt is on for the "Civil Serf" demon blogger of Whitehall', *The Times Online*, 9 March, Accessed 17 March 2008 from www.times-online.co.uk/tol/news/politics/article3512007.ece

Pahl, R. (2000) *On Friendship*, Cambridge: Polity Press.

Pettinger, L. (2005) 'Friends, relations and colleagues: The blurred boundaries', in Pettinger, L., Parry, J., Taylor, R. and Glucksmann, M., *A New Sociology of Work?*, Oxford: Blackwell.

Reynolds, T. (2006) *Blood, Sweat and Tea: Real-life Adventures in an Inner-City Ambulance,* London: Friday.

Richards, J. (2007) 'Workers are doing it for themselves: Examining creative employee application of Web 2.0 communication technology', a paper presented to the *Work, Employment and Society Conference (WES) 2007*, 12–14 September, University of Aberdeen, Scotland.

Richards, J. (2008) 'Because I need somewhere to vent: the expression of conflict though work blogs', *New Technology, Work and Employment*, 23: 1, 95–110.

Schoneboom, A. (2007) 'Diary of a working boy: Creative resistance among anonymous workbloggers', *Ethnography*, 8: 4, 403–23.

Schoneboom, A. (2007b) '*Hiding Out: Creative Resistance Among Anonymous Workbloggers*, unpublished PhD thesis, City University of New York.

Selwyn, N. and Robson, K. (1998) *Using Electronic Mail as a Research Tool in Education and the Social Sciences*, University of Wales, Cardiff, School of Education.

Simonetti, E. (2006) *Diary of a Dysfunctional Flight Attendant: The Queen of Sky Blog*, BlogBasedbooks.com.

Spencer, S. (2005) 'Illegal Blogging: Employee Bloggers are Loose Cannon that Can Go Off When Employers Least Expect it', *People Management*, 27 (January 27th), 18–19.

Sticker, B. (2007) *Walking the Streets (the Book, Not the Blog)*, London: Lulu.

Wallace, W. (2007) 'The rise of teachers' blogs', *The Guardian: Education*, 17 April.

Author Index

Subject Index